DEEP MOUNTAIN

DEEP MOUNTAIN

Across the Turkish-Armenian Divide

Ece Temelkuran

Translated by Kenneth Dakan

VERSO

London • New York

Original Turkish-language edition published by
Everest Yayınlari as *Ağrı'nın Derinliği* 2008
English edition published by Verso 2010
© Verso 2010
Translation © Kenneth Dakan

1 3 5 7 9 10 8 6 4 2

Verso
UK: 6 Meard Street, London W1F 0EG
US: 20 Jay Street, Suite 1010, Brooklyn, NY 11201
www.versobooks.com

Verso is the imprint of New Left Books

ISBN-13: 978-1-84467-423-7

British Library Cataloguing in Publication Data
A catalogue record for this book is available from the British Library

Library of Congress Cataloging-in-Publication Data
A catalog record for this book is available from the Library of Congress

Typeset in Bembo by Hewer Text UK Ltd, Edinburgh
Printed in the US by Maple Vail

To Mt. Ararat and to Hrant

Contents

Preface

WHAT STARTED OFF as a straightforward journalistic endeavor dramatically changed character with the murder of my dear friend Hrant Dink, a Turkish-Armenian proponent of meaningful dialogue between Turks and Armenians. Turkey had ceased diplomatic relations and sealed the border with Armenia in 1993. Despite this, intellectuals and NGOs in both countries had been engaging in cultural exchanges and there were calls to open the border. As a veteran columnist for the daily newspaper *Milliyet*, I was commissioned to travel to Armenia to record my impressions in a serialized article, published in May 2006 and entitled "Armenia: Our Most Distant Neighbor." My experiences in Armenia gave me a greater appreciation of the extent to which identity and national myths have obstructed dialogue. *Milliyet* sent me to France to interview leading members of the Diaspora in autumn of 2006, at a time when the French parliament was debating a law that would criminalize the denial of the "Armenian genocide." Some of these interviews were published in Turkey in December 2006. About a month later, on January 19, 2007, Hrant Dink was gunned down outside his office in downtown Istanbul. As a tribute to Hrant, I decided to write a book incorporating material from the original *Milliyet* articles, as well as further researches in America, home of the most vocal and politically active members of the Diaspora. My reasons for writing this book were twofold: on a practical level, I aimed to give the Turkish public as wide and as accurate a picture as possible of the varying views and feelings of Armenians in both Armenia itself and the Diaspora; on a personal level, it seemed important to me to recognize and express the extent to which I was bringing to the task less objectivity but more insight than would be the case for a Western journalist.

Ece Temelkuran, 2010

Acknowledgements

I would like to thank Theodore Zeldin for the questions he posed and the questions he encouraged me to ask myself; Dr. Kalypso Nicolaidis, the director of Oxford University's European Studies Center, and Dr. Sarmila Bose, the director of Oxford University's Reuters Institute, for helping me to "get away from home"; Mehmet Karlı and Gökhan Yücel for their recent help; Prof. Theo Vanlint, for believing in me; Susan Pattie, for her warmth and support; my "dear translator" and friend, Reem Abou-El-Fadl, for her contributions to this book; the writer Huberta von Voss, for enabling me to feel as though I had a home away from home in Berlin; Bernardo Dreano, for his wonderful stories; and Dr. Kerem Öktem, of the European Studies Center, for his insights on "dispossession."

I would also like to thank Sedat Ergin, the former editor-in-chief of daily *Milliyet*, for enabling me to set out on these journeys; attorney-at-law Fikret İlkiz, for protecting me from legal proceedings over my books; and my friend and editor, Çiğdem Su.

I am eternally grateful for the brilliant intellect and acumen of Özgür Mumcu, whom I met and married as I was researching this book.

Introduction

H E SAT DOWN next to me. He'd waited for an invitation, of course. But it was as though everyone knew that by the end of the night that empty chair would be occupied by a waiter in a blue apron encrusted with tomato seeds, a waiter whose approach was stealthy but whose words would become a rushing torrent.

He hesitated the moment he opened his mouth. When someone is afraid that they won't be able to express something they badly need to say and halts mid-sentence as though to catch their breath, I'm overcome by the impulse to reach out and touch them. I know what it is to be so afraid that no one will listen that your throat aches. It's always seemed to me that a simple touch will set things right. So I touched his arm, and he spoke.

Gathered around that table in a kebab shop in Oxford were a group of big-shot academics expounding on "the rise of nationalism in Turkey." And it was this subject, which he'd no doubt overheard, that our waiter had been rehearsing back in the kitchen. The social conventions of Turkey had been left behind: here, we Turks were on a more precarious but more equal footing. We were familiar. That's why the waiter made no introductions and waited for no questions. "This," he said in a halting voice, "is what I think."

Middle Eastern men tend to address the other men at the table even when it's to the woman present that they'd like to speak. He didn't want to be taken the wrong way, so he looked at them, not me.

"This is what I think: if we research the past of everyone in Turkey then we'll find out what race everyone is."

The "doctors" at the table, every one of whom had read stacks of weighty tomes on nationalism and ethnicity, and all of whom were firmly united in their conviction that everyone should be purged of nationalist sentiment of any kind, began pondering the optimum treatment for the ignorant waiter who'd suddenly appeared in their midst. After a moment I asked:

"Why?"

"Because then," he said, now looking directly at me, "because then it'll be clear that no one's pure. We'll see that everyone's got mixed blood. And that'll be the end of racism."

Having succeeded in getting everyone to listen, he breathed more easily as he continued. "I mean, look at me. I'm a Turk. But my mother's side of the family is Kurdish. And as for my father—well, that's a bit mixed up. My father doesn't have any relatives. They say he's from Erzurum, but he hasn't got any relatives. Do you see what I'm getting at, sister?"

I saw. But did he?

"And that's why I think my father might be an Armenian. And that's why I think they should research everybody and maybe we'll find out everyone's part Armenian, or Kurdish, or whatever."

"Why would it even matter?" asked one of the "doctors" in a bid to treat the outbreak of "racism" at his table.

"It matters because people wonder about that sort of thing. And they want to know," the waiter replied.

Then he added, "And what's more, people just need it."

Why? Why do people need it?

★

We live in a world of stories. And it is our curiosity about where we fit into those stories that compels us to examine the past—a past that is, for the most part, full of terrible secrets and much bloodshed.

"Dad didn't talk about it much. But my great uncles and elders would tell us stories. Nothing happened in our village. But in the Kurdish villages they filled baskets with Armenian children and threw them into the river. They took the women who were beautiful. They settled onto the lands that had been emptied. Our village didn't do any of this, of course, it was the next village over. And they took aside the men who would be useful, the craftsmen and such. Our village had [an Armenian] cobbler, for example. He must have been one of those people who said they were Alevi, or Kurdish, or Turkish, or whatever it took to stay alive. That's what I'm trying to say, that if you researched our roots you'd find that most people in Turkey aren't what they seem. We need to find out."

He didn't seemed at all fazed by what he'd said, by the inconsistency of his story, by the contradiction of having had an Armenian cobbler in his own village while claiming that everything had happened in the other villages. Perhaps he didn't see it as a contradiction. Like I said, the world is composed of stories. We've been brought up on them. We've memorized them the same way we've memorized our prayers. And we recite them without fully understanding what they mean, the same way we recite our prayers.

Because we all know what happens to people who try to change our prayers. There are no prayers left to mourn the dead. Perhaps it doesn't matter to the dead, but then the living realize that they, too, will be passing to the other side all alone. That's how the world terrifies us: by teaching us that if we change our prayers and our stories, then we'll die alone.

And that's why evil only ever happens in "the next village over"; blood flows over there, in that place of crime and pain and savagery. If someone were to say that any of it had happened right here, in our village, the story would change . . .

. . . and Hrant would die.

★

HRANT DINK

Campaigning editor assassinated
outside his Istanbul office

Hrant Dink, who was assassinated aged fifty-two outside the
Istanbul offices of *Agos*, the Turkish-Armenian weekly newspaper that he edited, was the most prominent advocate of mutual
respect between Turkey's majority population and its Armenian
minority.

Jonathan Fryer, *Guardian*, January 22, 2007

★

It doesn't rain in Oxford. It's more like jittery droplets suspended
in mid-air, and you bump into them as you walk. The rain
isn't straightforward, with a beginning and an end. For many
days I watched those droplets stream down the windowpane,
watched as the more feeble ones clung to the glass, not going
anywhere. So that's why people come here to study and write,
I said to myself. This is a place where even the rain takes its
time. So much so that I've grown irritated with the cars stop-
ping to let pedestrians meander across the street. I find myself
missing the chaotic order of Istanbul traffic, the streets streaming
with cars and people. Here and now, it seems very human, that
blind leap of faith, the untenable and misguided sense of trust
between driver and pedestrian. Far from home, you can find
yourself missing even the deadliest streets of your own country.
But why?

Why do we miss our own countries? Is it so wearying to be
a stranger in a strange land? Or is there something binding us
to our homeland? What is this anguished, compulsive love of
country? What is it, and why?

Our homeland is like a lover demanding our return each time
we part, but never pledging to return our love. Why do our
hearts always return to Anatolia, only to be ground to dust and
burned to ashes? Why do we love the people of this land just as
you'd love a systematically and brutally beaten child?

And how is our love different from the love of those who say they'll die for their country and will kill anyone who won't?

What distinguishes love of country from nationalism?

How should we love our country?

If it's true that some people are willing to die for their country, what makes us different from them?

The difference is that they know one story, and we know another. Their story tells them that love of country involves killing and death.

When people's stories diverge from each other, their flesh too is severed. Our stories are sharper than the sharpest cleaver. And when we kill each other it's usually over our stories.

These stories chronicle our land. They tell of a past and of a future, of land steeped in blood, and of a people at one with a blood-soaked land. They tell the story of a people who flourish like wheat, are cut down like wheat, again and again—always the same story. Perhaps the only ones who know the truth are the swallows that have been migrating over these lands for millennia. Perhaps the truth can be found in their eyes. We're made to memorize only those stories that enable us to kill each other. And for that reason, when tales of death and destruction are told here in these lands, don't ask: "How many more have to be sacrificed?" Don't ask: "How many more people have to die?" Don't ask, because we've memorized a story and it's a story that's always thirsty for more blood.

That's why we need to create a new story. We need to redefine what it means to love this country. If we don't, our children will kill and be killed. Blood will gush forth from these lands, and some of us will be destroyed by the stories we've memorized.

People write stories. But later on those stories begin to define the people. And you forget so completely the things that were left out of the stories that you can't even remember what it is you might have forgotten. It's like being told stories about your early childhood, stories repeated so often that you imagine after a while that you're remembering what happened, and even find yourself remembering things that never happened. That's the power of stories.

They're like the prayers memorized as a child: you imagine you've known them from birth. That's why it never occurs to you that these stories could change, could be narrated as something entirely different. All that you've been told has become so much a part of you that, when someone suggests the stories might not be true, you may even feel physical pain.

Did your mother lie to you? Did your father deceive you? That's what a story does: it binds you to everyone else who has memorized that same story. It defines you. If you betray your stories, you betray everything and everyone.

You have become the story; anyone who questions the story questions you. And if the story is changed, you fear they won't tell you the new version. It shakes you to your core. It's terrifying. And when people are terrified, they kill . . .

What is it that makes someone so terrifying they have to be killed?

Who has the most to fear from stories?

★

He sat down across from me. I suppose we both knew how the night would end, knew that we would broach the subject carefully but would then plunge straight in, and that, finally . . .

He started talking the moment he sat down. When someone's voice cracks under the weight of the story they're trying to tell, you can be certain they're telling you some uncomfortable truths. His throat constricted, seemingly at random but actually at certain words he found painful to pronounce. But we were both laughing. I was relating some of the frustrating moments I'd had while conducting interviews with Armenians, and we were both laughing. But we knew that, soon, we'd be crying. We knew, because we were drinking *rakı* and we were talking about our country. He was telling me about himself, stories I'd never heard. It was like he was taking the stitches out of his own flesh and using them to stitch up our country, but the sutures wouldn't take, they wouldn't hold, because of the stories we'd both been told. And as he spoke, it was as though his mouth was filling up with shards of glass.

Because his was a story of corpses and orphans. And when his voice trembled, we both knew that one of those orphans had touched his heart.

Was he outraged? No. Was he angry? Not exactly. He was just pouring out his grief, sorrow and suffering that had accumulated over a thousand years. And what he was really saying was, "How we've suffered together. Suffering that belongs to us all, just as the land belongs to us all."

He spoke of how much he loved this country; he said he would always stand by our people, his people—anguished and compelled.

"İsmail!" I said.

"Who's İsmail?" he asked.

"İsmail from the State Orphanage. At primary school he'd sit in the back. I don't know why, but I'd always go and sit with him. My teacher would make me move to the front, next to the tidy, hardworking, beloved children. It always upset me."

If someone journeys to the bottom of their heart, you too can follow their example and descend deep into your own heart and ascend with a story. And as you quickly rise to the surface you're not afraid of getting the bends, because you're not alone. There are two of you.

"You know," I said, "people don't want to listen to İsmail's story. If you so much as mention someone like İsmail, they tell you to come and sit up front. The world treats anyone sitting next to İsmail as shabbily as they treat him. They don't listen. Do you know what I mean?"

He did, of course. We clinked glasses.

"And that's why I keep insisting you should write a book," he said, "about Armenians."

"Get out of here," were my exact words. "I can't write a book like that. I'd be asking for trouble."

"Are you scared?" he asked.

"No, it's not that. There are so many people sitting in the front row talking about İsmail in the back row. I don't want to be one of them. I don't want to get involved in the Armenian issue. It's become an intellectual industry. And anyway, they'd never listen to me."

"You'd make them listen," he said.

"Leave me out of this, brother," I laughed.

"No," he said, "I'm going to persuade you. Come visit me next Wednesday."

But Hrant was killed.

Four days before Wednesday.

★

Oxford rain is insidious. After each rainfall, late at night, a night bird appears out of nowhere. It sings on its own all night long, with no one to listen. "There must be someone out there," it's probably thinking. The song is deeply touching, but it's also frightening because it makes you ask yourself questions.

And that's what makes some of us so frightening to others: their words touch us. It's not like the clamor of enemies, to which we're immune, and which leaves us indifferent. It's as if, at their gentle words, the stories you've memorized start to fall apart.

You know that their words aren't intended to wound or to accuse. They're simply pouring out their heart, their only expectation being that you'll share their pain and their darkness. Like you, their voices crack under the weight of their stories. And that's why their stories are so terrible and so threatening to ours: they're not calling anybody to account, they're singing the song of the night bird, graciously allowing you to ask yourself questions, and questioning themselves as well.

And that's why, on that night in Oxford, when the waiter in the blue apron said, "Because then it'll be clear that no one's pure. We'll see that everyone's got mixed blood. And that'll be the end of racism."

I said to myself, "That's why they killed Hrant. Because you've begun thinking like this. Because people like you have begun asking questions."

So why am I writing this book?

Because Hrant is gone and I'm alone with my grief. And for İsmail—especially for him.

And for another reason. I want to redefine what it means to love my country. Because I want to love my country along with all its truths and realities. Because I know it's possible. Because I know that, together, we can shoulder the heaviest truths. Because . . . Because, in the words of the waiter, "people need it."

People need a country.

Now some claim "countries will stop existing." Others tell us "we" has been replaced by "I." "It's time to bail out," some say, "and move to the West." But what are they going to do about that voice inside, the one they put there, the one telling us we need a sense of belonging? And even if we managed to silence that voice, what would replace it?

People need a common story.

Contrary to popular opinion, human nature tells us that it is better to sacrifice ourselves for the common good than to save ourselves and die alone. "I" always seeks to dissolve into "we." "I" stands ready to sacrifice for "us." The problem is that the stories upon which we've constructed our sense of community are themselves constructed out of blood. And so "I" bleeds, and so the land bleeds. And so those who seek to dissolve into a blood-free "we" are isolated and marginalized.

People need the truth.

"We" need stories that tell the truth about our land, our history, and our present. And we can only really reach the truth by weaving our separate truths and our separate stories together. Do I believe in storytelling even as blood is being shed across the world? Even as blood, power and violence are worshipped as never before?

Disputes create their own industries, and the glorified concept of "dialogue" often becomes a service industry. My travels around the globe have taught me that exchanging stories about blood, land, and pain over a cup of coffee is insufficient and does not mean that we can merge our stories into one. But we still need to talk, and we still need to arrive at the truth of our stories. If we don't talk, we lose ourselves in the stories we've memorized and in the lies we've memorized. So, we need to talk; not to fling the truth into each other's faces, but to merge our truths.

More than anything right now, we need to talk and we need to listen.

The story I'm going to tell in the pages of this book is about Armenians, but it is also equally about Turks. As I listened to them tell me things they may never have told anyone before, I found myself reconsidering what it means to be a Turk. The stories they told spanned different countries, and were not about yesterday's truths but today's. This book is a long letter addressed to everyone who has been sent away from Anatolia, forced to abandon Anatolia. How do we remember? How do we forget? How do we make peace? How do we learn to forgive? These are some of the questions I will explore.

This is the story of a journey of remembrance and of forgetting, and it's a story I would like to share with you.

Yerevan, 2006

PART I

"Young lady, at least we have a soul"

Chapter 1

"I didn't steal anyone's mountain"

THE SUN IS setting in Los Angeles, over Venice Beach. Off in the distance men beat drums as women dance, whisky bottles in hand. The ocean is a gray void. There's no horizon line: sky blurs into water. I've always wondered which one colors the other: did the sea decide to go gray? Or was the sky the first to sulk?

I'm feeling a bit washed out myself as I sit on the sand like a blurry photograph. Here, at the final stop on a long and difficult journey of terrible loss, I face the ocean smoking a final cigarette. Yurttaş is beside me, toying with his camera. He must be feeling a bit bleak as well. He breaks into a plaintive folk song.

That's when I see her, the young woman sitting alone a little further along. The moment the song begins she recoils, even as her head swivels to look at us. She's got wavy, light brown hair, like me. Her eyes are dark brown, like mine. We might even be the same age. Her nose, her mouth, her penetrating eyes—we have similar roots, it seems obvious.

She realizes she's been noticed and turns her gaze back to the ocean. But out of the corner of my eye I see her turn to look at us again and again, and I know that she needs to look just one more time. We've identified each other. It is clear to me in that moment that she is Armenian—now I understand her instinctive reaction to Yurttaş's song. Even if she no longer understands the language of the song Yurttaş sings, she knows it comes from the "old country." She tenses; I watch her. She feels troubled, irritated, and angry; then she refuses to let herself feel this way and lets it go. I can see it all, step by step, everything she's feeling. The cycle starts again: troubled, irritated, angry. It comes from the residual pain of something she hasn't experienced personally, nor her mother, nor perhaps even her grandmother; but it's running along her spine nonetheless. It's the long-ago suffering of others, and she doesn't know what to do with it.

Now, what can I say to you? Armenian sister of mine, what can I say?

Would you like me to apologize? Apologies extracted from the mob aren't genuine. Apologies come cheap in this day and age. "I'm sorry" can easily be written in the sky, just like that. When the smoke puffs of regret disperse, all is forgotten, if not forgiven. But then again, there are those German youths who grow up ashamed of their own language and go off to a kibbutz to make amends for the sins of their great-grandfathers. That would be a shame, wouldn't it? Or is that what you want? Shall my baby too be born into guilt?

In my country, people who demand respect for human dignity are still being killed. Do you know that even now children are being tortured? Dear sister, how do you expect a country unable to confront its present to feel pain that is a century old as acutely as you do? I won't mince words; I'll speak the truth. For it is also true that the massacre you mourn marks the point in history at which mass killings started to become routine in my country. Yes, my sister, it was in the summer of 1915 that the concealment of death scattered its first seeds.

And so it was that your great-grandmother and great-grandfather were scattered to other lands. Your people carried off their dead on their backs and re-established themselves far away. And, after a time, pain became the pillar propping up your homes, and to that pillar you clung. And your people were told that to release the pillar of pain meant obliteration. Determined not to lose yourselves, you clung tighter, in the same way that my people, afraid of losing their country, have clung to selective amnesia. This is what we, too, were told. Women like you and me bore new children, and the old fears multiplied. In the same way that I've been dealt an injustice by not being told the truth about the past, you've been dealt an injustice by being told too many painful truths of the past, repeatedly, and while still a child. We were babies once, you and I. Think of how we were brought up, both of us, on the stories they told. In truth, you had no interest in death, and I had no interest in lies. And now, on the shores of an ocean on the other side of the world, see how we look at each other, stealthily, out of the corners of our eyes. Just look at us, and see how we squirm.

Armenian sister of mine, what can I say?

I can tell you that I understand and that I feel for you. Sister, I want to speak with you. If it brings tears, so be it; but if it brings laughter, so much the better. I want everything to be remembered and to be made right, and when everyone has embraced and cried as much as they need, may everything be forgiven and forgotten. But not by concealing anything. I want words with the healing power of a mother's spit to make things right and to allow some things to be forgotten. There's more to you than wounds; there's more to me than blame. We're more than that, and that's not the way I want to talk to you.

Look at those black men playing drums. Look at the blonde women dancing. They know nothing about us or the century-old story that binds us. Every year, on April 24, your people shout as my people try to drown you out. The only thing they know, these men and women of different races, is that olive-skinned people are shouting at each other. They watch as we reduce our century-old story to: "It was genocide!"; "No, it wasn't!" In the face of that century-old story, we'd be the last two people on this beach to speak to each other. But it is also precisely because of that century-old story that we belong to each other in a way that no else here on this beach does.

Do you know what I'd like? I'd like to be able to joke with

you. I'd like you to poke fun at me, and me to be able to do it back to you. That's how much I'd like us to trust each other, and that's what's distressing me. I want to be like just anyone else for you, and for you to be the same to me. I want us to be ourselves.

Come to me with whatever you bring. We've been carrying our homes on our backs: let's take the weight off.

Let's know, let's accept, and let's share as we journey together through our shared history. Let's revisit the past. Then let's come to the present. Not as the selves that have been woven out of stories, but as our true selves. Let's wonder about and let's be amazed by each other. I want to meet with you in the purity of human wonder and amazement. In order to form these simple sentences I've traveled a difficult path. In far-flung countries I've spoken to men and women with faces resembling yours and mine. I'd like to tell you about the difficult journey that brought me to this beach and inspired these thoughts. Dear Armenian sister, I'd like you to do as I did and, unburdened of fears about your identity, set off on a journey toward me. I'd like us both to have children to whom we don't have to explain any of this. I'd like those children to encounter each other somewhere in the world and feel less lonely than we do now.

Those were the things I wanted to say. But I said not a word. We sat there in silence, each keenly aware of the other. We both turned our faces toward the ocean—water blurring into sky, no line on the horizon, fading into gray.

And so the journey ended on that beach in California just as it had begun on a hilltop in Yerevan—peering into the gray emptiness . . .

★

Pointing at an indeterminable point, our guide gabbles, "He came here for a week, just like you. When Armenia became part of Russia he wanted to see Mt. Ararat. But it was raining like it is now and he couldn't see a thing. That's when he said,

'You might be Ararat, but I'm the tsar. And if I've been unable
to see you, Ararat, well, you've been unable to see the tsar!
May you never again have the opportunity to see a tsar!' And
that's exactly what happened, because the Russian monarchy
was overthrown soon afterwards!"

His story over, we resume staring futilely into the gray emptiness allegedly containing the elusive Mt. Ararat. We share the
hilltop with Mother Armenia (Mayr Hayastan), the statue that
symbolizes Yerevan. Benjamin waits for us to laugh at his anecdote, but my companion, news photographer Yurttaş, is too
cross to laugh at anything. "I'm telling you, we've been cursed.
This rain won't stop for a week. If we don't get a photo of
Ararat that's the end of the series. This is the just the kind of
thing that happens when you get mixed up with Armenians."

The three of us stand there helplessly: Benjamin, who's absolutely certain he bears sole and full responsibility; Yurttaş, who
scans the horizon with a camera lens half a meter long; and me,
who's at least as angry with Ararat as the tsar was.

Every few seconds Benjamin says, "It was supposed to be
right over there," as though he's simply misplaced the mountain
and expects it to pop up any moment. He keeps wringing his
hands and, convinced that Ararat will soon make an appearance,
decides to keep us entertained in the meantime with the story
of his life. "I migrated here fifteen years ago. I'd planned to sell
women's underwear, but a single pair cost $2 and the guys here
only earn $3. So I wasn't able to sell any. I kept trying but, no, it
was impossible. Then they said they'd find me a wife. That was
a disaster, too. Why? I'm short, and the women are all so tall!
We had to meet with ten different girls before we found one.
The people here are poor, but they'll borrow and scrimp to feed
their guests. Phew! The dinners they gave me!"

Benjamin always has wet trouser bottoms because all the
trousers in Armenia are too long for him; he finally managed to
get married, but his wife is about to throw him out because he
can't make enough money; and he's not really a "fixer" in any

case. A series of coincidences brought us together. Even though he constantly takes us to the wrong places, interrupts serious interviews to opine to one and all, apparently believes that he needs to appear front and center in every photograph we take, and most definitely talks too much, we're unable to let him go.

"And, oh—let me add this. It makes no difference to the people of Yerevan. It doesn't matter if you're an Islamist or a communist. Or even if you're a Turk. Were you to go out into the middle of the street and shout, 'We're Turks!' they'd simply respond, 'Pleased to meet you.' And they're such a chatty people, ready to talk at a moment's notice."

Even though he's so talkative that we don't have a chance to think, we're unable to let go of Benjamin.

"You know the expression, 'little Switzerland,' and all that. Well, it really is like Switzerland here. All that's missing is money. But the guys at the top are lining their pockets something awful. Phew! If they stopped doing that and the economy improved, this place would be just like Switzerland."

As I was saying, we're unable to let go of Benjamin.

"Let's say there's a car collision, for example. You brace yourself for a fight, but what do you see? 'Ahbercan!' cries one of the guys. Phew! Then they hug each other. The people here are so calm. And they're well educated too. Take my wife, for example—she studied at a vocational technical high school in a tiny village. The women are all so strong. You've got to give them a house when you get divorced. No one harasses women on the street. They've got a nickname for the policemen here: '1,000 dram.' That's because they take a lot of bribes. If you hand over 1,000 dram, you can do whatever you want. Phew! Everybody owns their own house. If they had to rent, there'd be a revolution. They all got houses back in Soviet times."

We're unable to let him go—that's right. Because, when he's with us, he's far from Armenia and close to Istanbul. He has all the enthusiasm of a person who's found someone from back home and is telling them about the "strange" country in which he has spent fifteen years, and in which his children were born; "gossiping about the Armenians" with his "compatriots" is doing him good. The yearning for his old home takes the form of garrulousness, and he's so overjoyed to be with people from home that we just don't have the heart to leave Benjamin behind.

Benjamin's stories are endless, and the hilltop is unbearably cold. I take a deep breath and interrupt him with, "Look, Benjamin." Determined as he is to appear professional, his facial expressions give him away. "Benjamin, I've told you three times. We need to talk with people. We need to find out what it's like here so we can tell the people in Turkey, in order for them to have a better understanding of Armenians. This is going to be the first ever serialized article of its kind to be published in Turkey. The more people we talk to, the better. But you've taken us up to this deserted, bitterly cold hilltop. Tell me, Benjamin, what am I supposed to do now?"

He becomes even shorter; his trousers grow even damper. His face seems to curl into a ball and hide behind his large glasses. "It would have been nice to see Ararat," he says, his voice growing so tiny that his last words are barely audible: "It's decided not to come out again today!"

Benjamin studies the horizon and says the same thing he's been saying for days: "If only you could see it! Ararat looks so beautiful from here."

When we'd arrived in Yerevan that first Sunday, the city had greeted us first with this endearing Armenian, and then with the infinite grayness shrouding Mt. Ararat.

Benjamin is still burbling tales and anecdotes as we begin to make our way down the hill. Yurttaş pauses to light a cigarette, and says, "It really *is* beautiful here! Amazing!" Why is it so "amazing"? The only remarkable thing is that, despite the thousands of articles that have appeared in Turkish on Armenia and the Armenians, there are only a handful of people in Turkey who actually know what this city looks like. We all have opinions on Armenia, but none of us knows a thing about its inhabitants. Even more surprising, no one is curious. What is it about the Armenian issue that has prevented us from wondering about this city just across the border? How can our minds be so closed that we don't even have a mental picture of it?

Despite never having been to Paris, New York or even Bombay, you can imagine all three. But when it comes to Armenia . . . Are we "Turks" unable even to imagine our "forbidden neighbor"? Even worse, I, the author of many articles on the Armenian issue, find myself astonished by the beauty of this city, this European city seemingly exiled to the Middle East. Surely, the only way not to see that which is so close is to take pains not to look at it. Especially when you consider that the lights of Yerevan are plainly visible from the frontier city of Kars. Yurttaş stops and says he wants to take pictures of the city from the hilltop; I sit down and jot the following in my notebook:

> Distant lights are visible from the four corners of Turkey. In Van, someone sets a match to an aromatic roll-up and gazes out at the lights of Iran; in Urfa, someone looks at the twinkling lights of Syria as they wrap holiday gifts to send to their relatives across the border; a child runs to the top of a hill in Hakkari and looks out toward "Welcome to Kurdistan" on a sign at the Iraqi border; a woman in İzmir raises a glass of *rakı* in a wistful toast to those who made it to the shores of Greece and to those whose souls swim still in the waters of the Aegean. And then, the very next day, these same people from the four corners of Turkey all read incendiary headlines about their neighbors. Turkey is a country bounded on three sides by seas and on all sides by sorrow. Those who fled may well outnumber those who stayed; the dead certainly outnumber the living. We've become accustomed to not looking, even once, at the people who burn those lights on the horizon. Our closest neighbors are our most remote . . .

★

Yurttaş points at a missile poised on the hilltop. "Look," he says, "they've pointed that missile right at Turkey." He laughs and continues: "When you do your military service on Mt. Ararat they make you train every day for what to do if the Armenians attack."

He's barely finished speaking when a bird lands on the nose-cone of the missile, as though making a little joke. That bird stars in our first photograph from Armenia.

We can see the concentric circles of the city down below the hilltop, at the foot of which stands a statue of Alexander

Tamanian, the neoclassical architect who laid out modern Yerevan. A little further along is a sculpture of a fat cat by Fernando Botero. As we descend into the city we see other statues and sculptures, each of them a cultural postscript of a people: a pre-revolutionary statue of an elderly man handing out flowers to the girls of the city, a boy selling water, famous composers . . . The diversity on display here is pure poetry to me: the overwhelming majority of statues in Turkey are of Atatürk.

Noticing that I'm taking notes on the statues we pass, Benjamin reacts with the words of a poor man: "They pay a lot of money for those. Armenians are devoted to art."

Yurttaş stops next to a wall and takes a picture of an empty space ringed by stones. Benjamin laughs as he translates the inscription on the wall: "It says, 'We are grateful to you for helping Armenian families to heat their homes.' These people are hilarious!" He laughs hysterically: "They've put up a memorial to a tree they cut down. Ha ha ha!"

I watch Benjamin laughing at the naïveté of this city. It's clear to me that even though he's been living here for fifteen years he doesn't regard the people as his compatriots—as though his true countrymen live in the land of Ararat, in Turkey. Even though he's Armenian, he seems to feel he belongs to Turkey, not Armenia. He's not a *Yerevantsi*, he's an *Istanbullu*. I'm still considering the question of where he belongs when we walk past a line of shops selling souvenirs. He points to the pomegranate-shaped mementos displayed in the window: "The pomegranate is highly significant for Armenians. They crack open pomegranates by throwing them onto the ground for the bride. It's believed that the seeds that spill out will be the number of children she has, like some kind of fertility symbol."

I'm about to ask some questions about pomegranates when Benjamin turns flippant again. His approach to Yerevan isn't dissimilar to the way a Turkish guest worker might describe a German city: it's the derisive admiration of a settled stranger. Whatever it is that happens to people who are strangers in their homes or have homes where they are strangers, it's happened to Benjamin, here in Yerevan.

It could be because of the way you distance yourself from your home as you describe it to others. It's almost as though the process of constructing sentences to describe your home causes you to reconstruct your home. Benjamin must be having mixed feelings, hence the mockery.

We wander aimlessly through the streets and take more photographs. Why are all the men wearing black leather jackets?

On buildings made from tuff stone, traces of Cyrillic are still visible around the edges of signage using the Armenian alphabet. These days, it's the signs in Armenian that are being taken down to make room for international brand names written in English. What do Armenians think of this process of dismantlement? Or about the old women begging in English? Why have the cafés been partitioned into tiny rooms? What used to stand on the empty pedestal in the city center? Why do waiters sit down at restaurant tables when they're not serving? What's the meaning of all the primary schoolchildren gathered in front of that shop window displaying huge silvery cakes? Why do the jacket covers in the bookshop window feature pictures of hotels? Why are there no other statues with the aesthetic values of Mother Armenia?

Benjamin must have been telling the truth about pomegranates: we pass still more windows displaying trinkets and still-life depictions of the reddish fruit. What makes the pomegranate so important to Armenians? Is it because they've been scattered around the world like pomegranate seeds? Is it because their survival depends on multiplying with the fertility represented by the ruby seeds of this legendary fruit? Images of the city flash by as night falls in Yerevan. Benjamin goes home and, all on our own, we manage to find the liveliest bar in town: "Cheers." Inside, Latin music pulsates. On the wall next to a picture of Ararat is a likeness of Che Guevara. The manager, a long-haired rocker, comes up and greets us in English. We nod and smile. It's only after we've made small talk about music, Latin America, and so on, that he asks, "Where are you from?"

"Istanbul."

He frowns: "Did you mean to say Constantinople?"

"If that's what you'd prefer, so be it. We're talking about the same place, after all."

The frown deepens. He points to the picture of Mt. Ararat: "You stole Constantinople and you stole that mountain."

"Me?" I laugh. "I didn't steal anyone's mountain."

I wait for him to laugh with me. Clearly, that's not going to happen: "You're a Turk, aren't you?"

I freeze. A Turk?

"You're a Turk. You stole Ararat from us."

I scan his face for traces of humor. There are none. So I smile and point to the other picture, the one of Che: "Don't you think it's a bit strange, here in the presence of a man who spoke on behalf of mountains everywhere, to pick a fight over who owns one mountain?"

In independent Armenia, "Mother Armenia" has replaced Stalin

"Unless you recognize the genocide, please get out of my bar!"

I stare at him blankly. We leave. Yurttaş is fuming, but I'm too preoccupied by the manager's question to feel angry: "You're a Turk, aren't you?"

A Turk . . . Oh, how I've always managed to wriggle out of that one, with a joke and a smile, doing what Benjamin does, resorting to sarcasm and disparagement. A Turk . . . It's the Turks who laid siege to the walls of Vienna, who abuse the Kurds, who expelled the Armenians, who hail from a land of Turkish Delight and shish kebab, of moustaches and belly-dancing . . . Or at least that's what it looks like from the outside. But on the inside—well, the word "Turk" is loaded for this particular Turk. My leftist mother and her friends were tortured by men who called themselves Turks; from primary school through high school we'd assemble outside in the snow to hear rousing speeches praising our Turkishness; university classmates were beaten by young men convinced that the virtue of being Turkish outweighed all else, as were the armed men who stalked the streets with cries of "*Ya Allah bismillah Allahu ekber!*"[1] and who committed massacres in Anatolia in the name of Turkishness.

But most disturbing of all are the threatening letters that arrive every time I write an article about the Kurds, the Armenians, or the army: "You're a Turk, aren't you?" or "Aren't you a Turk?" The very question asked at that bar called "Cheers," and with the same fury.

Does being a Turk mean you're "one of them"? Is it possible to be a Turk without being a part of any of that? Why have I never referred to myself as "a Turk"? Is there something forcing me to be more guarded than a Frenchman or an Englishman?

Whatever my thoughts on being Turkish, there's no getting around the fact that here, in this country, I am without doubt a Turk. That's how they see me. I'm a Turk in Armenia every bit as much as a German is German in Israel, an Israeli Jew is Jewish

---

1   "In the name of Allah the greatest."

in Ramallah, a Frenchman is French in Algeria, or an American is American on the lands of the Native Americans. There are many more examples, of course . . .

To what extent do we share responsibility for the sins of the past? How should we feel about those sins? Do we need to feel anything at all about sins we ourselves haven't committed? What's the best way to listen to people who say the sin is yours as well? How do you talk to people who are angry at you before they've even met you?

I can see now that Yerevan is not going to be a city in which I can laugh and be myself. I'll always be a Turk here, first and foremost. And the moment they realize I'm a Turk, they will be Armenians . . .

And so it was that we were launched on a journey toward the hearts of Armenians and the Armenian issue. From that day onward, it continued as it had begun, as a bombardment. I had no idea when or where the journey that began in Yerevan would end, or what lay concealed behind that endless expanse of gray.

Chapter 2

"I'm a reporter from Alaska"

"IN YOUR COUNTRY you toast 'honor,' don't you? It
figures. After all, people raise their glasses to what they don't
have!"

My hand freezes in mid-air. The room falls so silent you can hear
the champagne bubbles popping one by one. Even the director of
the Genocide Museum, Barseghian Lavrenti, winces at his female
assistant's choice of words just as we are about to clink glasses. She
scans my face as though to gauge the damage she's done. I doubt
there's much to see: I didn't take it personally. Their silence suggests
I'm expected to say something, but nothing comes. I suppose I'm
still reeling from what I'd seen that morning . . .

★

As we climb up to Tsitsernakaberd, the "fortress of little swallows," as the memorial is known in Armenian, Benjamin points
to the other hilltops ringing the city: "The Anatolian Armenians
brought Anatolia with them: New Malatya, New İzmir, New
Sivas—the hills of the city are named after cities in Anatolia.
They call the memorial Swallow's Nest because the new arrivals
from Anatolia were like migrating swallows."

We wind our way up the hill. It's April 26 and the memorial
ceremonies held to mark April 24 are still under way. Busloads
of primary school children trudge up to the Fortress of Little
Swallows, flowers in hand. An eternal flame burns in the center

of the marble memorial. The children gravely add their flowers to the huge mound already there. When we say we're from Istanbul and we'd like to talk to them, they surround us, the expressions on their faces a mixture of suspicion and curiosity. It strikes me as odd that primary school children would automatically ask, "Do you recognize the genocide?" To my mind, it's a grown-up question using a grown-up word.

Which means, of course, that the children here are acquainted with the word "genocide" at a very young age, in much the same way that their peers in Turkey talk about how "we" defeated the enemy and established the republic. Long before they're old enough to grasp the concept of death, Turkish children have learned to say, "We drove the Greeks into the sea."

The school I attended in İzmir was called "September 9 Primary School." On that day, every year, they taught us once again about how the traitorous Rum[2] were driven into the sea. In Turkish, the expression literally translates as "poured into the sea." The phrase "the traitorous Rum were poured into the sea" was repeated so many times it became a kind of tongue twister, a meaningless string of words. What we didn't know was that the name of that school in whose yard we played hide-and-seek referred to an event that was a tragedy for another people.[3] Nor did we realize it was something we should know. I thought *Rum* was something poured into the sea, a bad liquid poured into the sea, where it mixes with the saltwater until, finally, it's

2   The ethnic Greek citizens of the Ottoman Empire and of modern Turkey are called "Rum."

3   Turkish forces regained control of İzmir (Smyrna) on September 9, 1922, more than three years after the Greek army landed troops in the Aegean port city. Most of Smyrna was destroyed by fire four days after Turkish forces reclaimed control. Turks claim it was part of a Greek "scorched earth" policy; Greeks claim that Turkish forces deliberately set fire to the Christian quarter (Greeks and Armenians made up the majority of the population of Smyrna in Ottoman times). Some 400,000 Christians were evacuated from the area. The city of İzmir has been overwhelmingly Muslim and Turkish ever since.

gone. I could see it in my mind's eye. Perhaps the children here in Yerevan have similar notions concerning the word "genocide." It might conjure up images unknown to grown-ups and forgotten by children before they become adults. Considering the effortlessness with which these children refer to a horrific massacre, they may regard Turks in the same way I regarded Ottoman Greeks: they may well imagine "genocide" to be some kind of monster.

They're all looking at me with the anger they've been taught. We're encircled by the rage and curiosity of children, and the ring is closing in on us. But we've got to hurry or we'll be late for our appointment with Barseghian Lavrenti, the curator of the Armenian Genocide Museum.

Awaiting us at the door to the museum, which is located under the memorial, is a young woman. She tells us she's the assistant to the director, but doesn't reveal her name. We're to walk down a long, narrow corridor at the end of which we'll reach the director's office. But she's in no hurry. She's anxious for us to see every detail of the museum. Because this isn't just any museum, and because we're from Turkey, the guided tour down the long corridor is fraught with deep meaning and mixed emotions.

First, we're shown a map etched in stone. On this particular map, western Armenia incorporates much of what the world knows today as eastern Turkey. I sense that I'm expected to fly into a rage; in fact, I've always thought people are too easily upset by lines drawn on maps, especially considering that most of us haven't even visited the places on those maps or seen how the people there live. We pass the map and reach the "documents" section. Document after document—all of them from the year 1915.

Something's odd. Something about the design and the approach of the museum is a bit strange. The focus seems to be less on the mourning of a painful tragedy than on the painstaking verification that the tragedy took place—as though, despite

Survivors of the events of 1915

the palpable fury enshrined within its walls, the museum awaits not Armenians, but Turks; as though all of the objects in this museum have been specifically selected and displayed to express and explain something for the Turks who might visit one day. The museum has the tone of an aggrieved and abused child speaking through gritted teeth.

The assistant director has fixed me with such a stern look that I dare not air the thoughts swirling in my head. The documents section is followed by photographs of people who are dying or have already died of starvation. As we pause in front of each one, the assistant director manages to make me feel as though I haven't remained in front of the picture for quite long enough. I want to inform her that there is no correlation between the time I spend gazing at these black-and-white images and my ability to appreciate and empathize with the suffering they capture. But what is truly puzzling is that, despite the fact that I'm looking at these photographs for the first time, I really am moving along rather quickly. Why is that? Am I disturbed at having been so

Today's children look at yesterday's

abruptly burdened with my Turkishness? Or is it simply that
the images themselves are so disturbing? Over the years, I've
seen many pictures every bit as horrific as the ones on the wall
before me now. I might have paused and gazed at them a bit
longer if it weren't for the sense of obligation: no matter where
my eyes land, I'm aware that the assistant director is constantly
studying my face, searching for something—signs of regret or
guilt? A tear, perhaps? What I feel at that moment is a disquiet-
ing sense of detachment, which is undoubtedly a reaction to
the theatrical situation staged by the assistant director and to the
emotional lines she seems to have scripted for me. I hasten past
the photographs.

I wonder what she's feeling? Her face is strained, the face
of someone too enraged or grief-stricken to speak, of someone who's afraid of losing control if she does speak. We reach
the end of the museum. An entire wall is covered by a life-
size photograph of children who arrived in Armenia after 1915.
Hundreds of children posing in rows for the camera, all of them

hungry, thin, and dark. All of them Anatolian. Our eyes meet. I know these children.

The children of Anatolia grow up early. It might be malnutrition, or it might simply be the kismet of the Middle East, these miniature versions of the faces of grown men and women. The faces of these little men and women suggest they know horror. Childhood deprivation and the denial of childhood itself could well be a fate worse than death, I think to myself, as I slow down to examine their faces, one at a time. But I can't allow myself to have an emotional moment in front of the assistant director. I keep walking . . .

At that moment there's no way for me to know that later, much later, under entirely different circumstances, I'll be studying the faces of these aged children. But I imagine, as I sweep into Lavrenti's office, that I've managed to sweep those images from my mind.

Our glasses are immediately filled with champagne. And, finally, the woman who led us down the corridor responds to my reactions in the corridor, or the lack thereof: "After all, people raise their glasses to what they don't have!"

When Mr. Lavrenti realizes I have nothing to say, he diplomatically interjects: "Armenian men always drink to beautiful women. Here's to your honor!"

Champagne is drunk and conversation is made, but I'm unable to concentrate. I'm thinking about the assistant director. I'd like to tell her that I understand how she feels and wish she wasn't angry. Mr. Lavrenti is still speaking: "We've been neighbors with Turkey for 700 years. We can't sever those historical ties. But neither can we distort historical facts. We underwent genocide, and we'll never forget. Throughout our 4,000-year history, our people have faced periodic persecution. For example, in the fourth century CE . . ."

Mr. Lavrenti embarks on a long history lesson as I mull over the behavior of his assistant. Even if I do think I've been treated unfairly, I still want the anger to dissipate. I know that anger can

mask tears, that anger enables us to remain unbowed by grief.
What I don't understand is her ability to internalize the pain of
something that happened long before she was born. How has
this pain been kept alive, so alive that she can be enraged with
someone she's only just met and knows nothing about?

A moment passes before I realize that the silence is my cue to
speak: "How long has the museum been here?"

Lavrenti has acted as curator for the museum and been its
director ever since it opened in 1995. In a sense, it's the reason
for his existence. That's why I ask, "How would you feel if
Turkey said, 'Yes, it was genocide'?"

"People don't want money or land. All they ask for is an
apology. The same way West German Chancellor Willy Brandt
apologized for the Jewish genocide. Nothing is more painful for
a victim than denial of the crime. Every year, 50,000 to 60,000
Armenians from the Diaspora come to this museum. I'm always
the one who shows them around. When they cry, I cry."

Lavrenti is as adroit as a politician at tailoring his message to his
audience. He moves on to historical and political developments in
a bid to persuade me personally: "Does the Ottoman government
of 1915 have anything to do with you? No. They mistreated
Turks as well. They authorized Kurds to kill Armenians. That's
why the Kurds attacked the Armenian villages."

As I struggle to follow this sudden pivot, Lavrenti softens his
voice and asks, "And anyway, what would happen if you just
apologized?"

It's time for my scene and I'm all alone. I'd been cast as a
"Turk" only the night before; today, I'm expected to apologize for being a Turk. I take a slow sip of champagne, and then
another. Sensing my discomfort, Yurttaş plays the "We're late
for an appointment" card, and we exit without apology.

As we step outside with Lavrenti, he waves at the rain and says,
"If only you could see it, Ararat looks so beautiful from here."

I now know that in Yerevan I will constantly be stalked by
my Turkishness and by the curse of Ararat. As we step outside I

come eye to eye with the female assistant. I wonder what it does to a person, living here among these pictures and documents, surrounded by death in the hush of a museum . . .

★

"If only you could see the beauty of Ararat from here."

Haygaram bursts into laughter at this greeting from Writers Union Chairman Levon Ananian, who receives us in a Russian-built wooden building, creaky and Kafkaesque.

Haygaram?

Haygaram Nahabedian is a lot like Yerevan: silent, unpretentious, and sophisticated. It was as though the city realized Benjamin could never do it justice and decided to send us a new guide. A young man, tall and taciturn. But before he decides to help us, we're interviewed at length to determine whether or not we're like previous Turkish journalists who "write articles about Yerevan without ever leaving the front of the Marriott Hotel" and "imagine there's nothing to Armenians but the genocide." He's a journalist who studied Turcology. When we tell him about our meeting with Museum Director Barseghian Lavrenti, he tries and fails to suppress a smile. "He's like that," Haygaram shrugs. "It's his job." We talk about the female assistant and the question of "honor," to which he says, "You shouldn't think everyone in Armenia is like that. But neither should you expect to find a single person who doesn't care deeply about the genocide."

Haygaram tells us we should talk to Levon Ananian, and an appointment is scheduled straightaway. As we walk into the room I'm telling him how we've been plagued by the missing mountain, which is why he bursts out laughing the moment Levon Ananian brings up Ararat.

The toppled Soviet regime is still being mourned in the Writers Union building, whose emptiness makes it seem even bigger and bleaker. Buildings that have been made redundant are like that—all their secrets sucked into the walls and locked away there. Ananian's room is located somewhere at the end of a maze of corridors. On the secretary's desk, next to an old rotary phone, rests a brochure listing the union's activities. It's obvious, though, that the words spoken in this building are no longer held in high esteem. Sitting in his spacious room surrounded by battered armchairs, Ananian is the proverbial captain who's going down with the ship.

Ananian not only calls for his secretary, he also turns on a recording device and explains, "Other Turkish journalists have brought me trouble. I hope you'll excuse me, but I'll need a record of everything I tell you."

"Couldn't you pretend for a couple of moments that I'm not from Turkey?" I ask him. "Imagine I'm a reporter from Alaska and, if possible, could we talk about Armenians in general before we discuss 1915?"

I briefly relate my experiences at the museum that morning. I emphasize that I want to write about Armenians, not necessarily what happened in 1915. Ananian smiles: "Young lady, you're like a swallow trying to migrate back and forth between our two peoples. But, as you know, your people and mine are shaped by destiny. There's no avoiding it."

I can't escape my destiny? Not even a little? Are our destinies shaped by the societies into which we're born? I turn these questions over in my mind as Ananian continues: "No matter what we do, the genocide will come between us. We can't really know the Turks, and the Turks can't really know us. But it's not the Armenians' fault. A society has to make peace with its history. They're now trying to debate this scientifically, at conferences. For us, the question, 'Was there a genocide in 1915?' is like asking, 'Did the Turks conquer Istanbul in 1453?' It's impossible to talk to Armenians without talking about the genocide."

"In much the same way, it seems we can't avoid talking about Ararat," I say. "How does it feel to belong to a mountain that doesn't belong to you?"

Ananian lights a cigarette. He exhales and purses his lips. "Armenians wouldn't exist without Ararat. You Turks call it Ağrı, even though it's written in the bible as Ararat." He grows agitated and his voice rises. "Every poem written in Armenian refers to Ararat. Even an Armenian living in the US carries Ararat in his heart." He sighs. "I wish they knew how we felt about Ararat. You can be certain, young lady, that if they did, even the most bigoted people in Turkey would be happy to bring that mountain to us, by the truckload."

In my mind, I run through the mountains in Turkey, most of them emblazoned with the star and crescent in chalk or white stone. No, I wouldn't want to raze Ananian's Ararat. That's why, at the entrance to the building, I have us pose in front of a picture of Ararat, that soaring mountain, rising layer upon layer.

I recall the pictures of hotels we saw on the book covers in the shop windows, and ask Mr. Ananian about them. He smiles ruefully: "Our people read a great deal. But the free-market economy has changed everything, of course. In Soviet Armenia, a book of poetry would have a print run of 40,000, a novel 60,000. Royalties were generous. But when we gained independence and state support ended, writers were forced to find people to finance them. Financiers attach conditions. That's why you see book covers featuring pictures of hotels, or anything else the sponsor demands. Ours is a country so poor it's being deserted by its own inhabitants. But we still write of the seas, keeping alive a time when this land of ours stretched from sea to sea. There's only one thing that's keeping this land alive: our emotions."

"Our emotions." The things I've seen are starting to make more sense. The memorials to trees that have been chopped down, Benjamin's Ararat, the female assistant director, the elderly women begging in English in front of the foreign exchange offices, the masses of flowers and children at the Fortress of Little Swallows . . . It's as though a people battered by repeated depletion and dispersion are replacing what they've lost with a mountain, with pain—with their emotions. And, as they are scattered to the four corners of the world, they believe that, for as long as that mountain, their focal point, is standing, they too will remain on the face of the earth. Deep inside is buried anguish that, until they receive an apology, will bind them ever more closely to their sense of self. The less I stand accused, the better I understand the hearts of the Armenians—or so I think.

As we leave Ananian in that building, so silent and empty of people, I feel the need to tell Haygaram how angry I am with journalists who come to Turkey for a few days and attempt to reduce its deepest complexities to a couple of sentences when they return to their own countries. We're both right to be wary of the journalists who visit our countries.

Haygaram is protective of his country, and that's why I trust him—because he doesn't simplify things when he explains Armenia to me; because he grows impassioned and explains things at length. Only by listening to someone who cares deeply about a country can you learn the truth about that country. That's why I trust him, and I think he begins to trust me the moment I tell him what went through my mind in the museum. Or it could be because I told him how upsetting it was to see elderly women begging in English. "The transition that has taken place after independence hasn't been easy," he says, "for any of us. It's been . . . strange."

He falls silent. Then he seems to cheer up as he comes up with an idea. "Let's get something to eat," he says. "There's a restaurant I want you to see."

★

"Soviet pacifiers! So durable you can use them for a hundred years!" As if the USSR Restaurant wasn't ironic enough, it's located right next to a Porsche dealership. The sign over the door is as red as the red Porsches on display. We enter . . .

If you'd like to send Stalin your "requests and complaints," there's a small suggestion box. The bill arrives tucked inside an

Back in the USSR . . .

old identity card, medals have been hung on the statues of Lenin, the menus are stamped "secret document," and to the right of the entrance there is even a cell for political prisoners. Inside the cell, a man in prison clothes sits on the bunk eating from a metal bowl. The walls are emblazoned with slogans poking fun at the Soviet-era mentality. Things like the pacifier and "the biggest microchip in the world is the Soviet microchip." A fitting anecdote comes to Haygaram's mind: "Sophia Loren arrives in the USSR. That part is true, the rest is a joke. Brezhnev asks, 'Is there anything you'd like, Miss Loren?' Sophia Loren replies, 'Yes, it'd be nice if you'd open up the borders, Mr. Brezhnev.' The general secretary comes up close to Sophia and flirtatiously asks, 'And why's that, Sophia? Is it because you want to spend some time alone with me?'"

Haygaram laughs and launches into the next one. "The reporters ask, 'Mr. Brezhnev, what do you do in your free time?' 'I collect all the jokes about myself,' Brezhnev answers. The journalists are curious: 'And how many have you collected to date?' 'Two and half prisons' worth!' Brezhnev answers."

We both laugh for a long time. In the days ahead we'll see that for many people the recent past isn't at all funny, but just for tonight, after a long, difficult day, we both need a laugh.

"Who did you say was playing tonight, Haygaram?"

"Arto Tunç Boyacıyan. The Armenian Navy Band!"

"Armenian Navy Band? But Armenia doesn't have an ocean!"

★

"I belong to myself," says Arto Tunç Boyacıyan. I think to myself: finally, someone I can talk to. I'm so at ease with Arto Boyacıyan, who, it turns out, is an Istanbul Armenian who spends his time traveling between Istanbul, Yerevan, and the US, that we practically pour our troubles out to each other like old friends. He sprawls in his chair, a man who has reached middle age but who speaks in the tones of a heartbroken child. As he speaks, at times he grows angry and at times his voice grows high-pitched with sorrow: "When I come here, I'm a Turk. When I go to Turkey, I'm an Armenian. They don't like me much here either. Some guy is sitting here with his pat political views, and you come along and say something that spoils it. If you make them uneasy, how can you expect them to like you? Something happened in 1915. A lot of people in my family died too. But right now, even as we speak, just outside of Yerevan there's a nuclear power plant. If it melts down there'll be no Armenians or Turks. I wish we could all be earthlings, citizens of the world. Damn it! We write all these songs but people don't change a bit. I'm a member of a minority because I'm Armenian; you're a member of a minority because of your ideas. What difference does it make? Anyone who's really 'human' is already in the minority!"

Pre-concert, under the harsh glow of the fluorescent lighting in the wings, Boyacıyan continues to speak as though I've touched a sore spot. "I want to live in Anatolia. You can build all the planes and missiles you want, but once you've lost Anatolia it's gone forever. That's why I'm building a house 150 kilometers from Yerevan. I went to İzmir, but it's not the same, and you can't find the flavor of Anatolia in Yerevan either. At least, outside of the city, you can feel the chill of Sivas. The smell of Anatolia."

In my role as fellow earthling I ask for his take on the elusive Ararat. "When I first came here I spent the night at a friend's house," he begins. "I saw this amazing picture of a mountain on the wall. 'Armenians produce great artists,' I said to myself. 'Just look at that painting.' When I woke up the next morning, I saw it wasn't a painting—it was a view of Ararat from the window. That's the day I understood why they keep talking about that mountain. It looks like a poem from here. I did my military service on Mt. Ararat, but back then I had no idea how important Ararat was. They feel they belong to that mountain. There's only one people in the world who feel like they belong to a mountain: the Armenians. So, let me ask you: Who owns a mountain? Is it the ones who have it within their borders, or is it the ones who feel like they belong to it no matter where in the world they go?"

Arto, who appears on stage in front of a people who belong to a distant vision of a mountain and, through his "Navy Band," tries to transport them to a nonexistent ocean, must be so tired of all the complexities and contradictions that when he performs it's in a language all his own, songs he makes up. Up on stage he speaks Turkish from time to time, and says, "Bush is cursed best in Armenian."

"Abush!" he shouts—the Armenian for "idiot."

As he sings this song without lyrics, his son, who has an American mother, joins him on stage and begins rapping with his African-American friends. The audience sings along with Arto and his son as they extemporize lyrics based on the Armenian alphabet, and with each new letter every face in the hall seems to light up. Why? Because each letter of that alphabet binds them to each other and to their own stories, in the same way Ararat and 1915 bind them. That script, created in the fourth century C.E., tells the children of Yerevan that an

Armenian hip-hop artist who lives in the US is coming from the same place they are. Their expressions of joy are from the recognition of the old stories and the ancient letters. And as these youths smile delightedly, spellbound by these characters seventeen centuries old, I wonder where they feel they belong.

All of us, all the children of the world, are taught a story that tells us where and to which particular set of sorrows we belong. They're so intent on passing along these stories, which take on an increasingly epic character, that it's easy to poke fun at them. But once you begin to do that, you become distanced from the feelings and sense of belonging they seek to instill. And now, in Armenian, as they sing this avant-garde folk rendition of the Armenian alphabet, where do they carry the stories they've learned? Are they as distant from the things they've memorized as we are from the things we've memorized?

Chapter 3

"Don't you ever get tired of the 'genocide issue'?"

"I'VE ALWAYS KNOWN. I don't remember when I first found out about it." Natalya stares off into the distance, lost in thought for a moment, before adding, "I do remember, though, that when I was still very young my brothers often played a game called 'What we'll do when the Turks come.'"

The six university students gathered around the table scour their childhood memories for a few minutes. But not a single one of them is able to remember exactly when they first heard the word "genocide" or first learned that Turks were "terrible." All of them, however, are absolutely certain that they knew about the events of 1915 long before they studied them as part of the official curriculum for eleven-year-olds. They think long and hard, but it's as though they're trying to retrieve something from a bottomless well.

Their uncertain silence is in striking contrast to the chatter of the well-prepared students who have assembled in the hotel lobby. The women are all well groomed, smart and confident, the men assertive and sharp as tacks. In keeping with the serious nature of this interview with a Turkish journalist, some of them even carry dossiers. But the crisp, razor-sharp creases soon disappear. When the meeting begins and conversation suddenly turns to the personal, we all, myself included, find ourselves in uncharted and unanticipated territory. They fall silent, these young men and women in their twenties, all of them at an age when life and language are taken more seriously than ever before, and probably ever again. And only a moment earlier they were speaking with such passion, on any subject that came up.

Gayanen, Gor, Aram, and Hovhannes are studying international relations; Hovseph, a Syrian Armenian, is majoring in politics; Natalya hopes for a degree in Intercultural Communications. It's clear they all love talking about politics, but the uneasy silence indicates that they've never considered the questions I pose. How did they learn about the genocide? Who told them? How were they told, and using what words? How did they feel the first time they heard this tragic story? Is there a traditional way in which it is passed along to the next generation?

They're dumbfounded. They're dumbfounded by the realization that they don't know the answer to any of these questions. Or by the realization that what I speak of is "acquired" knowledge. Gayanen is the first to acknowledge that she is a stranger to this knowledge so central to her core being, and says, "Yes, first we learn that Turks are the enemy. But we later learn, of course, that ordinary people are never the enemy."

The silence continues, however. Hovhannes closely follows Turkish politics, and has a more diplomatic approach than the others. He changes the subject: "Armenia is a very new country, and a very young one. We're building an interesting future. Sealed borders, clashes, pressure applied by Turkey—I can't say the future looks bright, though."

Now that the conversation is on safer ground, Armen joins in: "By placing the genocide front and center, we're making closer relations impossible. As a country with limited choices, our first priority should be to open the border with Turkey. Sooner or later, Turkey will acknowledge the genocide anyway."

The rhythm of the conversation hastens the approach of the moment when the words "border" and "genocide" are pronounced, as though a button has been pushed in each of the students. They begin debating among themselves, with familiar words and arguments that are just below their skins and flow easily from the tips of their tongues.

Natalya: "If they haven't acknowledged it for a hundred years, they're not going to acknowledge it for another hundred years."

Hovseph: "But we haven't had an independent state for the last hundred years. That makes a difference."

Natalya: "But would it be right to open the border even if they haven't acknowledged the genocide?"

Hovhannes: We want a bright future for our children, don't we? The way to ensure that is to establish relations with Turkey."

Hovseph: "Of course no one's going to attack anyone when the border's opened. But Turkey's concerned we'll demand some of their territory. If anyone here expects them to give up land, they must be crazy."

Gor and Aram, both of whom have maintained a tense silence throughout the discussion, finally speak up: "What do you mean, crazy? Yes, we expect to get our land back. And no, we're not sitting at the table with Turkey until they recognize the genocide."

"I agree," Aram says. "Unless we make our demands clear, nothing will happen. A nation that forgets its history can't progress. If a people forget their history—"

Gayanen interrupts: "As you can see, we have a serious sense of responsibility while we're talking to you. If we say we're willing to put the genocide issue to one side, we'll feel as though we're betraying ourselves."

Everyone falls silent again.

Finally, Hovhannes laughs: "What color are your ultranationalist wolves? Was it green, or was it gray? Oh, that's right, they're gray. Well, we've got our own 'wolves'! Don't pay any attention to them, though. Your *bozkurt*[4] are no more representative of Turkey than those of us demanding land are representative of Armenia."

---

4   Grey Wolves (*Bozkurtlar*) is an ultranationalist youth organization of the Turkish Nationalist Movement Party.

As we step outside together, I find myself wondering if it would ever be possible for us to distance ourselves from the stories we've been taught. Can they be extracted, those stories driven deep into our psyches? We're walking toward the empty pedestal in the city square, I and those young men and women who may have imagined they'd moved beyond those sentences, but who consider too much distancing to be a form of betrayal. Levon Ananian was right—the destiny of our homeland is carved into our backbones. And in the Middle East, our lot has always been blood and the sword. There's no escaping it; and even if we do break free of our destiny, we'll bear the scar they call "betrayal," or endure a sense of "homelessness" as debilitating as a missing vertebra.

I'm distracted from my thoughts when Hovhannes points to the empty pedestal, and I finally learn its secret: "The best statue of Lenin in the whole Soviet Union used to stand there. Now he's stretched out on the ground behind the museum, resting!" They tell me that in 1996 there was a huge political debate over whether or not to scrap the pedestal as well. What appears to be the pedestal is in fact what was left after the marble plinth was removed. Rising from the pedestal is a multimedia advertising panel, the victory flag of the free market economy. They joke about the Soviet era and we all laugh. Encouraged by their jocularity I summon up the courage to ask, "Don't you ever get tired of the way the 'genocide issue' is always bearing down on you?"

Silence . . .

Clouds of suspicion darken their faces as they remember, once again, that I'm a "Turk." I change the subject in record time. "I really do hope you'll come to Turkey one day, to Istanbul of course, so I can get you a glass of *rakı* . . . somewhere on the Bosphorus . . ."

They're drifting away, but they turn and glance back at me from time to time, and I'm left with the reproach in their eyes and the knowledge that I've hit a nerve. They walk off in heated debate, also leaving me with their misgivings over whether it was a betrayal to talk to the kind of journalist who would pose a question like that.

Societies keep their pain fresh in the tender flesh of their children, just below the surface of their skins. Suddenly I remember the "liberation from the enemy invader" re-enactments held across Turkey. Each of our liberated cities stages a re-enactment in which some of the children play the part of the enemy while the other children take the role of the heroic Turkish soldiers who saved us from the French, the English, the Armenians, and the Greeks. In order to leave no doubt as to the identity of the bad guys, the enemy is always portrayed as a subhuman creature. The children are made to watch as good triumphs over evil, and what the children learn from these spectacles is this: we're good; they're bad.

If Turkish children were asked when they first learned that Armenians were "bad," their silence would be as telling as that of their Armenian peers.

An old photograph flashes before my eyes. I must have been about eight. We were about to re-enact one of those scenes of liberation, but when one of the boys was told he'd be a Greek, he started crying. He didn't want to be a "traitorous Greek." I can still remember the words with which our teacher comforted him: "It's just for fun, sweetie. And only for fifteen minutes . . ." I remember how he relented when told it was only for fifteen minutes, and the way the other children gave him pitying looks for having to become a "traitorous Greek." Perhaps something similar happened to those young men and women in Yerevan, something that got under their skins long ago and made them mistrustful of even fifteen minutes of joking around with "the enemy."

★

"It's impossible for them to make light of it or to tolerate anyone who does. The boundaries of acceptable humor end at the genocide."

That's the response of Istanbul Armenian and *Agos* newspaper cartoonist Aret Gıcır when I tell him about the icy reaction to my question. And this from a man who arrived in Yerevan to study art, and who doesn't hesitate to lampoon many subjects sensitive to Armenians. Subjects such as Ararat, or the longing gazes directed toward Turkey, or being a minority in both countries, or the conservatism of Armenian society. "The women are completely liberated, but the men are still macho. Real men don't sweep the streets, for example. Why do you think they all wear black leather jackets?"

That's right—why is that?

"Because if they wear any other color someone might think they're homosexual. It's only recently that the men began wearing the color blue. In the Soviet era, blue was supposedly favored by so-called 'sexual deviants.'" Even though Aret himself is Armenian, he's still able to see things from the outside, because he's from Istanbul. "Armenians in Turkey wouldn't be caught dead anywhere near a police station; they'd be terrified. That's why they keep their heads low. But when I came to Armenia I saw Armenian men fighting and swaggering for the first time. It's their country, and I suppose that sort of thing's normal, but I'll never forget the first time I saw an Armenian shouting and carrying on. I said to myself, 'Wow, what kind of an Armenian is that!' And have you noticed the way the cafés are all divided up into small rooms?"

I have, actually. What's the meaning of that?

"I suppose it's a need for privacy, left over from Soviet times. The old fear that someone might overhear what you're saying."

Even though Aret's been here for a long time, he still finds it strange and pokes fun at much of what he sees. "You'll have some guy talking about small Anatolian cities, like Tokat or Sivas. You'd think he was describing Paris. Tokat's nothing like Paris, of course, but they don't realize that." They don't realize it because the Armenian-Turkish border is "officially" closed. Unofficially, it's open—but not to just anyone. Who manages to cross the border? We'll soon find out, but for now, Aret continues to talk about how it feels to be an Istanbul Armenian in Armenia: "I don't feel as though I belong in Istanbul; but I don't belong here either. I'm a man without a country. I suppose that's true for a lot of Armenians." Once again, he refers to the question I posed to the students: "They take the genocide very seriously because their pain hasn't been recognized. They still feel like victims."

Another reason the youth of Armenia have internalized the events of the past is that the closure of the Turkish-Armenian border has hindered access to the wider world. Aret tells me that many Armenians have indexed their personal plans, including weddings, to the likelihood of the border with Turkey being reopened. A "border prayer" is even recited.

How? Like this: "Every morning, I pray to Jesus that the border will be opened!"

Anait's face has a radiance all its own. She's a stocky, powerful woman—"sturdy as the state," as the saying goes. But her voice is soft. Even though she runs the showiest shop in the marketplace I visit with Aret, her manner is unassuming. In this marketplace selling clothing and textiles from Turkey, she opts to speak in halting Turkish as she presides over the wares she's brought all the way from the Istanbul district of Laleli. "We're on our own right now. But when our neighbor opens the border it'll be good for us and good for you. The economy turns on trade with Turkey. Every time they say they'll never open the border we have a heart attack. Talk to them. Tell them how difficult it is for us to go through Georgia."

Officially, the only way to cross the border is by plane or by crossing into Turkey via Georgia. The Armenians who pass through Georgia are subjected to lengthy customs controls and forced to pay bribes. As one of the oldest "traders," Anait has repeatedly endured both procedures. She started going back and forth to Turkey in 1993. At first, she brought car parts to Turkey, traveling through Georgia to Ardahan. She'll never forget her first trip: "I was terrified. I didn't know anything about the Turks. Would they attack me? Then the bus broke down in Ardahan. The bus was full of women. A Turk came and gave us some sliced watermelon and cheese. He had the bus fixed. He didn't ask for money. 'Sell your goods and pay me on the way back,' he said. Now 90 percent of the goods here are from Turkey."

"If there were a hundred in 1993, there are a million now," Anait says, referring to the number of traders traveling back and forth from Turkey. "Turkish goods are all good quality," she adds, before telling me that her dream is for her unemployed son to go to the Aegean resort town of Marmaris the following summer and find a job in a hotel. She grips my hand at one point, and exclaims, "It'll be great when the border's open! For you and for us!" "Tell them," she seems to be saying, "tell them to open the border right away." Anait talks as though the border issue is completely unrelated to the "genocide issue," as though Turkey is even keeping the border closed because it doesn't know about the sufferings of Anait, and if they only knew what Anait has had to endure, surely they would throw open the border gates immediately. In reality, of course, Anait can't have forgotten that the dispute over the "genocide issue" is the main reason the border remains sealed. Poverty, a jobless son, and the challenges of navigating the Georgian border have taken their toll on Anait. This is a case of the reality of poverty trumping an abstraction like betrayal. Would others be willing to betray the pain inherited from their ancestors to alleviate their own poverty here and now?

★

"You're like a long-suffering saint," I tell Alla, whose large eyes well with tears. As she weeps, Armenia seems to weep. Neither of us speaks for a moment. A moment earlier, however, she'd been making some very astute observations.

"Bangladesh" is what they call this district of streets pocked with mud-puddles, scattered reminders of the poverty that is everywhere apparent. I'm here to meet with Alla, a mathematics and theater instructor, and Rozanna, a high school basketball coach, at the only structure in Bangladesh with any claim to charm: a one-story school with a broken bench in the yard surrounded by dilapidated public housing towers. In front of the school a diesel-driven ice cream machine rests on a motorcycle. A group of teenage girls queue in front of the machine, which makes as much racket as a whole factory. The girls are all wearing cheap, gaudy garments of the sort sold by Anait. The brightly colored ice cream clashes with the paint on their faces, which is an inexpertly executed imitation of the makeup they've seen in magazines. The bell rings, and we follow the chattering crowd of schoolgirls inside, where Alla and Rozanna await us in the principal's office. Alla is forty-four. She has the upright bearing of all teachers in the Middle East. At first glance, no one would ever guess that for the past fourteen years she has been trying to bring up two children on her own, and has been made to pay heavily for the misfortunes of her country. The woman standing before me in the principal's office has nothing to say and no troubles to relate. She seems prepared to provide only a few terse responses before she excuses herself, leaving the presence of the journalist who has suddenly appeared in her school. I mention the girls eating ice cream in front of the school—their makeup, their clothes, their high spirits, the way in which the turmoil following independence has apparently brought "color" to their lives; "I suppose," I add, "that their mothers haven't experienced the changes in quite the same way." She motions toward her face, her clothes, her hair. And it is only then that she speaks, as though forcing the words through a hairline crack in her stoic veneer. "An entire society is struggling to ensure that its children remain ignorant of the difficulties we all face," she says, and begins telling me her story.

"My husband and I are university graduates. Before independence he was working as an engineer. But we all lost our jobs. There's nothing my husband didn't try so we wouldn't go hungry. He even went to Turkey to bring back goods."

Her voice falters but her face tells me that engaging in the "suitcase trade" is almost as bad as going hungry. She regains her composure and continues. "These are the growing pains of a new country. We'll get through this, of course. But . . ."

But?

"We had no idea it would last this long. I just can't see my way through to the end of this anymore." Her face falls. She's about to move on from her country to the depletion of her personal reserves of strength. "I'm able to have a short holiday and see my husband on the children's birthdays, at New Year and during summers. But our relationship remains strong. This is the best it's going to get, and we have no choice but to endure. It's more of a partnership than a marriage. My husband takes care of the children's financial needs, and I handle their emotional needs."

At the word "emotional" something snaps inside her; her eyes fill with tears. When I compare her to a saint, she smiles, but when she speaks again her voice is thick with emotion, and halting. "We've solved our financial problems. They can be solved. But it's not so easy to maintain human relations. It's been fourteen years since we lived together as husband and wife. Can you imagine what that's like?"

Rozanna is touched by Alla's words and by the tears in her eyes. Rozanna separated from her husband for similar reasons a year ago. Her husband, who's also a basketball coach, is currently selling furniture in America—the same way Alla's husband, who's an engineer, sells flowers in Russia. And again, just like Alla, Rozanna has two children. But she's still young and, judging from her expression, she expects the situation to improve before she runs out of strength. She's conscious of Alla, whose eyes are full and whose hands have fallen to her lap, so she doesn't want to appear to be too cheerful. Still, her eyes sparkle as she tells me that her husband will soon be returning. She doesn't see the look Alla gives her, but I do. "These are still your best days," Alla might be thinking, "wait until you can no longer remember his face, his voice; just wait until you grow old . . ." Rozanna is telling me how much she misses her husband and the plans she has for what they'll do with the children when he comes home; the moment her gaze shifts to Alla, she collects herself, as though ashamed of her joy and youth. But when her eyes move away from Alla and off into the distance, her face starts glowing again, her voice gets louder, and the words come faster. Rozanna is off and running, and doesn't hear Alla murmuring to herself.

"Later, you get tired of waiting. Life passes."

Rozanna doesn't hear her because she's too busy talking about how her husband is coming for the New Year, and how, in any case, she might take the kids and join her husband in America, where there's a school they can go to and, in any case, he'll be visiting soon . . . Alla retains a silent, skewed smile, probably because she wouldn't forgive herself for putting a damper on Rozanna's cheerful patter.

In Armenia, where nearly every family has a member who works abroad, it is women like Alla and Rozanna who are afflicted by the country's most severe and least visible problem—like saints sleeping alone. When the bell rings, both of them automatically produce compact mirrors and refresh their makeup. Alla laughs at her reflection: "We're the compulsory heroes of Armenia. But we've got to keep it from the children. It's always that way, you know—whenever there's a common problem, women do most of the heavy lifting."

Heads held high, the two women head for the doorway. The door's opened and the clamor of children spills into the room, like cold water splashed onto their faces before they step out onto the stage.

Perhaps one day a statue will be erected in Yerevan to them as well. And the inscription might well read: "Many thanks to the lonely women of independence, those compulsory saints."

Is it possible, after a time, for people to forget why they feel pain?

Alla, Rozanna, Anait—not one of them mentioned 1915 or the "genocide issue." Everyday heroes bear the weight of history too, even if they have no time to remember why they do so. And true heroes are almost certainly too busy with the stuff of life to realize how heroic they're being—because, in Alla's words, "Life passes." Students in their twenties are unable to appreciate this as much as women in their fifties. As life passes you by, the reserves of passion that fuel heroism become depleted. And, just as Lilit will say tomorrow morning, "You can't live and breathe pain every day."

Chapter 4

One, two, three . . . Long live the Turks!

IF AN ARMENIAN were to lose their way one day anywhere in the world, they'd be able to locate the capital of Armenia by consulting the map of their heart. They would navigate toward it by reference to the coordinates of pride and fear, of mourning and loss.

To the north of Yerevan is the Mother Armenia statue; to the south, the Fortress of Little Swallows; to the west, Mt. Ararat. In the same way that the city is landlocked, it is also locked into its coordinates of meaning, especially those of pride and mourning. The city expands in concentric circles, and the outermost of the circles of meaning ringing the city passes through these points to the north, south, and west. Perhaps that's why the people look so worn out, I think to myself, because they're locked into these coordinates.

"No, not at all," says Lilit Bleyan, "we don't live and breathe the genocide." Lilit is a director at the Center for Open Dialogue. Founded as an antidote to the closed political culture of the Soviet era, the Center is a non-governmental organization dedicated to promoting dialogue both within Armenian society and with Armenia's problematic neighbors. Although still a young woman, Lilit has a four-year-old daughter who looks like a miniature version of herself. The girl is named Arax, after the river that flows along the Turkish-Armenian border and, in Lilit's view, unites, rather than divides, the people of the two countries. Arax scampers along under the high ceilings and over the parquet floors of the Center for Open Dialogue, her pattering footfalls echoing through the wooden building and drowning out our voices. Then she pops up out of nowhere, widens her eyes, and cries, "Surprise!"

Every time she utters the word, one she's probably just learned, we have to feign astonishment; in between all these "surprises," we need to discuss politics. "Support for the Armenian Revolutionary Federation, a party that has made the genocide the centerpiece of their policies, stands at about 6 percent. And their support continues to erode. I ask you to draw your own conclusions," says Lilit. Then she tells me something that is discussed among Yerevantsi, but isn't normally revealed to a "Turkish journalist" in Armenia. "People have slowly started discussing whether Armenian politicians might have shared some of the responsibility for the events of 1915. If this new willingness to question the past were combined with positive overtures from Turkey, we'd have the opportunity to foster dialogue between our two peoples."

I tell Lilit that, as I was on my way to Yerevan, my only thought was that the people of our two countries, who have been made to believe that there is only one subject up for discussion, would need to start talking again, come what may. I also tell her that I believe that the initiation of dialogue unrelated to the events of 1915 will eventually enable our people to discuss those painful days as well. I ask her how my idea would be viewed in Armenia. She replies, "There are many other things that we can and should discuss. But when we start with the genocide we find we can't talk at all."

Lilit and I are unable to have a more in-depth conversation. Not only does Arax insist on singing a Greek song for us, we're scheduled to meet other people here at the Center. Perhaps it's for the best: thanks to Arax, we talk not about 1915 but about things like the best age for a woman to have children, and whether or not it's a good idea to start a family early. We talk about Arax, and we talk about life. She flows through our conversation like the river that is her namesake, sweeping away the debris of the past, which is a subject for another day.

I watch Arax running along the wooden floors, and I wonder to myself when she'll begin hearing stories from 1915, and if she'll be as eager to sit in my lap and sing Greek songs once she's been incorporated into her people's painful past.

In Turkish, "destiny" or "fate" is referred to as *alın yazısı*: "the writing on one's forehead," the inscription present at birth. Perhaps societies, too, have an *alın yazısı* from which we're exempt until we've grown up enough to leave our childhood behind. Perhaps one of the rites of passage is to be branded with this sense of historical identity and societal destiny. But, unlike *alın yazısı*, can a society's destiny be changed?

As we learn the letters of the alphabet, we learn that other alphabets are not like ours, and with each new letter we are drawn further into the shared destiny of the people who use those letters and who speak that language. We believe we're simply reciting the alphabet, but what we're actually learning is that we were born as a constituent part of a people.

A song suddenly springs to mind—a song that rhymes in Turkish and which I chanted as a child, long before I started school, never realizing what the words really meant:

> One, two, three; long live Turks
> Four, five six; Poland's gone under
> Seven, eight, nine; Germany's swine
> Ten, eleven, twelve; Italy's a fox
> Thirteen, fourteen, fifteen; Russians stab backs
> Sixteen, seventeen, eighteen; we'll beat you up
> Nineteen, twenty; that's the end of the song!

How on earth do I know the words to this song? How did I learn them, and when? Why didn't I notice how appalling the words were? Was I the same age as Arax? I'm still turning this over in my mind when our guest steps into the room.

★

"We have no diplomatic relations, and the border is closed. But everything's open for business!"

Economist Aram Safaryan is the producer and presenter of the "Freedom of Speech" and "Political Dialogue" programs on Armenian State Television's Channel 2. He's animated and has a bit of a belly, suggesting he's a man who enjoys the good things in life. His attire catches my attention. It's nothing like the drab clothing inherited from the Soviets, which is all I've seen men wearing for days. He sports a shiny tie, a chic suit, and the latest designer glasses. He talks about the border as I look him up and down. "But we managed to get a visa in just twenty minutes. And goods from Turkey are on sale everywhere," I say.

Safaryan bristles with annoyance. "You're right, the borders are always open to businessmen. But the thing is, not everyone in Armenia is a merchant!" I can see that he's annoyed not by my question, but by the subject in general. He's unable to sit still, and springs to his feet as he explains, "Annual bilateral trade stands at $120 million. Of that, Armenian exports are worth $1 million, while imports from Turkey are worth $119 million! Why would Turkey want to change anything? Meanwhile, here in my country, 49 percent of the population lives below the poverty line."

He tells me that Armenians are masters at concealing the poverty and privation that lies behind the magnificent stone facades of Yerevan: Armenians have historically had a close relationship with concealment. I listen attentively as Safaryan presents me with a rapid-fire rundown of why Turkey and Armenia need to establish direct relations. "Neither the US nor the EU can bring Turkey and Armenia to the table. Turkey views Armenia as an extension of its own Armenian population. But we're a young, independent country. If Turkey stopped seeking the support of the US for entry into the EU and focused instead on playing a dominant role in the Mideast, it would get into the EU a lot more quickly. Armenia should be more than a dumping ground for cheap Turkish goods."

Selling goods in Vernisaj

Safaryan has a point: the aesthetic charms of Yerevan are certainly in contrast to the unlovely goods flooding into the city through the "suitcase trade." It's also true that the cheap shops of Laleli are in a sense dictating, through the traders, what Armenian women wear. I understand why he's angry. "Armenians shouldn't be made to wear clothes that no one would wear in Turkey. Authorities continue to turn a blind eye to the suitcase trade, which has squeezed out the small investors so vital to a commercial market."

Safaryan talks as though relations can be changed tomorrow, reeling off concrete examples. "Armenia earmarks $50 million a year for investment in advanced technology. Turkey could establish a Silicon Valley here, like the one in the US. Major investments could be made in energy. But unless diplomatic relations are established, none of this will happen."

According to Safaryan, 80 percent of the uPVC windows, nearly all of the paper and cellulose products, and all of the chocolate in Armenia come from Turkey. Even so, formal diplomatic relations have not been established. Safaryan thinks the time has come for a "formula" to be devised concerning the "genocide": "Turkey should grant the Armenians who once lived in Turkey, and their heirs, the right to live there again. Those Armenians should have the right to live in Turkey on the condition that they don't demand the return of the land they inherited from their ancestors." I point out that the land is not as they left it. Safaryan responds with: "It's only because they're forbidden to return that they imagine it's so wonderful. If they visited the places they used to live they'd be back in Armenia within fifteen days! But, then again, if we turn the page on enmity, it will create a revolution in the Armenian mentality."

An intellectual in a country that's shedding population because of the sealed border, Aram Safaryan sounds angry and must be feeling frustrated. Like all of the intellectuals living in the republics of the USSR, he's been forced to watch as everything the people own is put up for sale. And what's more, you don't have to be Armenian to be upset at the sight of Vernisaj, where people sell everything they have for next to nothing, only to take the proceeds to a country that doesn't even officially recognize them to buy that country's cheap goods for resale in their own country. A handful of medals sold in exchange for a 100 per cent polyester blouse! Perhaps the "Armenian mentality" has already undergone more than enough "revolution" for the time being.

That could be the reason the waiters sit at the tables when they're not serving. The rapid transition to capitalism has worn them out, and they need to rest at the old communist-style tables. Or perhaps they haven't yet grown accustomed to the fact that not only have their time and labor been put up for sale—so also, in a sense, have their energy, their gestures, and their behavior.

Having left Aram and Lilit, we're wandering the streets when an elderly woman in front of the gate to a huge Soviet-era street market shows us the candied eggplants she's selling. Frankly, they don't look like anything we could eat. "Maybe later," we say as we walk past her. Yurttaş finishes taking pictures in the marketplace, and we're on our way out when that same woman, selling those same candied eggplants, calls after us in a trembling voice, "But you said you'd buy some!" Hers isn't a vendor's insistence or a marketing tactic: she genuinely can't understand how we could get her hopes up and then fail to buy anything. That's how the people here are growing accustomed to the free market: uncomprehendingly, compulsorily, with voices that tremble.

We walk through Vernisaj, looking at the dignified poverty of the artists. "Hello," someone says in English. I look at him. He smiles so warmly that I nearly forget that he was one of the students who declared, "We'll take back our land, of course." Now, he smiles with the bemusement of a young man, uncertain of where to put his hands or what to say. He asks how we are and if we need help. Then he wishes us happy wanderings and walks away, occasionally looking at us over his shoulder and smiling.

The heavy despondency pressing down on Yerevan seems lighter after the sudden appearance of the young man, in whose face I'd caught glimpses of rage and curiosity, pride and gaiety, bereavement and the desire to live in the present. Like so many young men in the Middle East, his face too was a study in complexity. It wasn't long before he'd disappeared into the busy streets.

Yurttaş is snapping photos of the painters and their pictures. They're selling their wonderful paintings for such low prices that we're both too embarrassed to buy one. It seems somehow shameful—as though we'd be taking advantage of these gifted, educated, elegant people. We probably owe our sense of shame to our Middle Eastern backgrounds.

But we soon encounter a face that's as Middle Eastern as ours.

"To live without sitting at the table of tyrants and to regard each day with the wonder of a newborn child—that's what the people of Armenia are trying to do." Smoke streams out of the mouth of Armen Elbakian, followed by one of the most moving lines in Sufi mysticism. A dramaturge who has also directed theater for many years, Elbakian has the classic features of an Armenian: the distinctive nose, the piercing eyes. Flitting across the planes and curves of his expressive face are comedy and tragedy, as though he's on the brink of a joke or about to burst into tears. A skilled actor, he appears to have been expecting us, even though our arrival at the theater and request for an interview was sudden and unannounced. He smiles at this delightful coincidence and, with next to no questioning of our identities and "Turkishness," speaks easily and at length in his role of interviewee.

The sound of chattering children comes from the auditorium. They're waiting for the curtains to open on a puppet show. Many of the chairs are broken, the hall is small and gloomy, and the curtain is tattered. "They'll be watching *Don Quixote* in a few moments," Elbakian says as we walk through the crowd of children and are received in his office. Artwork, mirrors, cigarette smoke, and that magical aroma, a mixture of face powder and wood, found in all theaters. Elbakian must have assumed that the size of the audience had caught our attention, for that's where he begins.

"In the Soviet era the theater was inexpensive and for everyone. Children were taken to the theater, whether they needed it or not. It's no longer compulsory, but even if our audiences are smaller than before, at least I know that only those who truly need the theater come here." Elbakian smiles at the sound of laughing children, and closes the door. "There'll always be a need for theater—always," he says, with a meaningful glance at the door. His lips curl into a mischievous smile, as though he has a secret he might share. What could it be?

"As you know, the Armenians were stateless for centuries. And we had to find a way to preserve our language—you know, to resist assimilation. It was the church and the theater that prevented us from being assimilated."

The church—that's right. I know how important religion is in the daily lives of Armenians. So why haven't I seen any churches in Yerevan? I'm trying to answer my own question as Elbakian continues: "It's the same for all stateless peoples. The theater preserves your language and your identity. People who have always had a state wouldn't understand. Theater as philosophy creates a hero for its own time, around whom people unite. Heroic catharsis helps the people to find answers to the questions of their times."

So, who is the hero of Armenia and of Yerevan, a city that expands in rings and whose coordinates are privation, poverty and pain?

"The people of my country love plays. They also love the play of human interaction. Armenians love the transparent depths. But this country is going through a period of transition. The twenty-first century hero of the Armenian people has not yet emerged. Still, we go on playing the part of Don Quixote! What else can I say!"

We laugh along with Elbakian.

"For Armenians, who or what is the Dulcinea for whom Quixote fights?" I ask. And that's when Elbakian takes a deep breath and a long drag on his cigarette, before answering, "To live without taking a seat at the table of tyrants and to regard life always with the wonder of a newborn child—that's what the people of Armenia are trying to do."

I continue the theme he says he enjoys so much: "And the windmills?"

He remains in character, and replies, "Freedom is sometimes like a raging river—it brings mud as well. In ages past, humanity needed to believe in thorough knowledge and deep understanding. The prophets emerged when the waters of that river were stilled. The enduring meaning of humanity must be protected from the mud of the raging river."

The sudden hush in the auditorium suggests that the magic of the theater is at work, as it has been for millennia. Colorful lights, painted players, and incredible puppets have transformed the tiny stage into an imaginary kingdom. Don Quixote is mounted on horseback and trying to convey to the children the enduring meaning of humanity by fording a raging river of exchange rates, Laleli polyester, and women who've learned to beg in English. The children, most of them the same age as Arax, are laughing now. They don't know it yet, but the more they laugh, the more they're filled with a truth higher than the destiny of their people, a universal truth. That's what Elbakian was talking about when he referred to "deep knowledge." And as they watch and laugh, they're infused with it—with this healing power, and with the knowledge that it doesn't matter which people, faith, or ethnic group they belong to, because they'll be in the minority no matter where they go. But, at the same time, they'll be part of a wider humanity that is greater and more ancient than their own culture. And it is in the name of this allegiance to a higher humanity that they will work for a better world, and perhaps even meet, one day, with the children of peoples they've been taught to regard as enemies. There will never be many of them; they'll always be in the minority. And they'll think thoughts similar to mine: Can I affect the destiny of the society in which I was born? Should I? What if they squeeze me into a corner, as they've done to so many others?

★

"All I'm asking is for a tiny favor. If those guys weren't with her I'd have spoken to her myself long ago."

A woman sweeps the statue erected to Tamaman, Yerevan's planner

Yurttaş has fallen for a girl. In a twist of fate, we see the girl first in the evening, in the hotel lobby, then again late that night at a jazz bar. Convinced at first sight that she's been sent from above, Yurttaş spots her making for the door of the ladies' room, directly behind us, and is determined to make me introduce him. Matchmaking is top of the list of things at which I'm hopeless, and do everything I can to avoid—but there's no getting out of it. Finally, I go into the ladies' room and up to the girl. Unfortunately, or perhaps fortunately, she doesn't speak English. French? Russian? I don't speak either of those languages, so we end up gesticulating ridiculously and at length. The lovers had managed to exchange glances in the lobby, so she certainly knows full well what I'm trying to get across, and seems at least as upset as Yurttaş that I'm proving to be so useless. So piteous is the look she shoots at Yurttaş that even I feel bad for the "separated lovers." But back to her table she must go, to the company of a bunch of men her father's age and to a growing heap of plates of fruit and bottles of whisky and champagne. The girl is becoming less and less visible; once in a while she turns to look at us, but the beefy man sitting next to her squeezes her so hard she looks like she's suffocating. She shrinks smaller and smaller at the side of her companion, most likely a wealthy man she's just met. Yurttaş keeps drumming on the table, an abstracted staccato that is out of time with the music. I decide to turn my attention to the stage.

It might be impolitic to admit this, but, as I scan the faces of the musicians and the members of the audience, most of them male, I'm surprised that those faces could belong to people who play, or who appreciate, jazz. In order to understand why I'm so surprised, I review my visual codes. Who do these men look like? The men in the southeast of Turkey. Men from the village. So familiar are some of the faces that I imagine I recognize a couple of them. In fact, one of them is the spitting image of a friend from Erzurum, a friend whose family is devotedly Muslim and avidly Turkish nationalist. When I realize why I'm so surprised, I'm stunned. Because it could mean . . . yes, even I might know Armenians who remained in Turkey, converted to Islam, and became "Turks." But if that's true, why haven't they told me? Do they even know? Or could it be that they know, but have decided to keep it a secret?

"Don't you think these guys look like our Easterners? One of them looks exactly like a friend of mine from Van." The moment Yurttaş corroborates my impression, an expression pops into my head—a phrase I'd forgotten I knew: *Kılıç artığı*, literally, "the leftovers of the sword," a reference to the survivors of a conquered people; more specifically, a reference to the survivors of 1915, the ones who didn't flee and weren't exiled. The ones with concealed pasts.

We stare at each other. He seems to have reached the same conclusion: there's a lot we don't know. I say "seems" because we don't talk about it. It's strange—neither of us says a word. Instead, Yurttaş changes the subject to the girl, and we talk about her all the way back to the hotel. He keeps joking about what a hopeless friend I am and how he'll never again agree to be my traveling companion.

We enter the hotel and step into the lift just as the door is about to close. And inside the lift we find . . . the girl, her back to us, her eyes on Yurttaş' reflection in the mirror. She shrugs and lifts her cupped palms, as if to say, "What can I do?" The man at her side sways drunkenly as he searches for the right button. This girl embodies the fate of a country beyond rescue, no matter how many Don Quixotes come charging along. The fate of her people dictates that she be squeezed into a corner. And just as she is squeezed into the corner of the lift, others—the ones who escaped their destiny by surviving in another land—are squeezed into a corner of a different kind. That girl and the "leftovers of the sword" in Anatolia share the same silence.

Outside the hotel, barely visible in the gloom, an old woman in a Soviet-era apron is sweeping the street. She sweeps in no particular direction, her twig broom scattering the dust to and fro. But as I watch her I feel likes she's sweeping the corners of my mind. In the darkness of the night that old woman becomes the missing coordinate: to the north, Mother Armenia; to the south, the Fortress of Little Swallows; to the west, Mt. Ararat; and, somewhere to the east, an old woman who has no idea where to sweep the mud brought by a raging river into this city of concentric circles . . .

Chapter 5

"If 'genocide' is in quotes I'll get around it"

"IT'S IN MEMORY of Red Monday," Haygaram tells me on the phone. "We all used to clean the streets together, one day a week. Some still keep the tradition alive. But you said you saw her in the night, didn't you? Interesting. The poor old thing must be a bit confused."

"And there's the question of the churches, Haygaram. Why are the churches hidden away? I've noticed that they're all concealed behind other buildings."

I sense a smile on the other end of the line. "That's because all through Soviet times, in order to protect religion and places of worship, the tactic was to hide churches by surrounding them with other buildings. That's why you don't see any. There'll definitely be a church wedding tomorrow—you can go and watch." Haygaram has been speaking quickly. He asks, "You're going to the May Day celebration, aren't you? You need to hurry."

"Why?"

"You'll see soon enough!"

Yurttaş abandons what's left of his *ser surç*—Armenian for "sweet coffee"—and we rush out into the street. Benjamin appears in the distance, hitching up his trouser legs as he scurries toward us. The three of us run through the streets of Yerevan. "It's not over yet," Benjamin assures us, breathless and unconvincing. We arrive at 10:15 and, yes, the ceremony began at

10:00 on the dot, and is almost over. The hundred or so people gathered in front of a statue of Alexander Miyaniskan, the first president of Soviet Armenia, are obviously listening to the final speaker. I expect Benjamin to translate for me but, for all the attentive squinting and pricked ears, his mouth remains firmly closed. It's not his fault this time: the words spoken into the megaphone are barely audible. On the periphery of this small square located at a crossroads, cars whiz past, rubbish is collected to the mechanical clamor of garbage trucks, and lorry drivers slow down to stare at the crowds without bothering to turn down the music blaring from their open cab windows. Everyone—those assembled in the square as well as the passersby—probably already knows by heart the speeches coming from the megaphone.

May Day in Yerevan

They're huddled together in the center of the city. Children smile in imitation of photographs of the jubilant Soviet youth of old and release balloons at the wide pedestal of the statue. The uniformed men and women are practically leaning against each other to remain on their feet. Most of them are war heroes from World War II. When their right arms become too heavy to wave their Soviet Armenia flags, they lean on their canes and switch hands. There are a few placards bearing the names of the home regions of the Soviet Communist Party members; they, too, struggle to remain upright in the crowd. Every May Day, medals that no longer find buyers in Vernisaj are affixed to the chests of those who come to this square to stand at attention to ever-diminishing applause. No one cares about them. The inhabitants of this city are still warm in their beds, making the most of their day off. The ceremony is soon over, and the weary Soviets sink onto the nearest bench.

Elderly people with long stories to tell and few people to listen to them are the same all over the world. But it's even worse in Yerevan, where the tellers know for certain that absolutely no one in this city is interested in their tales. When they see the camera in Yurttaş' hand they're eager to pose with their medals and to explain to us why their tales are still valuable—even before we ask . . .

"Talat Pasha was a Jew in any case; we all knew that." Arshak Sarkisian, whose sunken chest is hidden behind medals, breaks into Azeri Turkish the moment he hears we're from Turkey. "Turks would never have committed genocide like that. The Young Turks were all Jews. They're the ones who set Armenian against Turk." I'm reminded of Museum Director Barseghian Lavrenti, who implied that the Kurds were the real culprits. What's going on here? Why would Armenians try to absolve the Turks of responsibility? What kind of psychology is that?

An elderly woman next to Arshak Sarkisian, whose show of patience has only served to emphasize her own impatience to speak, finally has her say. "The Turks actually like us better than the Azeris." Her name is Bapian Annik; she's eighty-four. She turns to show me the medals on her chest and waits for me to ask about them. Those medallions represent a lifetime; I ask about them, of course. "I'm a heroic worker. I worked in the chemical industry for forty-eight years. They used to honor workers at thirty years. These medals are what I got for being a hero of the workers."

Considering they've given their lives for these symbols and wear them still, I suspect they're disappointed with the ceremony. Bapian Annik surprises me: "It was a very fulfilling ceremony. Fulfilling for the soul." She smiles, unwavering in her pride. Perhaps people of her age have a different take on life; perhaps, from where she's looking, the Yerevan of destitution and multinational billboards isn't even visible. Ironically, the audience at the ceremony listen to the speeches of their old supervisors with their backs turned to the flashy, gleaming building that is the new City Hall. And the uniformed speakers to whom they listen so attentively no longer scare a soul.

Most of the people who come up to us smell of vodka. Even if only for a few moments, I want to share with them the tragedy of their lives. The only photographer on the scene is Yurttaş, and they're so happy to see that he's still taking pictures that we find it impossible to leave—not just yet anyway. I sit down on a bench between an elderly woman ånd some children. Lacking a common language, the children and I can only exchange smiles, but I do understood that they're asking where I'm from. "Istanbul," I say. The woman next to me suddenly starts shouting and clapping her hands. She thrusts her face toward mine: "How dare you call our Constantinople 'Istanbul!' How dare you say 'Istanbul'!"

We beat a hasty retreat. When we look back, we see Bapian and Arshak are waving goodbye and, I suspect, scolding the woman for having driven off the only photographer to take their pictures.

"Did you make it?" Haygaram asks. "We did. Don't even ask what happened! I'd forgotten for a few days, but now, thanks to one of them, I remember that I'm a Turk, once again." Benjamin gives an exaggerated account of the women who rebuked me, distancing himself from their "shameful" behavior by acting utterly "amazed" that such a thing could have taken place. Haygaram listens calmly, glancing at me from time to time, familiar enough with Benjamin now to filter out much of what he says.

We exchange knowing smiles, but Haygaram feels called upon to explain, yet again: "You understand, don't you? It's the expectation that Turks will do what's morally right. People expect it as an act of courtesy. They expect recognition of their ordeal and their pain. For them, it's more of an emotional issue than a political one. And the longer it takes for that recognition to happen, the angrier they get. They get angry at all Turks."

I tell Haygaram that I thought the anger was coming more from the Diaspora Armenians. He shakes his head: "The idea that the Diaspora Armenians are exaggerating the issue and that Armenia is more concerned with bread-and-butter issues is propaganda circulated by Turkey. You won't find a single Armenian who doesn't expect Turks to acknowledge their suffering and history. You won't find a single one, anywhere in the world. Nor in Armenia. But Turkey is trying to present this demand for acknowledgement as a form of nationalism, and seems to think that we've adopted a hard line on the genocide because what we really want is land. You believe that because you don't have the opportunity to hear anything to the contrary."

At the approaching footsteps of a middle-aged man who is obviously not a local, our Ararat brand cognac shudders in the glasses resting on the hotel lobby end table. That the newcomer is a businessman is indicated as much by his smile as by his gold ring. "Excuse me. I don't wish to disturb you, but . . ." he begins, in Turkish. As he asks permission to sit with us, he sums up the situation with a joke: "How do you spot the Armenian in a crowd? You don't have to. He'll soon come up and introduce himself."

Arto Bülent Kilimli has come over because he heard us speaking Turkish, and because he heard Haygaram mention the word "diaspora." An old Istanbul Armenian who has obviously been eavesdropping on us for quite some time, he cracks a joke about 1915 the moment he's seated. "I never knew my grandfather. Come to think of it, nobody my age did. All right, let's say my grandmother was an immoral woman. But surely we didn't all have immoral grandmothers!"

Haygaram laughs, but he's visibly displeased that Kilimli has burst into the discussion with his jokes. I assume Haygaram's antipathy is for strictly personal reasons until I learn more. When I ask Arto Bülent Kilimli, who lives in Paris as a member of the Diaspora, if he's in Armenia on business, he blurts out what Armenia means to him. "For me, Armenia is a tourist spot. Why would I invest here? To lose money? The corruption here is incredible." Haygaram has obviously had it with these well-heeled, sitting-pretty businessmen from the Diaspora. "The Diaspora expects special business incentives to invest here!" Kilimli ignores Haygaram as he confides in me, his fellow *Istanbullu*. "They're new to capitalism here. They don't know how to do business," he says. "And anyway, I feel more at home in Turkey than I do here." Kilimli, who's arrived in Yerevan

A heroic worker after the May Day ceremony

to take in a few plays and a few museums, shows me his tickets. "How could I expect to belong here? Look at the way they've written the title of the play we're going to. I don't even understand their language. They speak a different kind of Armenian here. In any case, if there's a problem it's because of the people here who've lost their connection to Turkey." He's referring either to Haygaram or to Armenia as whole. That's how the argument begins. Both of them blame the other for the failure to reach an understanding with Turkey.

Which means that there are tensions between the Diaspora Armenians and the Armenia Armenians—tensions I'm seeing for the first time. I'd always assumed that all Armenians were united on the subject of being Armenian. It's only some months later that I'll get a better understanding of the implications of these divisions and tensions. For now, I look at Haygaram's face as he struggles to remain composed but grows increasingly agitated the longer he talks. Haygaram might agree with some of the less favorable comments Arto makes concerning Armenia, but he's not about to let some rich Armenian merchant from Paris criticize his country. Oddly, these two Armenians, who live on opposite sides of the same continent, are not able to communicate in Armenian, but only in Turkish.

As they talk, I think of the Young Turks mentioned at the May Day ceremony. I'm surprised I never wondered about the role of the Young Turks in the events of 1915 when I was in Istanbul writing articles about the Armenians. My lack of interest is certainly strange. It's as though I've been programmed not to feel any curiosity. I know terrible things happened, but a part of me doesn't want to learn any more. That might be because I'm not prepared to deal with yet another thorny issue related to being Turkish. And anyway, nothing I learned would change anything. After all, the old suffering has become loaded with new meanings. For Armenians, the events of 1915 are about core identity; for Turkey, Armenians' allegations are considered to be politically motivated. I've hesitated to get mixed up in any of this. I put down my lack of interest to the awareness that blood has been shed in the lands of Anatolia throughout history, thus further legitimizing my indifference. Are we obliged to know all the details?

I think back to the many articles I've written and the many interviews I've conducted on the Kurdish issue. In certain parts of Turkey, too, some were angry with me for being a Turk. Over the years, I learned that I needed to make angry Kurds trust me, both as a journalist and as a person. But theirs was a different kind of anger. We may often be at each other's throats, but Turks and Kurds are brothers. For all the bruised feelings and pent-up rage, for all the accusations and blame, the person posing the questions and the person answering them has a shared sense of "us." It's not like that with the Armenians here in Armenia. At some point in history our relations took a wrong turn and were frozen in time. We no longer recognize each other. Perhaps that's why I felt closer to the elderly people. They remember faces like mine and the language I speak. Perhaps that's why, even if they've suffered the most, they're still willing to forgive the Turks. That might be the reason they'd like to believe that the Young Turks were Jewish. Younger Armenians are much more foreign to me, both because they've learned only one narrative from the preceding generations and because, unlike the elderly people, Anatolia never worked its way under their skins. It's impossible, of course, for youth to understand the ancient Anatolian equation of brother pitted against brother. It would take the old-timers an entire lifetime to explain the peculiarities of that particular equation . . .

"Did you hear me?"

"*Efendim*? Yes?"

I haven't been listening for some time, so I have no idea what Arto just said.

"I was just saying you might come to Paris one day. To talk to the Diaspora."

I mumble something like, "Yeah . . . sure." I dismiss the possibility because something's troubling me. What's more, here, in Yerevan, I've had my fill of posing questions to people programmed to hate me, and I doubt I'll ever do anything like this again. There's also the question of my return to Turkey. How am I supposed to write about Armenia without using the word "genocide"? I could get out of it by putting it in quote marks, I tell myself. At first I think of this merely as a tactic to salvage my article. What I don't realize is that my hesitancy to get further involved and my reluctance to write down the questions inside my head mean that I'm, in effect, putting everything I've seen inside quote marks. And I'm most definitely not going to Paris.

Chapter 6

"Open your bags, please!"

FOREHEADS PRESSED TOGETHER, the bride and groom are making their vows. A Hummer is waiting at the door to whisk the newlyweds off to their honeymoon and, according to Benjamin, Armenian women have only recently begun wearing miniskirts in church. And yes, the church is indeed surrounded by buildings and visible only from one side. It is the architecture of a people who have learned over perhaps thousands of years how to lead lives of concealment. How to conceal themselves, and how to multiply like the seeds of a pomegranate . . .

★

I associate the homes of elderly women with the smell of cookies. A smell warm and tender—like cookies dipped into tea. And it's this warmth that brings out the child in visitors. In some homes, there's no place for good and bad, right and wrong. There's room for everyone in the embrace of elderly women who have grown old in goodness and squeezed several lives into one lifetime. So many things have collected in this embrace, in this house, that you might find your own life here—answers to your questions, stories to ease your mind, a kind word to lift your spirits. You find your path smoothed and your obstacles removed, just like those moments in life when a cookie dipped into tea is exactly what's needed to set things right.

Silva Gabudikian serves Ararat cognac and pomegranate wine

After finding the building we'd nearly given up for lost among the unlovely housing towers, we make our way up uneven stairs and past raw concrete walls to meet with an elderly woman seemingly untouched by mortality. That's how eighty-four-year-old Gabudikian has been presented to us: the oldest woman poet in all Armenia! They tell us other things about her too: The poet who foresaw post-independence! A national monument! The most lyrical poet in Armenian! A living legend!

But when the door is opened and the nurse leads us to her side, we're greeted not by a down-at-heel, forgotten old woman, but by a *grande dame* who revels in the finer things of life. Beautifully arranged on the table are cognac glasses, a bottle of Ararat cognac, cakes, nuts, hors d'oeuvres, and a bottle of pomegranate wine, just in case. Silva Gabudikian seems as eager as the journalists from Turkey to see that last bottle opened. I'd intended to maintain a respectful distance—that was the plan, anyway. But I'm so mentally drained that I begin the interview more in the vein of pouring out my troubles to a grandmother. It was wrong of me to expect to understand the people of a country in a single week. But the newspaper expects me to have unraveled the hearts of the Armenians in that amount of time. Ararat is important not simply because it's mentioned in the Bible, but because the Armenian people trace their origins to Noah's Ark, which is said to have landed on Mt. Ararat. That legend is in turn connected to Hayk, the patriarch of the Armenian nation, and it is while looking toward Ararat that this proud people, who at the crossroads of history have repeatedly faced annihilation, vow that they will exist on the face of this earth for all eternity.

She's probably amused that I'm now talking aloud, largely to myself, spilling the contents of my muddled head onto the table for all to share. She starts laughing. It's with that know-ing laugh that she carefully pours out the cognac and raises her glass: "*Barev!*" she cries; "Hello!" Yes, I need to slow down and collect my thoughts. Go slow, I instruct myself . . . I'm still bringing my glass to my lips when, just like that, she downs hers in one.

She waits for the sweet fire to slide down her throat, pauses for a moment to savor the sensation, and begins to comfort me—yes, as a grandmother would: "You've arrived here at a difficult time, young lady. This country has seen its whole way of life changed. And then came the war in Karabakh. Then the earthquake of 1988—50,000 people killed, half the country destroyed. Aid was delayed because of the closed borders. On the day independence was declared, no one expected that our troubles would last for fifteen years. Young lady, we lived without electricity for four years. This country lived in candlelight for four years. We all went to bed fully dressed. One out of four of us migrated. And you, young lady, are trying to understand the soul of a people that has just gone through all of that."

The soul of a people

She carefully refills her glass. Although she's smiling, it's plain to see that the health concerns caused by her recent heart attack fade into insignificance compared to the sorrow of speaking about her people. The rain begins again. In a voice roughened by sips of her second cognac, she continues, "So, you want to understand the soul of Armenia? In that case, I'll have to tell you a four-thousand-year-old story. We'd better hurry up and finish our cognac." After the second cognac is finished she no longer sits with the hunched back of an old woman, but as she might have sat in the 1950s—one elbow resting on the table, the hand holding her glass extended, eyes fixed on a point somewhere in the distance. "Only a people with a soul are able to come through dark days. Our soul"—she pauses, and looks directly into my eyes—"and yours as well, young lady, have been through rough times. But you know, at least we have a soul, your people and mine."

Her words transform this house lost in the outskirts of the city into a house of fables; the room in which we sit slowly becomes the center of the world. Each word falls onto the table like a stone. Her sips of cognac are slowing. She's like someone who's crested the hill and is now on level ground, slowly walking. She looks me in the face and smiles for a long time. She definitely sees something in my face—something from long ago, a struggle in the distant past, a breeze, something missed and wistfully remembered. But instead of talking about any of that, she begins to cross-examine me: "Did you visit any villages?"

I'm about to say "It's been raining for a week . . ." when she takes me by the hand and leads me to the villages. "If you go one day you'll see shepherds and milkmaids. When you ask them their names they'll say 'Ophelia' or 'Hamlet.' I know, you're here to ask questions about the genocide. But there's more to life than pain. We also care about the good things in life. This is a country that translated and read Shakespeare two centuries ago! That means something—something important."

"But isn't the genocide issue the key to understanding

Armenian identity? Doesn't this identity forged out of pain mean that even the identity of the children yet to be born in this country has already been determined? Isn't it an injustice to those children?"

"Young lady, you don't yet understand the meaning of 1915. It concerns the entire Armenian community. Other people may not be able to live with their own national issues. But a person who doesn't know about this issue and doesn't feel it inside cannot be considered an Armenian. You're right—it may be an injustice. But people need to feel connected to each other, any way they can." She stops and looks at Yurttaş. She directs her question at him, not me: "Did you know Nâzım—Nâzım Hikmet?" Yurttaş smiles and looks at me for the answer. I simply tell her our birth dates. She takes a big swallow of cognac and grows old for the first time. "Excuse me. It's a psychological thing. People don't realize how old they've grown. You think everyone's seen what you've seen." Then she turns to Yurttaş and says, "You look a lot like Nâzım!" Silva has a flirtatious look now, because she's describing Nâzım's hair, his eyes, his form and figure—the way she once raised a glass in his honor in Tiflis, and how he called her "the most lyrical and beautiful poet in the Soviets." It's as though the portrait of young Silva on the wall is coming to life, and she's kissing Nâzım on the cheek like she did every time they met. I know that's what she did because her cheeks, wrinkled as they may be, are blushing pink.

Perhaps old people harbor shelters created out of good times. The doors of those shelters are thrown open when they need to relive those wonderful memories. Perhaps when people return from those wonderful memories to their real ages, they return even older. When Silva Gabudikian starts talking again, she's now older than she was a moment ago. "I used to joke around with Nâzım. Whenever we met I'd say, 'Give us back our land.' He'd smile and reply, 'After the revolution!' That's how we'd joke with each other. Once day he said, 'Our two communities are so intermingled there may even be an Armenian in my family.' To which I responded, 'You may well be an Armenian!' 'What makes you say that?' he asked. And I said, 'Because you're a genius!'" She glances out of the window. For a few minutes, the rain does the talking. Then she murmurs to herself: "The old days . . . Now we spend our time looking at our grandchildren's pictures. What were we saying?"

Our glasses are filled with cognac once again, of course. I ask, "So, do you think Yerevan was better in the old days, or now? Do your grandchildren have a better life, or do you?"

"We suffered the pain of the migrants from Van and the cruelties of the Stalin era. But the joy of victory in World War II made us forget all our problems. The current generation has never seen the good side of the Soviet era. The system we have now is good for the children of the wealthy but, as you know, young lady, this is a poor country."

Silva Gabudikian has a face that reflects whatever her people experience. That's why, behind a glass of cognac, her face seems to grow pinched all of a sudden. I swear, her fluffy, curly hair fades and goes limp. And it's when she talks of "the ones that went away" that the creases in her face deepen the most: "For the past fifty years the propaganda has been that we were calling on all the Armenians in the world to come and live in these lands. There was Victor Hampartsumian, the founder of astrophysics, the pride of our people, and the symbol of our pride. We used to say, 'This is a place where the stars speak the language of Hampartsumian.' But everyone's leaving now. They all keep leaving . . ." She looks like she's about to cry. She collects herself, and continues. "My poems were for the people. Don't imagine that I'm a nationalist. But a person who doesn't love their own people can't love other people."

Silva Gabudikian still actively loves her people. Her most recent political activity was to cite widespread corruption as the grounds for rejecting a state order of merit. But it's not politics she enjoys discussing, it's love poems. "All the women in

Armenia have memorized my poems. Could there be a greater source of pride?" she asks between sips.

And finally, the bottle of pomegranate wine is opened as the conclusion to a natural process. In the expectation that it won't be long before we're all drunk, I ask Gabudikian the question I most wanted to ask: "And Ararat? What about the Armenians' Ararat?"

She pauses for a moment, goblet in hand, wine-red refractions playing along her palm. "Ararat . . . Ararat is a mountain we're unable to reach. The longer we're away, the more beautiful it becomes. Our hearts are buried at its foot." She stops looking at the glass or through the window into the distance and, once again, her eyes pierce mine. "Young lady, Ararat is a matter of height for you; but for us, it's a matter of depth!"

As she waits a moment for me to absorb the meaning of her poem, she merrily fills our glasses, gives me a smile, and raises her glass high with the words, in Turkish: "*Hadi*! *Eyvallah*! Drink up!"

★

The sky clears for the first time in a week. Drunk on Silva Gabudikian's hospitality, Yurttaş insists we immediately climb the hill on which Mother Armenia stands and take a photograph of Ararat.

"There's no need for that anymore," I say, "we've seen Ararat."

We stand at the window with flushed cheeks and gaze off into the grayness where Ararat is supposed to be. For a split second we catch a glimpse of the outline of the mountain. Then, naturally, the rain starts again. Benjamin mutters to himself, as usual: "If only you could see it. It would have been great to see Ararat . . ."

I can't get angry at him anymore. I smile and say, "Ah Benjamin, you never did find that Ararat for us!" I scribble a few lines into the final pages of my Armenia notebook:

It's just as well Ararat didn't reveal itself to us. It's a wise mountain; it must know best. Most likely, that magic mountain wants us to see not the mountain itself, but what the Armenians see in the mountain. Once it was certain we understood, it shrugged off the clouds, winked, and retreated into nothingness again.

My country . . . So many hearts are buried there. And far away, they remember those barren lands with great affection and deep sorrow. And with each passing day, the steppes become more beautiful to someone far away. We don't see you and we don't hear you, but we know you were once here with us. Otherwise, why would elderly men in the southeast—amazing, I only remember this now—declare, unprompted, "These buildings were made by Armenian master stoneworkers. No one since has been able to create such beauty." Or why would women fanning themselves on their balconies in the summer heat of İzmir keep saying, "The Ottoman Greeks always left space between the buildings for the sea breezes to cool the city. Ah! Look at the city now!" My grandmother from Fethiye would always talk of "the ones who went away." "It was from them that we learned how to cover mattresses with sheets and how to make pickles," she'd say. Why did I never ask her about "the ones who went away"? Why is it only now that I remember these things I never realized I'd remembered? It's as though information stored somewhere in my body is being awakened.

The heart of my country—so many hearts buried here. In fact, everyone here knows about "those who went away" and keeps them in their own hearts. In fact, everyone knows without knowing that the ones who went away are raising their glasses, somewhere far away, to these lands. They know what lies beneath the soil, at the foot of the mountains and of Ararat. In silence. The people remember in silence—in absolute silence . . .

Countries never forget. Neither does the soil. Memories can't be erased. They simply know what needs to be remembered, deep down . . .

★

"Open your bags, please!"

"Could you open your bags, please?" Such is our greeting, from a plainclothes policeman, on passing through Turkish customs.

"What for?"

"We need to search your bags."

Military coups have taught us something: plainclothes policemen don't like questions. What's more, when you're worn out from a week in Armenia, the only thing on your mind is getting out of the airport and to your home as quickly as possible. Rather than putting up a fight, you simply allow the bags from the "suspect country" to go through the x-ray machine and wait patiently in the hope that the ordeal will soon be over. But if you're like me, you might ask something along the lines of, "To date, has anyone ever tried to smuggle in a bomb or anything else from Armenia?" Silence. Of course, you might be feeling insistent: "I'm only asking because . . ." At the policeman's utter lack of a response of any kind, my question trails into silence. The expression on the policeman's face has become even more forbidding, possibly because I'm now suspected of "discouraging suspicion of Armenians." He nods a curt thank you, and we get our bags back.

"When we came back from northern Iraq they took us to the exact same checkpoint, remember?" asks Yurttaş. "These *random* searches always seem to find us." Two undercover cops give us such a chilling look that we remember where we're from and where we are. In just the same way the bar manager at "Cheers" decided that calling his Constantinople "Istanbul" made us too Turkish, the looks of the cops here in Turkey suggest that we aren't sufficiently Turkish. We walk under a sign proclaiming: "Welcome to Istanbul!" And I'm suddenly struck by the thought: "I'm going to have to rephrase all of those interviews."

Chapter 7

My "appealing" Armenians

"HOW COULD YOU make Armenia so appealing?" "It's bad enough you went there; why'd you write about it?" "How could you call Ağrı, our highest mountain, 'Ararat'?"

There's a lot I don't understand about people. Despite the books I've written and the dozens of speeches I've made in dozens of halls, there's still so much I don't understand.

When the articles I'd written about Armenia were serialized in the newspaper, I had new cause to be perplexed. The e-mails I received were similar in tone: "Why are you writing good things about them?" "Why do you present those people as good?" They were mad with rage. They couldn't understand how I'd returned from Yerevan without beating anyone up, and I suppose that was the reason they wanted to squeeze me into a corner and beat *me* up.

As a journalist, I tend to get entangled in subjects that invite a beating. I'm no stranger to threats, anger, and raw nerves. But there was something different about the reactions this time. They weren't arguing; they weren't telling me their own thoughts; they weren't cursing me as they spouted slogans. They simply didn't want to hear what I was saying—as though I'd opened a door, and they wanted to slam it shut. They were scuffling with my words. Peevish as children roused from a deep sleep—cranky, fretful children.

And I'd been so careful to protect the newspaper as I "rephrased" the interviews. The word "genocide" always appeared in quotes. It's true, though, that I eschewed the expression cooked up by Turkish officialdom: "so-called genocide." In fact, I'd wanted to write neither of "genocide" nor "so-called genocide." My intention had been to find a third way: to seek the truth through a language that would reframe the terms of the debate by sidestepping loaded political terminology.

★

"Thank you very much. A lot of bad things happened in these parts. Then the Armenians were gone. It's a pity. Good work."

That was it. An e-mail that, however brief, had probably been mulled over for days. A grandfather out east had asked his grandson to write it. Neither of them signed it, though. Among the correspondence I received from young people passing on the memories of their grandfathers and calling for the border to be opened, this letter stood out. It was a short note from someone who had a lot to say, but no idea how to say it. As brief and meaningful as that wink Ararat gave us just before we left Yerevan.

I wondered to myself why, during my hundreds of visits to provinces in the east, I'd never thought, even once, of asking anyone about any of this—even though I knew full well who built those stone buildings, and also knew, in general terms, that there had been great cruelty. So what was the reason for my apathetic silence?

I thought of the reliefs on the walls of the Armenian cathedral on Ahtamar Island in the middle of Lake Van, of the churches hidden away in the side streets of Diyarbakır, the decaying stone edifices in Istanbul . . .

★

"They did some great work, didn't they sister?"

Bored of being stuck in traffic in the sweltering heat, the taxi driver leans his chest against the steering wheel and cranes his neck to get a better view. He's looking out at the darkened stone buildings of Harbiye.

"Excuse me?"

"Those buildings all belonged to Armenians—did you know that? Just take a look at the new buildings, though. You'd think they'd take the trouble to do it right. If they don't know how, they could at least take care of the old buildings—not let them fall apart. Know what I mean? But they don't do that either. Turks just tear things down."

"Are you Armenian?" I ask the amateur architect in the front seat.

He's alarmed: "Of course not! I'm a Turk through and through, praise be to Allah! All I meant was, those buildings are something else. That's all I meant."

"What happened to the original owners of those buildings?" I muse aloud, as a little experiment. Silence. He's switched off, like a computer rebooting. Then:

"What was that street number again, sister?"

"Drop me off right over there, please," I tell him, "in front of Sebat Apartment."

The taxi driver watches as I enter one of those wonderful stone buildings. Am I Armenian? Did I really think he was? Is he tutting to himself even now?

"Ohhh!" Hrant exclaims at the door, as always—arms open wide and squeezing tight, as always.

"You're going to break my ribs one of these days," I grumble.

He laughs away my protests, takes my arm, and leads me to his office. "Your articles turned out well," he says. "Let me take you out to eat. We'll go to an Armenian restaurant together."

"Don't even mention the word Armenian to me. I've had it," is how I begin telling him of my adventures in Armenia and the reactions upon my return to Turkey. We find a lot to laugh about. I suddenly remember those familiar faces in the jazz bar and the conclusion I drew that night. "Not a day goes by when someone doesn't come to my office," he says, "carrying a letter or document written in Armenian. 'Could I be an Armenian?' they ask me. It's begun happening more and more frequently over the last few years. Interesting." He tells me that some of the people we've met or know are actually Armenian "converts"— a famous old musician; the father of a close friend. I'm surprised. I'm sure my friend never mentioned anything of the kind. But in any case, what's there to say? Does it matter? But why did my friend never bring it up?

"Have you heard about the French bill?" he asks.

"What bill?"

"The one they're bringing before the French National Assembly in September or October. It makes it a crime not to recognize the Armenian genocide. Can you believe it? They're out of their minds. And the French are going along with it."

He's angry. But we eat, and time passes, and he's in high spirits when we go our separate ways. As I walk down the stairs I call back to him: "By the way, Hrant, no one will be asking you for a guide again. Your guy sold us out and we got stuck with Benjamin."

His laughter rings in the stairwell of the old stone building.

I've never had much time for this interest in ethnic roots. It's always seemed to me to be like a ball of wool batted about the post–Cold War world. Various peoples become entangled in it, blood is shed over it, weapons dealers grow rich off it. I'm a democratic socialist who, by definition, is internationalist and liberated from such notions. But what about the taxi driver's silence? And my own curious lack of curiosity? The buildings and the people without a past—deprived of a past. There might be something to this.

Those were the days I'd begun recalling the things my grandmother used to tell me. She'd talk about a strange place we came from, was always emphasizing that our family was *saraylı*, or attached to a palace in some way. Years later, she'd toy with a ruby ring of mine and say, "All those pearls and diamonds got lost on the way." Which palace was she talking about? The way to where? Why did she come to Anatolia, and where did she come from? As she recounted her past, it was always like a fairytale. But I remember the exact point in her life at which fiction turned into fact: when she became one of the first teachers in the new Republic of Turkey; when the last of her beautiful daughters was educated—at a train station, everyone crying; Atatürk dead and grandmother crying her eyes out. The latter part of her story was always full of chronological events, but her early past remained as distant as the lands beyond Kaf, that mythical mountain range of sparkling emeralds and jinns.

It's like that for most of us in Turkey. Our elders always come from someplace else, or there's a sudden dislocation in their stories, which are always either too sketchy or overly embellished when talking of those days of pearls and diamonds, of purple grapes and emerald-green fields. The stories are repeated and repeated, and we find our link to the past is a fairytale. It's got nothing to do with you—it's the stuff of fairytales, the half-real, half-remembered murmuring of grandmothers and grandfathers. It doesn't need to be remembered; it's never been forgotten because it never truly existed. And when you ask what *really* happened, eyes glaze over, like those of the taxi driver. Because Turkey is a country that strides forward, chest out, shoulders back, eyes gazing determinedly ahead without a backward glance, like a young man who thinks he'll never grow old.

We've formed a strange relationship with our "official" Ottoman past. There are good sultans and bad sultans; dates to memorize; any number of mad sultans to learn about; a palace whose decadence is symbolized by the turtles trained to wander among the merrymakers with candles atop their shells. By the time you've finished high school you're so fed up with having to memorize dates and names that you can't stand "history." The past is something memorized for exams, and has absolutely nothing to do with you.

And furthermore, so much is happening in Turkey at this very moment, so many jarring changes, so many bloody stories unraveling. There's a natural reluctance to sort through the old account books when we're so busy filling up the fresh new pages of the present. The old sheets of paper are as dog-eared as the left-hand pages of the notebooks of primary school students. Our eyes are trained on the right-hand pages: cool, white and inviting.

Over time, the vacuum created by this truncated understanding of history may fuel interest in a distorted or salacious version of the past. Bestseller lists might feature titles like *Ottoman Sex* or *Love in the Harem*. You could find yourself peeping through a keyhole at a version of your own history and culture that is as alien to you as the "Turkish apple tea" European tourists delight in. Even worse, when historians enamored of our imperial past inform us that "minority subjects of the Ottomans enjoyed blissful, carefree lives," you might believe them.

As a progressive fighting for change in your ill-starred country, you've always felt quite removed from that blood-spattered enigma we call "Turkishness." You may not even refer to yourself as a Turk, just as some Germans avoid the term "German." And since you're "not all that Turkish," there's no need to acquaint yourself with the Turkish past. And what's more, it's exhausting.

Being a Turk is exhausting. We struggle each and every day to stay on our feet. Three coups; political Islam; the Kurdish problem; multiple economic crises; sexual inequality; a foreign policy that teaches us to feel under constant threat due to our "special geopolitical position"; the inexplicable notion that we are a country without parallel or equal; our tragicomic isolation among the nations of the world; the fervor whipped up by every international football match, as though we're off to storm the gates of Vienna again; those modern-day Ottoman conquerors, the young men who manage to steal the hearts of tourist girls; and a gutter press that in blazing headlines heaps praise and congratulations on every Christian who converts to Islam and gets Turkish citizenship . . .

Policies concerning Turkey's past are as confused as those concerning its present, for which reason our view of our past is somewhat blurred.

And then, suddenly, up pop Armenians demanding you give them an "apology." For whose crime? Why us? We weren't even there. What do they want from us? We didn't do anything to them . . .

The act of remembering takes two. If there's no one to remember with you, the things you remember never existed, never happened, vanish. A nation can opt to forget en masse. Eventually, not a soul will remember what happened. And those few who do still remember might send a brief e-mail, unsigned, to someone who's trying to remember with them.

Yes, the land does have a memory, but it is made up not of the recollections of individuals, but of the concerted efforts of a people who have decided to remember. Otherwise, even things that are impossible to forget—like the stone buildings that can't help but be visible—create a vacuum in the collective memory. "Armenians once lived here . . ." you begin, and the rest of your sentence is sucked up by the current version of history. Leaving behind "the eternal sunshine of the spotless mind"— the blinding gleam of an unsullied past.

Yes, the land does have a memory. It lies under a mountain somewhere, dormant until the time comes when children know they have nothing to fear from remembering. Perhaps that's why some mountains are higher than others: they harbor more memories in their depths. And Ararat, as every schoolboy knows, is Turkey's highest mountain.

PART II

"Numbed by the constant accusations"

.

Chapter 8

"Paris is going to be great—just great!"

IT TOOK DAYS for me to write anything. Not because I didn't know what I wanted to write; on the contrary, because I did know. I was back from Paris, but my serialized article still awaited my labors. First, I would have to write down my thoughts on the subject. And because I knew what I needed to write, I couldn't write anything at all.

I couldn't write because, on June 1, 2005, a new law, Article 301 of the Turkish Penal Code, had made it illegal to insult Turkey, Turkish ethnicity, or Turkish government institutions. A sword now hung above the head of anyone who criticized the rising tide of conservatism and nationalism in our country. Anyone who so much as mentioned the existence of ethnic, religious, or ideological minorities had become the "legitimate" target of ignorant, ultra-nationalist groups. I was among the writers being targeted by the nationalist and conservative press and their internet sites. But it was hard to take them seriously. The accusations flung at writers were so primitive, so intrinsic to fascist discourse, that there was no way to engage with them. The charges brought against writers for the crime of insulting Turkishness were surely too absurd to lead to any indictments by the public prosecutors. Those of us writing articles about these rapidly developing events felt like goalkeepers parrying direct shot after direct shot. It was becoming increasingly difficult to remain calm and steady. In retrospect, it seems obvious that we were headed for a tragedy. At that time, however, we simply didn't want to expect the worst; things were difficult enough as it was without prophecies of doom.

I was unable to write. Because, since I'd rushed back from Paris and speaking with the Armenian Diaspora, it was becoming increasingly difficult for me to put into words all I'd seen. Because my journey was as it should have been.

A true journey doesn't answer a traveler's questions; a true journey changes the traveler's questions. And I now had a whole new set of questions. When people demand the return of a country described in the tales of their grandfathers, what, exactly, are they demanding? Why do they weep as they talk about that country? How can a country just a three-hour flight away seem so remote? Why are they afraid to go to Turkey? Is it going to Turkey that they're afraid of? Is the rage of victims directed only at the perpetrator? What are the corrosive effects of rage on reason and sensibility? Are we obligated to share the pain they suffer? Can an issue that has been so politicized be expected to invoke personal feelings? What did I feel now, after my visit to Paris? What was this sensation of being weighed down? What should I do to feel less burdened?

It wasn't the questions themselves that were exhausting me. It was fear of the way they were forming, of the answers filtering through, of having to write it all down. Or of being unable to write it all down . . .

The newspaper had already suffered a backlash over the Armenia series. And then there were the dangers associated with portraying as "amiable" the far less amiable Diaspora.

I braced myself for the likely reaction: *How dare you cozy up to the enemy! And then you shamelessly write it all down! At a time like this, when the French parliament is passing a law against Turkey, surely the only words to describe the Diaspora are "traitorous" and "backstabbing"!*

I could easily anticipate what would happen. And I knew that no matter how carefully I watered my words down, I would be unable to prevent it. I was unable to write because I was squeezed between the things I'd seen and the things I couldn't and shouldn't write. Here's what I wanted to write:

It's time we recognized the sufferings of others—without having to declare one side wholly guilty, the other side wholly innocent.

But we must first have the courage to understand that perpetrator and sufferer are bound together—only when we're courageous enough to understand this will the stores of hatred dissipate.

In 1915, a dark summer was lived in these lands. Who was guilty, who was stronger—it's been talked over for ninety years. We've always known that something shameful happened that summer, but as we debated the terms we'd use to describe what happened, we glossed over our own need to mourn. Even though we know that everything uprooted and lost to this land leaves a legacy of pain—we know that all too well—what we don't know is this: we're still not talking; the ghosts are talking on our behalf.

Decency demands kind words in response to suffering. Only shouters resort to words that are sharp and crude. In order for sharp words to be replaced by true words and for the whisperings of ghosts to be replaced by the words of the living, the time has come to talk with Armenians and the Diaspora. Those children of ghosts . . .

Because those who assault writers as they're hauled into court are no more representative of my people than those who chant "Recognize the genocide or get lost!" are representative of all the Armenians living in distant lands. The deafening chants on both sides have enabled "our" dead to become bargaining chips on the desks of European diplomats and in the corridors of think tanks. Our ghosts are being picked apart to prove the guilt or innocence of one side or the other. Perhaps that's why they're so angry.

We're weary of all this. In the distant lands in which they've settled, they're tired of living with the dead. Here, we're worn down by our muteness. And our enemies are feeding on our fears.

Is it better to confront fear head-on, or is it better to go slow?

Should a child scared of the water be tossed straight in, or be given time?

If we're tossed into the deep end, do we really learn to swim, or do we become so terrified that we never wish to confront our fears again?

When I look at the streets of Turkey, the second scenario seems the truer. That's why I think stories should be told, but slowly and by degrees. If the label we attach to our pain makes it impossible to discuss that pain, I think priority should be given to our stories, not to our terminology. We need to develop a common story before we decide on a title.

I hope you're amazed by the stories I tell. I hope you wonder at the people I've met. Let's put our ghosts to rest. Because, whether we realize it or not, we've been living in a land where the ghosts are doing the talking. It's exhausted you, me, and all of us.

★

The words above weren't part of the plan. The plan was what Hrant told me when I returned from Armenia: I'd do interviews on the French bill and see how the harsh policies of the Diaspora were straining relations between Turks and Armenians. Hrant was angered by the bill proposing to criminalize "genocide denial." He even said that if the law passed he'd go to France and proclaim that "the genocide never happened" as an act of protest, whatever the punishment. "They're doing anything they can to obstruct dialogue between our people," he said of France when I visited him to ask for some advice. But he was also pleased that I would be talking to members of the Diaspora. "It'll be good, really good," he kept saying.

"It'll be great, just great," Yurttaş kept saying. In November 2005 we'd been in Şemdinli interviewing people on the Kurdish issue after a suspicious bombing and subsequent popular uprising in that eastern city. In July 2006, we'd traveled together to Lebanon. There, as we'd found ourselves without a guide, conducting interviews in a bombed-out Hezbollah-run hospital in southern Lebanon, Yurttaş had grumbled, "Why can't we ever go to a normal country?" That's why, when we returned to Turkey and I told him we'd be going to Paris, he broke out into "Ooh! Champs-Élysées!" immediately after sighing: "At long last, civilization!"

Back in those days, Yurttaş' idea of civilization was a place where bombs didn't go off and where you could sit with freshly polished shoes sipping a cup of coffee. Paris would most definitely meet his criteria. As Yurttaş brushed the Middle Eastern dust off his lens and his shoes, I asked Hrant for the names of the people I should interview and made certain that, this time, we'd get a competent guide and fixer. "Isabelle's an amazing lady," Hrant assured me, "You'll love her." I had no idea what awaited me in Paris in the coming days, or the circumstances under which Isabelle and I would meet in Istanbul some months later.

Chapter 9

"There are three kinds of Armenian"

"DIDN'T I TELL you? Look, here you are, in Paris."
I'm too busy spilling things on a tiny French table in a café across from the Gare du Nord to respond with anything other than "Uh-huh—yes." Which had more or less been the extent of my response to the person in the lobby in Yerevan— the same person now sitting across from me in Paris. Flushed by his vindication by fate, Arto Bülent Kilimli is feeling rather self-satisfied.

"I told you so back in Yerevan, remember?"

"I do," I say. The Armenian issue had been a bit much, and I hadn't been keen to come here. That I'd begun to feel a bit confused and had even considered dropping the project is something I'm unable to confide at that moment, at least not to him. I settle for: "Yes, you're right. You win!"

Further delighted by my ready admission of defeat, he asks, "All right—so what shall we do now?"

Mr. Kilimli may speak Turkish with an elegant Istanbul accent, but he's an Anatolian at heart. Paris is his home; we're his guests.

"But we," I say, referring both to Yurttaş and myself, "we've got to meet with our guide in a minute."

"Hmmm," he reluctantly assents, as I hastily add, "But I'd like to meet and talk whenever it's convenient for you."

He's smiling again. "We'll go to my house. I have some fascinating things to show you. Then I'll take you to a restaurant, followed by a bookshop. And after that . . ." Our program has obviously been prepared well in advance; he was simply waiting for an opening. As I fidget in the face of this outpouring of Anatolian hospitality, Yurttaş squirms at the cramped table, which is what he'll do at every café in Paris. Mr. Kilimli begins to dispense general information about the Diaspora. We're told in which neighborhoods Armenians live, instructed on how to behave when visiting those neighborhoods, and advised to solicit shopkeepers for their views on Turks before revealing that we've just arrived from Turkey. "You see, there are three kinds of Armenian: the first kind are those with ties to Turkey; the second kind may know nothing about Turkey, but harbor no particular antipathy toward Turks; as for the third kind, they're scared of Turkey even though they've never been there. You need to determine which group people belong to when you speak to them."

Scared? Scared of what? I don't have a chance to ask Mr. Kilimli this because, having observed how frequently I've been consulting my watch, he himself quickly rises to his feet. "Call me, then. The minute you call me I'll come and pick you up, wherever you are." As he shakes my hand he says, once again, "See the way I knew you'd be coming here? Armenians are like that: once you meet, you never part."

There's nothing to do but smile and nod in agreement. After all, he was right that I'd come to Paris and right that the Armenian issue would continue to haunt me. As I watch Mr. Kilimli walk off, it occurs to me that I've overlooked an important detail: his name. When we spoke in Yerevan he told me that he wished to appear in my articles as "Arto Bülent Kilimli," emphasizing that if I mentioned him I was to use the Turkish version of his name. I'd done as he wished. But why? As someone who insists on the Turkified version of his name, which category of Armenian does he fall into? What's the story of this cheerful merchant? And does it answer the question of his name?

"So what are we doing now?" Yurttaş poses this question in the aggrieved tone of someone who has been sitting at a cramped table for far too long.

"We haven't got a single Armenian," I say, "and we won't be meeting with our guide for a while yet."

"I get it," he mutters. "We're just killing time."

"Wrong again," I say. "We'll do what all Turks do upon their arrival in Europe."

"And what's that?"

"We'll find some Turks."

★

"To my surprise, that woman was terrified! I didn't realize it at first, but she was truly terrified of Turks."

Metin Ümit is telling us about his encounter with an Armenian woman as he escorts us through the Turkish quarter, which resembles all the other Turkish neighborhoods in Europe. In Turkey, this kind of undiluted Turkishness can only be experienced on certain corners of certain neighborhoods in certain cities. These unrepresentative immigrant quarters must be the reason that Westerners tell visitors from Turkey that they "don't seem Turkish." In fact, I remember a certain young female journalist who so prided herself on the "compliment" of not appearing to be Turkish that she responded, "Thank you very much!"

European Turks also have an issue with not appearing to be overly "Turkish." It's a complex psychological issue.

Metin Ümit, who's busily greeting acquaintances as we stroll along the pavement, doesn't look particularly Turkish either. Even so, we find out that he's sufficiently Turkish to terrify some Parisian Armenians.

Metin Ümit is the director of ACORT, the Association of Citizens of Turkish Origin. An organization that has thrown off the outdated sectarianism of left-wing culture, ACORT encourages residents of Turkish origin in France to participate in the life and politics of their adopted country. The emphasis is on political activity within the framework of "civic rights" rather than through the prism of religious or ethnic differences. Metin Ümit's association is working for change not in distant Turkey but in France, where he lives. Perhaps that's why Ümit, who has worked to distance himself from notions of nation and nationalism, is still trying to understand the reaction of the Armenian woman who confided, when they met, that she was afraid of him. He finishes telling us the astonishing story of that woman, laughs, and adds, "We invited her to some of our meetings and evening activities. She was overwhelmed when she came. She even embraced me and cried."

But according to Ümit, the Armenian Diaspora in Paris is not at all inclined to throw its collective arms around the Turks in a similar show of emotion. "In 2001, as the French National Assembly was passing legislation recognizing the Armenian genocide, our association adopted the position that Turkey should open the pages of its history to discussion. Naturally, there were negative reactions from Turkey; we'd expected that. But what we hadn't anticipated, and what was so astonishing, was that the Armenian Diaspora rejected any kind of dialogue with us."

Ümit says that not only did they fail to get a positive response from Turkey and the Armenian Diaspora in Paris—they also had to contend with "angry Turkish youth": "Whenever a memorial ceremony is held for 1915, nationalists from Turkey arrive in Paris to stage counter-demonstrations on April 24, to declare the genocide 'a lie.' Young Parisian Turks also go and participate. Most of them have no idea what's going on and know nothing about history. But these youths are simmering with a rage related to the problems of migration and poverty. They hear about the demonstrations, and off they go; they're looking for something or someone to shout about in any case. So they shout, and then they go home. Demonstrations like these feed on the anger that comes from the poverty here. But it's precisely because of these demonstrations that the people of France believe that all Turks insult Armenians."

Ümit says that the approval of a bill to criminalize "genocide denial" has only served to further sharpen the lines of conflict, and expresses his belief that Turks, along with the Armenians both in Turkey and Armenia, should react as one to the bill: "A public outcry led to the repeal of a new law stressing the 'positive role' of French colonialism. This law can be repealed as well."

But the representatives of the Diaspora are absolutely determined that the law should stand. Why?

"Because the Diaspora in France doesn't feel the need for a future that includes Turks, whether it's the Turks in Paris or the ones in Turkey. For that matter, I'm not sure they even take the Armenians in Turkey into account. Or at least that's how it appears to us. That's why we need people from Armenia to come to Paris and speak with the Turks here; we need the Diaspora to see that dialogue is possible. Europe needs to see that the Diaspora is pushing for these laws out of self-interest—that they're prepared to sacrifice the Armenians in Turkey, and that they don't attach much importance to the Armenians in Armenia either."

Ümit has adopted a worldview in which no one is "all that Turkish" or "all that Armenian," for which reason he believes in dialogue and compromise. But it's clearly not that easy for a Parisian Turk like him to find a Parisian Armenian counterpart. And the reason for that is that the Turks in Paris are far from home and cling to their Turkish identity, while their Armenian counterparts are most likely filled with the rage brought on by "homelessness."

"There sure are a lot of barbers around here that do dread-locks." Yurttaş is right. After Ümit leaves us on our own in the Turkish district, we notice the peculiarly high number of hair-dressers offering a hairstyle that is anything but "Turkish." In front of the shops are lines of west Africans. It isn't long before we realize that Turks and Africans have been brought together here in Paris by the common fate of poverty. The necessity of sharing a neighborhood has made them "brothers in destiny."

Which is similar to what we saw in Armenia. In order to avoid economic collapse, the Armenia Armenians recognized the need for good relations with Turkey and the opening of the border, and were making an effort to get along with that land of painful memories on their western border. For the Armenians here in Paris, of course, the situation is different: they don't need Turkey, and they don't need to speak to impoverished Turkish immigrants in order to confirm the events of 1915. But what about the Armenians in Istanbul? If the French senate passes the bill criminalizing genocide denial, will the Diaspora Armenians not need the Armenian community in Istanbul—a community Hrant Dink has warned could face grave consequences if the law passes? Does no one care about the prospect of Istanbul Armenians leading lives full of tension? From what Ümit has told me, the representatives of the Diaspora here are concerned only with themselves and with persuading the French to ratchet up the political pressure on Turkey. What about the other Armenian communities and the official "recognition of the genocide" for which they're lobbying various legislative bodies around the globe? Which of their needs would such legislation address?

The consequences for Turks have already been most unpleasant. Armenians, as well as all of the countries that have passed these laws, have been identified in the popular imagination as enemies in a "world that hates Turkey." If the aim of these laws is to encourage Turks to "confront their history," it's failing; it's only causing them to retreat even further into their own homegrown discourse. If the aim of the international community is to isolate Turkey, Turkish politicians will be only too happy to cooperate by affirming that familiar slogan: "The only friend of a Turk is a Turk." There will only be more anger, more deeply entrenched and willful ignorance and blindness, and more hatred: that has been the emotional response of the average Turk. Laws intended to force a people to remember are proving to be most effective at causing them to forget.

And what about the Armenians? The Diaspora Armenians— how do they translate their sufferings into other languages? As they explain what happened to people who know nothing about Armenians and Turks, and as they seek to demonstrate yet again the veracity of their claims, what do they feel? Are they pleased with the decrees and laws their lobbyists help to craft? With having their ghosts picked apart in the corridors of power? Are they all agreed that this is the only way?

My phone rings. Hrant had said Isabelle Kortian would be of help, and she's waiting for us right now in Montparnasse. She's waiting for us in a café, and she's tense. I suspect she doesn't trust us, even though we have Hrant as a reference. She's not going to help us. Just as I feared, we Turks are required once again to pass through multiple layers of security tests before we're deemed trustworthy. To make matters worse, each time I tick off the name of someone I'd like to interview, this attractive woman immediately responds with, "Difficult," "Very diffi- cult," or "Next to impossible." No, she's not going to help us. She's clearly anxious to get rid of us. And all of this is happening because we're Turks. Damn it!

"Excuse me for being in such a hurry," says Isabelle, "but I'm dealing with some health problems." She has no idea how mortified I feel at her words. The Armenian-Turkish issue has so permeated my perceptions that I'd forgotten people might be in a hurry for purely personal reasons. Running through my mind is Armenia, all the interviews, the reactions to my articles, and, finally, the Armenian woman Ümit told me about—the one who was frightened of Turks.

It's not easy to rid yourself of the destiny of your people and the shadows that destiny creates. Even as you pride yourself on having slipped free and fault others for not doing the same, you find yourself tripped up by your own misconceptions.

"Could you give me until tomorrow morning? I need to

reach the people you've mentioned." My guilt-tinged response to Isabelle is overly courteous. We make our farewells.

Yurttaş is reveling in the polished shoes and the French cafés. When he's not busy cracking jokes, he silently admires the animated French girls walking past us. I wonder if these girls are even aware of the Armenian resolutions passed by the legislative assembly elected to represent them. Do they care to know? Both Turks and Armenians have strong if divergent feelings on this subject. Do those French girls feel anything?

That's when I have an idea. "We should call Bernard," I tell Yurttaş.

"Who's Bernard?" he protests. "Why can't we just hang out for a while!"

"Bernard," I inform him, "is the most amazing Frenchman of all time!"

I try to remember when I last saw him. Was it at the Social Forum in Brazil, or was it at the one in India? Perhaps I was changing planes in Bahrain? Or was it in Istanbul? A former activist deeply involved in the French demonstrations of '68, Bernard has a brilliant mastery of national issues from China to the Amazon, and manages to make his explanations as fascinating as they are insightful. Not only is he the perfect person to tell us how the French and the French intelligentsia view the Armenian issue—his work at an NGO umbrella organization gives his words added weight. Bernard and the Armenians . . . "Hmmm, this should be fun," I assure Yurttaş with a smile.

"I hope you're right," he says, before repeating what he always says when we start working like crazy on the first day of a trip: "And no working like crazy this time."

No, of course not . . .

Chapter 10

"If I don't say 'genocide' I won't be able to look myself in the mirror"

"**P**OUF!"

The Gallic exclamation originates somewhere in the vicinity of Bernard's moustache and beard. He shakes his head from side to side, raises his hands into the air, and assumes a disheartened expression even as it's clear he's about to tell an amusing anecdote. "Stupidity! Sheer stupidity!" he cries.

What he labels stupidity is the French law, but Bernard is equally scornful of the botched "dialogue meeting" between the Turkish and Armenian communities living in France. The meetings were supported by the Helsinki Citizens' Assembly within the framework of the "Gamatz Gamatz" project,[5] but when Armenian radio announced that these meetings were being "organized by the Turks!" the Armenians decided to boycott them. When the reason for the cancellation was announced, Turkish nationalists upped the ante with an attempted raid on the radio station. Typically, Bernard, who was one of the organizers of the meeting, narrates the entire affair as a drawing room comedy with a surprising dénouement: "And so in the end, dialogue took place not in Lyon, but in another city;

5 "Gamatz Gamatz," which literally means "slowly, slowly" in Armenian, started as a youth seminar in the Turkish city of Antakya in 2005, and evolved into a project that scheduled regular discussion groups for Turks and Armenians.

and not between Turks and Armenians, but between Turks and Azerbaijanis!"

Bernard's narrative is a bit difficult to follow, what with all the slamming doors and dramatic monologues, but the moral of the play is clear: encounters between Armenians and Turks tend to produce rather unsatisfactory results. "The Turks accused the Armenians of not talking to them. The Armenians then spoke to the Turks, but only of the genocide, and thus considered themselves exonerated of the charge."

What about the French? What did intellectual circles make of the debate between the Armenians and the Turks as the law was being debated in the assembly?

"In this particular match we, the French, were confined to the bench!" Bernard shrugs, smiles, and adds, "Which is probably just as well. Because none of us have ever fully considered the issue. The arguments and the proposed law have forced French intellectuals to give serious thought to the Armenians for the first time. And to tell you the truth, no one has the faintest idea what to say. Everyone's aghast, because this law is so obviously ridiculous!"

"Just a moment," Bernard murmurs as he digs into his bag and produces a copy of *Politis*.[6] He shows me an article on the subject in the latest issue:

> Only hard-line Armenian nationalists want this law. It's obvious that the law disturbs the Armenians in Turkey and would impede historical research. This law will simply fuel the agendas of national-ist Turks and Armenians. This law will deal a death blow to efforts to uncover the facts surrounding the historical events whose memory it claims to want to preserve. But I know that, in Turkey, Kardeş Türküler will continue to write songs with lyrics from Armenian poet Charentz. And I also know that this will far better serve the future of Armenians and Turks than this stupid law.

★

6   A weekly left-wing newspaper in France.

Isabelle freezes. She's wondering how to translate the question I've asked; perhaps she's considering not translating it at all. But it's too late. I may be speaking English, but the term ASALA (Armenian Secret Army for the Liberation of Armenia)[7] is easily identified in any language. Aran Toranian, who is sitting directly across from me, immediately understands what I'm asking. Without waiting for a translation, he shakes his head from side to side several times.

"No, I wouldn't say I was a member. But I had close ties to ASALA."

Toranian might be sitting across from me denying with a straight face that he was ever a member of ASALA, but every article about him says otherwise. According to numerous sources, his political activities began while he was studying law at Sorbonne University, when he became the leader of Mouvement National Armenien, the political wing of ASALA. But now, this placid, middle-aged man seated in a Parisian café holding a copy of *Nouvelle Arménie*, the magazine of which he is editor-in-chief, is acting as though none of that ever happened. Furthermore, he seems to believe he needs to explain what ASALA was all about.

"As you might know, ASALA disbanded itself. And I abandoned ASALA when they began advocating 'violence against violence.'"

Although reluctant at first to speak on the subject, he suddenly begins speaking unprompted, leaning over the table and gesticulating as he tries to make himself understood. "ASALA is not the be-all or end-all of the Armenian issue. There used to be a wall of

---

7   An international terrorist organization founded in Beirut in 1975, ASALA was responsible for at least eighty-four incidents in over a dozen countries, primarily targeting Turkish diplomatic staff and their families. As part of their stated campaign "to compel the Turkish government to acknowledge publicly its responsibility for the deaths of 1.5 million Armenians in 1915, pay reparations, and cede territory for an Armenian homeland," ASALA killed forty-six people and injured 299.

silence concerning the genocide, both in Turkey and France. At first, the organization played a constructive role in tearing down this wall. More accurately, we had no other choice. The issue had been swept under the carpet, and we had to expose it. Turkey continued to execute a policy aimed at silencing the Diaspora, and, starting in the 1970s, this same policy was used to exert pressure on the French government. This continued until the 1980s. Before ASALA, no one was talking about the Armenian issue. Once ASALA had served its purpose, there was no reason for me to support them. After that, our mission was to disseminate information and to work for recognition of the genocide."

Toranian has dedicated himself to just that for thirty-five years. But why?

"Our mission is never to forget, and to put a name to what happened. For us, 1915 is a historical legacy, and we have to acknowledge this legacy. But, even more importantly, I've taken a vow. Saying 'genocide' allows me to look myself in the mirror every morning. But my dreams aren't what they used to be, of course."

Toranian takes a short breath and, adopting a surprisingly conciliatory tone, returns to his past. "Everyone has a dream. My dream is for Turks and Armenians to create a common future, which will only be possible through the establishment of a common past. Even if we can't change the past, we can create a future free of animosity."

With the conversation having suddenly taken a conciliatory turn, I ask him whether the Diaspora is really determined to engage with Turks. I also mention the differences in approach between Armenia and the Diaspora.

"There are, of course, practical reasons for Armenia and Turkey to forge a shared future," he says. "But for the Diaspora, Turkey is nothing more than a country that eradicated its people and for ninety years has engaged in propaganda claiming the genocide never happened. The Armenian community here isn't powerful enough to combat an entire country."

"There are many people in Turkey who think otherwise," I tell him. "In fact, the majority of people think that lobbying by the Diaspora has cast a shadow over Turkey's political future."

Toranian rejects that notion. "It's typical nationalist propaganda to claim that the Diaspora is powerful. If the majority really believe that, it's due to the manipulation of the ruling classes. But of course we're active. We're struggling for a cause. If we appear to be so powerful to Turkey, it might be because we're fighting for justice."

He speaks so knowledgeably of Turkey that I ask him if he's ever visited, even if in secret. He falls into his longest silence since the interview began. "That's the most difficult question of all. One day, when they erect a memorial to the genocide—which means a long time from now!" I'm surprised that he talks about Turkey, a country last seen by his grandfather, with such feeling. What about Armenia? Are his feelings for that country as strong as they are for Turkey? The words he chooses to talk about Armenia strike me as formal rather than at all emotional. "It's a wonderful country. Naturally, I'm pleased that the nation of Armenia exists over there. It's a concrete manifestation of the existence of Armenians. A ray of hope. We in the Diaspora are helping Armenia more and more. But we also have a lot of work to do here."

When I point out his lack of passion in discussing Armenia, Toranian seems troubled. "It's difficult to be a member of the Diaspora. Our sense of dispossession has caused us great suffering. We've always felt the need for a motherland, for our own country in our ancestral lands. You can't possibly understand what it's like." Toranian talks about his grandmother from Van, his mother born in İzmir, his family abandoning Istanbul. And he hasn't seen a single one of those cities! He seems to tremble at the very mention of a visit to Turkey. How odd that this former member of a violent, armed organization would be scared of "ghosts." It's truly hard to believe he was involved even to the slightest extent with an organization that assassinated Turkish diplomats and their families, and that detonated a bomb at Orly Airport. Perhaps rage can mellow over the years into something else. The days when Toranian "suffered rootlessness" and fed on rage in order to look himself in the mirror seem distant indeed. He shows us the last page of the magazine he edits, slowly, eagerly.

To Yurttaş' shouted instructions, I pose on the pavement with this mild-mannered man and ask myself what exactly ASALA thought they were punishing Turks for as they were gunning down Turkish diplomats. Were they simply avenging what had happened to their grandfathers? Or did their rage originate, at least in part, somewhere inside themselves? There was that woman Metin described, the one scared of Turks; and now there's this strapping man standing next to me, the one visibly shaken at the mere thought of visiting Turkey. What are they afraid of, really? Is it the Turks, or is it something else? I have to wait for a few more days to get an answer to this question.

"Good-bye, see you," he says, cheerfully squeezing my hand. Perhaps, having found a Turk he could really talk to, a tin soldier has just turned into a real person in Toranian's mind. And that's why the smile spreading across his face seems so very human to me. It's a childish smile—connected, somehow, to childhood.

And what about me? If I were the child of one of the dozens of Turkish diplomats killed by ASALA, would I have allowed Ara Toranian to take my hand? I'm not sure.

The interview successfully concluded, Isabelle is breathing more easily. She's astonished that Toranian has spoken so freely. We have no time to discuss it: she's still in a hurry. "You'll be meeting with Alexis Govjian—in an hour, at Café Le Select," she says as she runs off. I'd decided not to jump to conclusions after learning of her "health issues," but her brusqueness is still making me tense and reserved. I can't shake the impression that she's keeping her distance, even as I see that she has something she wants to say. And perhaps she will, in a few days.

In this land of cafés, Yurttaş and I seem to be continuously shuttling between them, confronted by an endless stream of talking faces. As I wait to interview the next face, I glance at the photographs on the walls of Café Le Select. There's one of Hemingway, brandishing a cigar and defying the world. I'm so engrossed in the photos that I don't notice the stealthy battle underway between Yurttaş and the waiters, all of whom have apparently taken a solemn oath to uphold the French language. By the time I notice, it's already too late.

"I'm telling you, I don't speak French. *Allahım yarabbim ya!*[8] *Un café s'il vous plait!* I'm saying '*s'il vous plait*,' *arkadaş!*"[9] He turns to me. "He knew exactly what I meant! What a joker!" This battle will continue for days. Yurttaş is convinced that French waiters are slothful, ill-tempered to a man, and absolutely loathe him.

The faces blur: Hemingway, who, back in the day, sparred in boxing matches so he could drink at Café Le Select; Yurttaş, who's seeking any pretext to quarrel with the waiters; and Ara Toranian, who's busy grappling with the ghosts of a country he's never seen. Land, bread, power, and being wired to throttle someone over their pronunciation. I don't understand any of it, perhaps because it's these types of men who have built the world of today and who have written all the subtexts. Were women able to rewrite history, who knows, perhaps the final lines of the latest chapter would end differently. Perhaps things would be a little less bloodthirsty. And perhaps I wouldn't feel at all guilty for having empathized with Ara Toranian. Perhaps . . .

"I hope I haven't kept you waiting for long."

Alexis Govjian releases a string of courtesies as he sits down. I miss most of what he says because I see Özgür through the window, walking past. Özgür and I will get to know each other much better at a later date, but this young doctoral student in International Law at the Sorbonne will tell me the funniest story I've ever heard about the Armenians the very next night.

8   "For God's sake!"
9   "Buddy."

Chapter 11

"We're passing on traditions, not rage"

"NO, I CAN'T speak it. I've forgotten. It's better like this." It's only near the end of the interview, when Alexis Govjian begins telling me his personal history and reciting the names of various Istanbul districts, that his fluency in Turkish emerges. I break into Turkish, but he continues in English. "I've forgotten," he insists, "I don't remember anymore." Is it possible to forget the language of the country in which you were born and lived until the age of seventeen? Has he so thoroughly abandoned the country of his birth as to believe he's even forgotten the language?

"I would never have left Turkey," Govjian says, "if I'd been able to talk about the genocide."

The dark suit, the soft-spoken manner, the ability to deliver even the harshest words with a smile—what we have here is a political organizer. Someone whose job is to sway people. Considering the ease with which he unhesitatingly responds to my questions, this is a man practiced in the talking points of genocide. Govjian is speaking on behalf of a confederation of 200 different Armenian organizations, including churches, schools, charities, and youth groups. He begins by expressing not his personal views, but those of the Armenian Diaspora in France. "The members of the Diaspora here don't hold to account the Turks that are alive today. But we have a history we need to share and discuss. Why, ninety years later, is Turkey still at exactly the same point? That's the problem. And now they've gone and formed the Talat Pasha Committee."

Govjian explains how they're combating the Talat Pasha Committee, a lobbying group that presents ultra-nationalist arguments to defend Turkey's official policy against the Diaspora. One day one side applies pressure on a local municipality, at which the other group digs in its heels, which leads to a demonstration the next day, followed by a counter-demonstration, then protests and petitions—and on and on.

So great is the growing zeal with which he elucidates these intricacies, I forget for a moment that we're discussing a great tragedy. I glance up at the photograph of Hemingway the pugilist, at that ecstatic expression of manhood unleashed. The fast-talking Govjian is looking more and more like that photo by the minute. I ask him about the bill that would outlaw "genocide denial," and mention how Hrant Dink criticized it as certain to harm the Armenians in Turkey, in particular, and dialogue building in general. "If the passage of this law really does harm the Armenians in Turkey, it will demonstrate what a poor record Turkey has when it comes to the treatment of its minorities. That should concern not only the Armenians but every democrat in Turkey."

A supporter of the bill, Govjian has a ready response to any of my questions on the issue, with arguments and positions well prepared in advance. He sums up the reason for his support as follows: "We want this law to counter ultra-nationalist Turks who demonstrate against Armenians in France. We want it to protect Armenians in France." We both know that the law will affect the lives of the Armenians in Turkey as much as it affects those of the Armenians in France. He's right, of course, to criticize Turkey on the subject of rights and freedoms. But he can also foresee the negative impact the law will have on Turkey's Armenian community. But Govjian is resolute. "Like I said, that's Turkey's problem. I wish we didn't need this law. But it's the Turkish nationalists who have forced our hand. They exaggerate the power of the Diaspora, even going so far as to claim that Orhan Pamuk won the Nobel Prize because of us—as if we spoke to God every day. We're not as powerful as Turkey thinks. Yes, I support this bill, but denying the genocide doesn't make someone a criminal: it makes him an idiot."

"That attitude suggests you're not the advocate of dialogue with Turkey that you claim to be," I say.

Govjian laughs. "It isn't an issue between Turks and Armenians," he says. "It's a political issue."

And thus Govjian makes his position crystal clear. I argue that stripping politics of a human face is wrong, that such an approach is ultimately dehumanizing, that it obstructs dialogue. Govjian lays his cards on the table. "So, we should just talk about other things. That's all very well, but we won't get anywhere by sidestepping the most important turning point in our history." He pauses, and adds, "The Diaspora is Anatolian!" That he says this in France, in English, and as someone who has retreated as far as possible from all things Anatolian, is of course the height of irony. My face must have betrayed my bemusement, for it is now that Govjian decides to tell me his own story—in English, of course.

"I was a student at Pangaltı Lycée, in Istanbul. Neither my mother nor my father had ever told me about the events of 1915. One day, we were discussing the famous Armenian composer Komitas during a literature lesson. I was fifteen at the time. I asked my teacher why so many of the prominent Armenians had been killed in 1915. He told me to come to his room after the lesson. My friends all thought I was in terrible trouble. When I went to my teacher's room, he said, 'I'm going to tell you something, but you're not to tell anyone else.' That's when I learned about what had happened and the deaths. When I got home I asked my mother about it. Without a word, she took me by the hand and led me to an old man who worked as a caretaker at the Armenian cemetery in Şişli. He told me about those days. And that was the day I decided that future generations had to learn what I'd learned. When I came here to attend university I was finally in a place where I could speak freely, and took up this cause."

So when did he tell his own children about 1915?

"I told my sons when they turned twelve or thirteen. But I also explained that the things I told them shouldn't make them angry with all Turks."

"Is that possible, Mr. Govjian?" I ask with a smile.

"We don't teach rage. We simply pass on a tradition. And it's something we have to do." Perhaps feeling he's strayed too far into the personal, Govjian repeats, "This isn't an issue between Turks and Armenians. It's a political issue."

★

"We haven't taught you any of the marches or made you memorize revolutionary poems."

That's what my mother said when we were growing up. I suspect she wanted to share the secrets of raising good children with her children. "Some teach those things. But they've always seemed silly to me." It's true. My brother and I weren't at all like the other children our age born into left-wing families after the 1971 coup. We hadn't learned the marches, the poems and the slogans.

We're the gendarmes, the socialists / Your only true friends . . .

The catchphrases and watchwords were like toys designed to help alleviate the sorrow of a revolution that never came. Eyes fixed on a point in the distance, they'd show off their skills and hold dear to what they'd learned by rote.

May first! May first! Holiday of the worker and the proletariat!

My brother and I weren't taught these things. But as we began learning to read, we'd look at the spines of the books in the library:

"Le . . . Le . . . nin. Lenin! Tr . . . Trot . . . sky . . . Trotsky!"

For children just learning to read, those unattainable books are strictly for adults, and retain a totemic quality even much later in life. They belong always to the world of adults. Only later, when grown-ups can't answer your question, and the answer is found in the encyclopedia, does the knowledge contained in those leather-bound volumes suddenly seem accessible.

Nobody wanted us to read those books, and neither my mother nor my father explained to us what had happened before the coup of 1980.[10] But you find out even if they don't tell you—because the faces of those shot dead are shown on television. Sometimes your mother and father jump up in horror; at other times you understand from the expressions on their faces that those faces on the television don't belong to "one of us." No one explains a thing, but if you pay close attention you'll find out who "they" are and who "we" are. You also learn that we are good and they must be evil—because they kill people who look like your mother and father . . .

Early one morning, an eight-year-old girl on the day of a coup, you now understand the meaning of the expression "the break of dawn," and you also understand that evil has overrun the city. You'll have to grow up fast and save the city, and your mother and father. They're listening to the radio, clinging to each other for support. Wreaths of cigarette smoke swirl against the indigo sky of daybreak, like water swirling whitely in a glass of *rakı*.

★

Water is swirling in a glass of *rakı* as you sit at a table on a university campus with friends raised just like you, and you sing folk songs together for the dead men and women who were revolutionaries, just like your parents. You grieve. You grieve as you sing dirges for those young men and women, those leftist

10   Politically motivated civil unrest caused at least 5,000 deaths in Turkey in the late 1970s. The military overthrew the civilian government on September 12, 1980, and restored order by detaining up to 650,000 people, of which 230,000 were tried, 14,000 were stripped of their citizenship, and fifty were executed.

progressives, now dead. Why? Because young people have been killed? Is that the reason? Because the people of your country have been killed by fascism? Is that the reason? Because people like your mother and father have been defeated? Is that the reason? As you sit at that table with everyone else, nothing said, how do you know you're all mourning the same thing?

There's more to it than that. There's the knowledge passed on to you as a child. Whether you realize it or not, it's been internalized and it's shaped your beliefs and attitudes all through your life. It's the distinction between good and evil. Even before you were old enough to work out the words on the spines of those books, a sense of good and evil was passed on to you, without a word being spoken. Much later, you cry not only because a certain person is dead or because a certain group has died at the hands of another group: you cry because "evil" has prevailed over "good." You're good; that means you've been defeated too. But who taught you that? How did they teach you? Who told you that you must always defend good against evil, and when? As you take part in demonstrations at university, you feel as though you're a continuation of your parents, doing your duty to defend what is good, just as they did. This is your duty to your mother, and to your father, and to what's right and good. And now, even if they telephone from a distant city and half-heartedly attempt to dissuade you from going to a demonstration, it's as futile as trying to make you unlearn something—because you're "good" and on the side of what's right. Can you possibly go over to the "bad" side? This is what it means to be part of a family.

★

In the dark blue of daybreak cigarette smoke is swirling, like water in *rakı*. You're mourning the grandfather you never knew—the grandfather forced to leave his country because he was Armenian, like you. You sit alone, grieving, because when you were a child you saw the grown-ups sitting and talking at night about the old times and the old country. Some of them cried. You see your mother. She's upset, because she's good and there are bad people who make her cry. And so it is that children grow up to save their mothers and fathers one day—sometimes from the fascists, sometimes from the "terrible Turks," but always from "evil," whatever that might be. It's through their mothers that children learn what must be done.

In the same way I'm now compelled to write articles demanding an accounting for days I myself haven't experienced, they're trying to pass laws in the French Assembly for their mothers and fathers. Every April 24 they shout in the streets, and each time they're recreating the "good" in themselves and the "evil" they're combating. So, instead of passing laws, debating historical details, and conducting lobbying activities based on opposing views of times past, could we perhaps discuss all of this in more depth?

Were those now living in the ancestral lands of the Armenians in eastern Turkey to try to remember what has caused them to "forget"—that is, to "remember" only in a certain way; were an Armenian to try to remember what it is that makes him weep for a land he's never seen—perhaps then we could gain a better understanding of how our present selves have been shaped, and how we've internalized "good" and "evil."

★

"Most of my generation left because of the events of September 6–7.[11] Otherwise, why would I have left the joys of my country?

11   The homes, businesses, and churches of the ethnic Greek population in Istanbul were targeted by mobs on September 6–7, 1955. To a lesser extent, the Armenian and Jewish minorities were also subjected to indiscriminate looting and arson. At least fifteen people were killed, and over 5,000 properties were damaged. The mobs are believed to have been trucked into the city by a counter-insurgency organization that also planted rumors that the Turkish consulate in Thessalonica, the birthplace of Mustafa Kemal Atatürk, had been bombed. The previous year, Greece had appealed to the UN for self-determination for Cyprus, which had been under Ottoman control from 1571 until 1915, when the island was annexed by the UK.

To tell the truth, the events of 1915 seemed far away to us. But I was totally traumatized by the sudden attacks on us over those two days in Istanbul in 1955."

It's only near the end of the interview that Varujan Srabian tells me this, and only after first talking about "politics." The middle-aged man sitting across from me in the café explaining political details didn't look at all like the type of man to become emotional. His words suggested he preferred not to discuss the personal. But he was a graduate of Robert College, in Istanbul. He'd arrived in Paris at age twenty-five. He'd become politi- cally active, along with Chirac, in Union Mouvement Populaire in 1976, and in "Armenian politics" starting in 1994. Srabian continued to follow a liberal democratic line as a member of Ramgavar, an Armenian political party active both in Armenia and among the Diaspora. After serving as party general chair- man from 1995 to 2005, he became director of the Chobanian Institute, which he'd founded in 2004.

"Chobanian was born in Beşiktaş, Istanbul, in the 1870s. At the age of eight or nine he began translating from the French. The Armenian Committee, which was formed in response to the slaughter of Armenians by the Hamidiye Brigades in 1895, sent him to Paris to explain what was happening in Anatolia. He told the intellectuals of Paris about it. In 1954, he died in Paris. We established the institute on the fiftieth anniversary of his death, around the same time that Turkey was resuming accession talks with the European Union. We felt that the French press didn't know enough about the Armenian issue, just as they hadn't back in Chobanian's time. Chobanian wrote that the French govern- ment had ignored the letters sent by the French ambassador in Istanbul. And so we established the Institute to reveal aspects of historical events that have been ignored or concealed."

So that's why this French citizen withdrew from national politics, joined the "Armenian lobby," and began working to shape attitudes concerning the events of 1915. Like everyone else involved in that cause, he's angry at Turkey, but is also trying to understand Turks.

"It's normal for Turks not to know anything, and to be shocked when they find out. But to deny . . ." He falls silent. It's as though he remembers that he's talking not to a citizen of France but to a Turk, and he begins explaining not from the "outside" but from the "inside": "I know how difficult this is for Turkey, psychologically difficult. I know that."

And that's when he begins telling me his own story. It happens every time. Every Armenian I've spoken to has begun with the "standard" approach tailored to the French, and then switched their approach somewhere along the way. It's even more striking when the person who does this has once lived in Turkey. "I didn't know anything about what it meant to be Armenian until I turned twenty-five. It was here that I learned. It was here that I read things written by Armenians. And I have to admit that the first books I read weren't particularly objective, and dwelt only on the sufferings of Armenians. It wasn't what I read that made me so angry; it was the fact that I didn't know anything. I'd completed university, but I didn't know a thing."

Why didn't he know anything?

"Atatürk was the best thing that happened to Turkey. But he can't be criticized in Turkey. I'm a Gaullist in France, but I'm free to criticize de Gaulle. Atatürk and those who came after Atatürk rewrote history. Modern Turkey is rooted in a certain ideology. When I was young I thought that Turkey's greatest problem was religious divisions. But I later learned that the ultra-nationalism that feeds on the founding ideology is a greater problem. Currently, Turkey is simultaneously experiencing the twin dangers of religious extremism and nationalist extremism."

The Ramgavar Party[12] is more open to dialogue with Turkey than, say, the nationalist Hinchaks. That's why I ask Srabian what percentage of the Diaspora would be open to building

12   Also known as the Armenian Democratic Liberal Party, the Ramgavar Party was one of the first Armenian political parties to be established in the Ottoman Empire.

dialogue. "Fifty percent," he says, adding, "But you need to be careful when you use the word 'dialogue.' That word has a different meaning in different places. There's a major divergence of opinion between the Armenians of America and those of France. It's a difficult game, this. When we're talking to the administrations of the countries in which we live, we all have to explain in detail exactly what we mean by the word 'dialogue.'"

It must be tiring, I suggest, to explain all of this in a foreign language to people who know absolutely nothing about it. I also ask him what he means when he says it's a "difficult game." "It's a political game, of course. Take Europe and Turkey, for example: if the EU is opposed to Turkish membership because of religion, but is using the Armenian issue as a pretext, that would be duplicitous. There are three different games within the game: the game Europe is playing against Turkey, the game Europe is playing against its own people and the Armenians, and the game Turkey is playing against its own people."

He stops and waits for me to take notes. He smiles to himself, and suddenly says, "Citizen, speak Turkish!" He studies my face to see if I understand the reference, and understands that, yes, I do remember reading about this nationalist slogan.[13] "It was even forbidden to say 'mama.'" For a moment, neither of us speaks. A serious expression suddenly spreads across his face as he steps out of his own life and back into the political arena. "Our slogan is this: 'To forget is betrayal!'" He repeats that last word: "Betrayal!"

As Srabian talks, where is he coming from? Where is he going to? There's obviously more to this "difficult game" than the war of strategies among the political actors. There's also a personal element. And, like all political activities and movements that fail to account fully for the human element, we find we're at

---

13   The "Citizen, speak Turkish!" campaign aimed to broaden the use of Turkish in the 1920s and 1930s by pressuring non-Turkish speakers to speak Turkish in public.

the mercy of the corrosive interplay of the political and the personal, the external and the internal. A single word can lead us to personal reflection, but the fear of becoming overly personal can cause us to grasp at one of those external words—the ones that draw us back into the world of the political. A familiar face or a kind word can transport us back to a time when we were still internalizing "good" and "evil." But the fear of going soft can suck us back into the political realm, to the hard and fast rules of the "difficult game." And as for the place where, and the moment when, "good" and "evil" were embedded within—that journey to the heart of the Diaspora will have to wait for another day.

Chapter 12

Good vs. Evil

"NO, NO! I didn't say anything like that."
In fact, I'd asked him several times if he was speaking on the record. "I don't want you to be upset when it's published," I'd said. Even so, he was furious when the newspaper published a transcript of the following lively interview in Paris. I sent him a letter asking which part of the interview was objectionable; he never responded. And the reason he didn't respond was that I'd written exactly what he'd said. In the following pages, I've decided not to reveal the identity of the person in question, but to reproduce here his exact words.

I suspect the real reason for his anger was that he'd remembered something. He'd realized that his view of good and evil had crystallized at some point, and that he had unquestioningly maintained this view up to the present. Worst of all, he was shaken that he had revealed all of this to a "Turk." He was angry because he'd said things that shouldn't be said to a Turk. He'd shared his mother's tears with "evil." And the publication of this "betrayal" in the newspaper had prompted his very human reaction of anger, and in turn caused him to deny everything. What was it that he felt he had to repudiate? What was so terrible that he felt he had to contradict an interview witnessed by Isabelle, another interpreter, and Yurttaş?

★

It's a delightful French autumn day. The young people in the garden café are flirtatious and tipsy on wine, but our table is the scene of some tension. Yet again, naturally, we're discussing the Armenian issue. And however much the Armenian intellectual seated with us says he supports dialogue, he doesn't hesitate to add, "The Turks treated the Armenians like dogs." He knows that this Turkish journalist will be taking his words to "the Turks," so he adds a bit of sting even as he tries to be objective.

"Most Armenians have that attitude; they don't distinguish between the Turkish government and the Turkish people. As for me, I don't believe the Turkish people are in a state of denial—but their government certainly is. There are extremists both within the Diaspora and in Turkey. What upsets me most is that books on the subject aren't being read in Turkey. That bothers me. If more people read, they'd see things differently. I don't favor any restrictions on speech. And I regard those Turkish intellectuals engaged on this subject as my brothers. But both sides have their barriers, of course. I understand Turkish denialists. Several generations have been traumatized by this narrative. When the Armenians were massacred in 1915, the Turks treated us like dogs. We still bear the scars of that."

"So what's the barrier for Armenians?"

"When they told us about the Turks it was with hatred, because the ones doing the talking had experienced a massacre. That's why there are still people my age who haven't set foot in Turkey. But, as for me, I traveled all through Turkey twenty-five years ago."

"You didn't say 'genocide,' you said 'massacre,'" I point out.

"It doesn't make any difference." He shrugs.

"But," I point out, "it's that particular word that's causing all the hostility."

He dismisses it as semantics, and adds, "That term was coined many years later. But the Turks most definitely relocated the Armenians in order to exterminate them. That was, of course, their real intention."

I suggest to him that words bear responsibility for creating barriers.

"Each side has different code words. For example, there were Turks back then who tried to save Armenians, but not much is known about them. If they knew more about history, perhaps our codes would balance each other out." I ask him if he thinks this "balancing of codes" and dialogue is possible. He reflects for a moment. "It's a sensitive situation. Some Armenians would never agree to dialogue, and are others are prepared to moderate their language. In the final analysis, Armenians and Turks are in the same boat. But Turkey is living a lie. And they know they'll have to pay the consequences when everyone realizes they're resting on a foundation of lies. We can see that Turkey wants to be European, but that won't happen until it resolves the Armenian issue."

But doesn't he agree that the bill passed by the French assembly will make dialogue more difficult?

"Punitive laws are bad. But they're necessary sometimes. We, the Diaspora, have no choice but to support this law. Some Turks have exceeded the limits of free speech. Armenians can't be expected to tolerate that."

But most of the Armenians in Turkey oppose laws like this one. What does he think about that?

"I understand the Armenians in Turkey. But I haven't met a single Frenchman who doesn't agree that we need this law. We have been waiting for respect for ninety-one years. It's been a long time. I'm sixty-four years old, and I've been working for this since I was eighteen. I've been living in an atmosphere of genocide ever since I was eighteen. I also became a member of some ultra-nationalist organizations. But I've learned my lesson. I know Turkey blames the Armenian lobby for the genocide issue. But there's no monolithic Armenian lobby: each individual Armenian is a one-man lobby."

"What makes each Armenian a lobby?" I ask. "How could each Armenian become a lobby? I mean, can you dig deeper and explain what you mean?"

He carefully considers my question for a moment. And when he does speak, he's halting and tentative, which means we've entered uncharted territory. "As a writer, I've always written about exile. The poems I wrote at age twenty dealt with exile, even though I was born in France. The exile of my mother's family has worked its way into my consciousness. That's why I don't feel French. When I go to Armenia, I don't feel as though I belong there either. That feeling never goes away: we're like the world's homeless people. I suppose my mindset has been shaped by what my mother told me."

He doesn't expect me to ask a follow-up question. He reflects for a moment and begins speaking again, as though talking to himself.

"My mother and her family would sit and talk at night, here in France, with other people who were forced as children to abandon their village. They'd talk about that village as though it were perfect. After a while, they came to feel as though they'd been driven from paradise. That's how the ancient Armenian lands have come to take on legendary, mythical proportions for me. It's a vision, of course—a dream. And in any case, my generation is a generation of dreams."

"So you're chasing after dreams," is all I say.

"Back then, our mothers were deprived of their childhoods. Anyone who goes to Turkey sees that the places aren't at all as described by our elders. We've dedicated our lives to a mythical land. Frankly, that's why I think Armenians are a bit crazy: there's this bizarre idea that we don't belong to the place where we were born."

"And so is trying to salvage your mothers' childhood memories," I add. "Their descriptions of a country remembered from childhood can only be as objective as anyone else's childhood memories. It really must be a bit strange for a generation to base its realities upon the childhood memories of their parents and grandparents—and for those childhood memories to shape the lives of their own children."

He responds, "Their missing childhoods have obliterated my childhood as well. How could we possibly have lived our own childhoods, overshadowed as they were by our parents' childhood stories! I didn't tell my children about 1915 so they wouldn't have to go through the same thing. But my mother and my grand-mother have told them, of course. So now they know . . ."

The interview had begun normally enough, and I hadn't expected him to dig so deep. By the end, he seemed to be listening to the words coming from his own mouth—watching as the words welled up from deep inside. Words like an illusionist's handkerchiefs, one thought leading to another, one word tugging along the next. There was no telling where his words would take him. His mother's lost childhood—his own childhood—the lost childhood of a generation was devouring the childhood of later generations. So that's how the Diaspora was proliferating as "a land of lost childhoods." And that's why nearly all the Armenians of the Diaspora spoke the way they did—as if speaking of the sufferings of children.

I ran through all the people I'd interviewed—the ones in Armenia, in Paris. In all cases, the stories they'd heard as children had become part of their own childhoods, for all of them. And what's more, the childhood stories they'd been told had been expressed with a child's pain. The Diaspora was composed of children wishing to salvage their mothers' childhoods and trying to assuage unbearable pain. That was the source of the rage. If your mother had been robbed of her childhood, wouldn't you, too, advance into the arena with your sword drawn?

The suffering of children is always great, because children are so helpless. Perhaps that's why, whenever I speak to an Armenian, I'm told, "Turkey is powerful and we're power-less." Perhaps that's why their pain, however much it may be expressed in adult terms, is rooted in childhood.

What is it that makes people want to transmit their painful stories to succeeding generations? Why do people wish to pass along pain? *That* is the question.

★

"Then they took me and stuck a wire into my ear. 'That should open it up,' the prison doctor laughed. Ever since that day my ear gets blocked whenever I'm very upset. To stop me from hearing, probably. That might be why my ears first got blocked up when they took me in. So I wouldn't be able to hear anything."

I must have been in primary school the first time my mother told me about being a political prisoner in 1971, two full years before I was born. I still remember the minute details of her story, the exact words she used; how hot it was, what my mother was wearing, how embarrassed she was when her skirt rode up as she was being interrogated, the color of the eyes of the policemen who questioned her . . . I grew up thinking something similar would happen to me one day, fearing that it would happen, and always taking an interest in political issues so that, perhaps, it would happen. Perhaps I too am a child of loss—just like the Armenians, and like so many others. But my mother—why did she tell me all this when I was still a child? Didn't she realize how young I was? Couldn't she have anticipated that the glare of her story would cast shadows across my mind?

Victims heal by recounting what's happened to them. The act of recounting is intrinsic to the act of healing. By loving us unconditionally and by sharing the genetics of our pain, our children are the allies best placed to alleviate our loneliness. We release them into the future, these glass bottles into which we seal our hopes, our expectations, our dreams, and our vows. Perhaps that's how we avenge the injustices we've suffered. When we're unable to reach our tormentors, we share the victim's sense of isolation with our children, with our tribe. We create a new "I"—one who will one day get to our tormentors. This is a human and perhaps instinctive act of solidarity in reaction to the injustice and isolation dealt us by life. And as we reproduce, our pain too is reborn.

And so we continue to transmit our painful stories to succeeding generations, even if they feed on our childhood and devour our children.

★

Isabelle, Yurttaş, and I are walking past the Louvre. In museums, we seek to preserve and display all that is most valuable about our past. But where lies the repository for the detritus of human history and for our collective pain? Could it be our children? Could the millions of lives that aren't on display in museums be stored up in our children, within whose tender skins the old painful memories are kept fresh and alive? Children who suffer because they always feel they haven't suffered enough, children who don't realize that it can be as damaging to listen to tales of atrocities as it was to endure those same atrocities firsthand.

★

"I've got something to say." Isabelle asks for a cigarette. "There's this business of 'not a single Armenian opposes the genocide denial law . . .'"

A normally sedate woman in her early forties, she lights her cigarette with elegant rage.

"There's more to it than that. They all whip themselves into a fury as they talk about Turkey, as though the Turks are the only ones who've tried to silence us, but I don't understand why they always seem to forget what happened right here in France. They've apparently forgotten that it was in France that Armenian youths were rounded up and hauled away from churches holding memorials marking the genocide."

She seems to grow sad. She was silent during the Ara Toranian interview, silent when I told her about Govjian, and silent throughout this last, long interview, but she's speaking now as the "alternative voice" of the Diaspora. "They wouldn't allow people to speak up about 1915. For many years in France not a single soul listened when we talked about 'genocide.' In the late '70s, young people handing out pamphlets on April 24 were roughed up and arrested by the police. Now, for some reason, this law has caused everyone to forget all about that. Perhaps they didn't ban freedom of speech here, but no one published what we wrote about the genocide, or listened when we talked about it." Isabelle slows down but is still clearly agitated. "The anger within the Diaspora isn't directed solely at Turkey. They're angry at France too. Because even here, in the country to which they migrated and in which they settled, no one listened. But nobody's talking about that now, especially these days. Everyone's talking as though Turkish foreign policy is the only thing that has silenced us." Isabelle is full of passion as she continues: "But the facts need to be known. Armenians need to remember what they went through and what this country, in which they're citizens, has done to them."

I can see how enraged Isabelle is by what she sees as selective memory and the distortion of the truth. Remembering is more than simply dredging up the past. Remembering allows us to sort through the past and to cull the information we need to get through the present, in order to begin the process of forgetting. That's remembering.

From what Isabelle tells me, this "remembering in order to forget" is as important for the Turks as it is for the Armenians. Isabelle tosses her cigarette to the pavement and issues a smoky warning concerning the following day. "You'd better be careful. You'll be encountering the most charismatic Armenian you've ever met. I wouldn't want to be in your shoes."

Isabelle isn't the only person who's warned me about the "terrifying" interview scheduled for the next morning. But for now we've got a whole night ahead of us, and neither Yurttaş nor I wants to do another interview. It's time to have some fun.

Yurttaş attaches great importance to souvenir photos, so he takes a few shots of "Ece in Paris" and "Yurttaş living it up." "What are we supposed to show our grandkids?" he says. "Photos of our adventures, of course!" Yurttaş shows me the artistic photos we've taken for ourselves and the sensible ones

we'll show to others. There's me, in front of Jeanne d'Arc;
Yurttaş with a backdrop of the Eiffel Tower. How simple. And
not unlike the picture Turkey has of the Diaspora.

Many Turks view those in the Armenian Diaspora as the
well-heeled European enemies of Turkey—with an agenda
dedicated to obstructing Turkey and villainizing Turks.

Is there a way to tear up this picture and show them a more
complex reality? With so many one-sided pictures to choose
from, will anyone care to hear about a trip to Paris that hasn't
gone nearly as smoothly as the photographs would indicate? And
isn't that the reason we take these kinds of snapshots anyway, to
impress upon our memories the simple, flawless side of things?
Perhaps it's best that way for everyone. You can always simplify
the story to go along with the picture; in fact, most people
would be grateful if you did. But how to narrate an in-depth,
nuanced story for mass consumption? The "Diaspora Photo"
has been politicized and simplified by both sides, and no one
wants to listen to what's happening behind the scenes. Still, isn't
there some way to tell this story?

★

"You've got your work cut out for you—what can I say?"

That's what Özgür says—Özgür Mumcu, a doctoral candi-
date in International Law at Sorbonne University. We meet
after the Alexi Govjian interview, and now I'm telling him
how difficult it will be, after what I've seen of the Diaspora,
to write anything, as well as what happened after the publication of the serialized articles on Armenia. I finish giving him a
humorous account of the reactions I received, and now it's time
for everyone gathered at the table to try to remember their first
impressions of Armenians. Yurttaş repeats some of the street
slang disparaging Armenians, and I blurt out a childish rhyme I
don't even remember learning: "*Madem ki Ermeni'sin, istemeden
vermelisin!*"—which means, roughly, "Since you're Armenian
you've got to give it up, like it or not."

I'm sitting there overcome with disgust at how "nice" children like us learned this kind of nonsense, when Özgür lightens things up: "No one has a weirder story than me. I was reading *The Three Musketeers* back in primary school. For a long time afterwards I assumed d'Artagnan was Armenian."

Come again?

"Well, as you know, d'Artagnan is transcribed as 'Dartanyan' in Turkish. ASALA must have been active in those days—it was around the time I first heard about 'Armenian terrorists.' So what was I supposed to think? Armenians were bad guys whose surnames ended in -yan, and Dartanyan was obviously an Armenian. But, strangely, I loved that character. I knew I was supposed to hate him, so I kept trying to find something wrong with him. Oh, how I struggled with the Dartanyan thing. A heroic Turkish boy resisting an evil-hearted Armenian!"

We talk about how quickly children absorb notions of "good" and "bad," and how quickly a piece of information can lead to harebrained conclusions. Özgür tells us another story: "And I was terrified of hippies too!"

Why's that?

"I was terrified. I was watching TV at my grandmother's house one day, and the news presenter was talking about a horrific murder in America. They showed a photo of the killer, and he must have had long hair. Grandma cried, 'Oh those hippies—they've killed again!' I was scared for days that the hippies were going to come and get me!"

We all laugh hysterically at this image of young Özgür, scared of cutthroat hippies, prepared to wage battle against that treacherous Armenian terrorist, d'Artagnan!

Who knows what else would emerge if we dug even deeper into our childhood memories. But we have no time for that now. I have that "terrifying" interview to conduct the following morning, and even Özgür, who's always up for a good time, warns me: "Hey! Watch your step. You're going to be talking with the master rhetorician of French politics!"

Chapter 13

"I'm tired of living with corpses"

"FOUCAULT'S PENDULUM IS in there, isn't it?"

Yurttaş has developed a sudden and pressing interest in things intellectual, for which reason we're forced to make a quick pit stop at the Panthéon building. He's determined to figure out how the pendulum works. While he's busy, I decide to study the frescoes on the walls. I gaze at the face of a blond prince in a tent looking out at the "Orientals." Judging from the prince's expression, he's been taken by surprise. I recognize that look; I've seen it a thousand times. It's the expression the West assumes when confronted with the curious savagery of the East. It contains discomfiture, a sense of dismay at witnessing something so strange, the fear of imminent attack, revulsion, wonder, speechlessness—it's an extremely subtle and complex composite of these and other emotions. In Canada, it appears on the face of an ultra–politically correct American academician when I crack a joke. It's the face of the German security guard saying, "It's not my job to give you that information," when asked for directions to the toilet. I even catch a glimpse of it when the handful of change I give to a down-and-out Englishman contains too many small coins. It's a peculiarly wary look that leaves every Easterner with an impression of arrogance and condescension—even if no one says a word . . .

Is this the way the West perceives the Armenian-Turkish issue—as just another burden added to the humanitarian crises demanding its attention? As they listen to Turks or Armenians relate those bloody events of yesteryear, do they assume the perplexed and judgmental expression of those who have never known or been involved in human savagery? And how do Armenians feel when no one listens to them? Like Anatolians?

★

Isabelle and I meet at the party headquarters of Union Mouvement Populaire. She's more nervous about this "critical interview" than I am. "He speaks English, but he still wants me there to interpret," she says. Patrick Devedjian—the "eagle-eyed" Armenian of the French political scene; his grandfather a prominent Ottoman bureaucrat; French to the core, but with roots in Elazığ, a city in eastern Turkey; a famous defense attorney in an ASALA case; infamous in Turkey mainly for being the architect and most outspoken proponent of a law proposing jail sentences for "genocide denial." In Turkey's eyes, he's the "bad Armenian" who engineered the passage of that law in the French Assembly.

Devedjian is tired of living with corpses

Devedjian receives us in his office with a greeting that is courteous, but measured. His smile is that assumed by practiced politicians and businessmen—what can be called their "professional faces." It's unsettling, that smile, because it seems to conceal more than it reveals; confusing because it is, in the end, a smile. Devedjian's professional face is decidedly Parisian, but his bearing seems to reflect the deportment of his statesman grandfather. The moment we're seated, the game of political chess commences. I make the opening move.

"Some of the Turkish-Armenians are disturbed by this law. They're concerned that this law, which was introduced under pressure from the Diaspora, will close all channels of communication and sacrifice the interests of Armenians living in Turkey. The bill hasn't been received with much enthusiasm in Armenia either. What do you think? Would you agree that this bill, which is designed solely for the Diaspora, sacrifices the other Armenian communities?"

"Up until a year ago, I was opposed to this law as a restriction on freedom of expression. But demonstrations by ultra-nationalist Turks and the theft of the Armenian memorial statue in Lyon have caused me to change my mind. Turkey is implementing an active policy of denial. Armenian memorials have been vandalized. The Grey Wolves are responsible. Turkish diplomacy has indicated that these attacks are approved and supported by the Turkish public. Following those attacks, we couldn't be expected to enter into a debate over free speech. Our security was at stake. We needed regulations to keep Armenians safe from attacks in France."

"You say that freedom of expression is no longer of primary importance, but this law was going to contain an exception that you yourself introduced and defended, even if it wasn't accepted. Scientific studies were to be exempted, but you were unable to muster enough support in the assembly."

"I'll do everything I can to ensure that the Senate version of the law contains that exception. I expect consensus in the Senate on this point. It's necessary to safeguard the freedom of scientific research. And that will illustrate the difference between Turkey and France! As you know, Turkey has Article 301 of the penal code!"

"Yes, it was a hastily passed article opposed by myself and many others. But you've been working for a long time on this bill. Even so, in technical terms, it will be difficult to get it enacted into law."

"It hasn't been that long. It took us three years to gain official recognition of the genocide in France. We can wait for this law as well. And in any case, we've already been waiting for ninety years."

"You keep referring to 'we.' Is the Diaspora really that homogenous? Are you certain everyone in the Diaspora supports this law?"

"Even if the Diaspora isn't homogenous, the activities of the hard-line Turkish nationalists will make it so. Besides, Turkey certainly appears to be homogenous from the outside. It has been state policy to homogenize cultural differences. And furthermore, Turkey's refusal to open the border with Armenia has made its position perfectly clear."

"You're right, the points you mention make dialogue more difficult. But isn't it obvious that the law you're trying to pass will only solidify borders?"

"I don't think so. I believe that Turkey will change only under heavy pressure. And I'll say it again: we've been waiting for ninety years!"

"You've been living with ghosts for ninety years. Would you agree?"

"Just like the Jews. It's deeply traumatic. Every time I look at my grandchildren, I remember the children their age who were killed simply for being Armenian. You can't live with that pain every day."

"But you're doing just that and, in a sense, it's become the basis of your life. I want to ask you a personal question: Don't you ever get tired?"

"I do. Yes. Very much so. But duty calls. I don't want to live for another century with corpses under the carpet."

And that's the moment when the "eagle eyes" grow moist. Devedjian, a man renowned for his charisma and decisiveness, sits across from me with tear-filled eyes before, a split-second later, those eyes become sharp as an eagle's, and, after another second, the professional face is back in place. But we both know what happened.

As Devedjian escorts us to the door, he tells me how much he values the efforts of people who are working to foster dialogue, and commends me for the important job I'm doing. I stop and smile. "But, Monsieur Devedjian, you're the one making my job more difficult!"

We laugh and go our separate ways, professional faces intact.

As we leave the building I ask Isabelle, herself an experienced journalist, if the tears were genuine. "There's no reason for him to pretend!" she says. But she too was astonished at the sight of Devedjian's moist eyes.

I'm no longer surprised. I've seen the least likely candidates, men and women both, reduced to tears when speaking of 1915. What does astonish me is this: How can someone manage to cry during a "match"? What kind of match? A "genocide match"?

How would that work? Like this: "We started the match down 0–1."

That's what is written at the top of the web-page of the Talat Pasha Committee, the nationalist organization mentioned to me by Armenians in Armenia and France. At the very top of the page is the name of their "project": "Armenian Documentation of the Armenian Genocide Lie—the Great Project 2006." The mission of the Committee and its project is outlined as follows: "The publication, in the service of national interests, of documents pertaining to the Armenian issue; the organization of symposiums and campaigns; the dissemination for the benefit of international opinion, of documentation corroborating Turkey's national policy." The fundamental view of the Committee is that there are no problems between Armenians and Turks, and that "Western states are organizing a smear campaign against Turkey."

The project has a budget of TL2 million (approximately $1.35 million).

The Armenian lobby has formed similar groups. But the Armenians are well ahead in this "match" over pain and suffering: 28,000 scholarly works seeking to document evidence of genocide have been published; this compares to only 700 defending the official Turkish position that the Armenian deaths cannot be designated "genocide." Over the past four years, twenty-five scholarly works advocating use of the term "genocide" have been published in Turkey, despite their authors having been hounded by the law and labeled "traitors" by those who consider this issue to be some kind of soccer game.

What I read leaves me with a sense of despair. What's the use of shouting in vain and on my own from the stands, is what I think to myself. The field's been overrun—the fans have major financial incentives to shout at each other from opposite sides, and here I am trying to form a long sentence that no one will take the time and trouble to read. I think of Hrant. Who listens to him? When Hrant declared that if the French law was passed he'd personally go to Paris to "deny" the genocide as an act of protest, even some of his intellectual supporters in Turkey found him to be "overexcited." If even Hrant is facing that kind of isolation, how could I, a "Turk," expect anyone to listen to me?

I was growing gloomier by the minute when Arto Bülent Kilimli telephoned, his voice full of cheer. He gave me an address. I was expected there for dinner. He couldn't resist adding: "You'll be surprised!"

As indeed I was . . .

★

A bottle of Yeni Rakı, of course—what else!

"Now that's more like it!" exclaims Yurttaş when Marten Yorganz places the bottle on the table. Here in Paris, at the Armenian restaurant run by Marten Yorganz, he's finally sitting at a normal-size table, eating normal food and drinking normal alcohol. "I told you you'd be surprised," laughs Arto Bülent Kilimli; and then he tells us that his friend Marten is nothing like the other Armenians we've met.

As Marten passes out little plates of fried peppers, garlicky yogurt, white cheese, spicy tomato dip, and other ubiquitous Istanbul *meze*, we wait for him to come and sit with us. When he finally does, Arto explains to this lively, high-spirited man in his late fifties why we've come. "We're told that your generation left Turkey because of the events of September 6–7," I begin, "or because you weren't free to talk about the genocide. Which was the case?"

He smiles and dismisses the subject with a flourish of his hand. "In my case it had nothing to do with September 6–7 or genocide. I came to Paris to be the new Johnny Hallyday!" Many years earlier, Marten had won the Golden Microphone Song Contest (in which singer Cem Karaca was placed second) organized by Turkish daily *Hürriyet*. "I had a great life in Turkey. The girls were climbing all over me. Then I came here. Not a climber in sight!"

It must have been all the food and drink that made me do it. I suddenly blurt out the question: "Did you do your military service?"

"I did my military service here in Paris."

What?

"I cried and cried for my 'country,' and that's what I count as my military service."

Was he terribly homesick?

"That was part of it, of course. But the main reason was that I had a girlfriend back there. I loved her. But I left her behind in Turkey."

Did he ever see her again?

"No, not her—our lives have all changed so much, you see. But a few years ago I suddenly had the urge to go to Turkey. I missed the islands and Moda. The Şişli Club invited me, and I went. It was wonderful. Istanbul was looking good, and I said to myself, if they let Turkey into the EU it'll become even more beautiful."

In an effort to turn the subject to more serious matters, I say, "The people your age that I've spoken to have told me that they got in touch with their Armenian-ness in France, and that being an Armenian became more important to them here. What about you?"

Marten holds up his arms and shrugs. "No. I felt more Armenian in Turkey. There are hardly any proper Armenian churches here, or schools. Those who stayed in Turkey are more Armenian, if you ask me." He becomes more subdued, somber even. "How could I not love Istanbul?" he asks, adding, "They're my friends there!"

When I bring up the matter of the French law, he's visibly upset. "Carrying on and shouting isn't going to get us anywhere," he says, and closes the subject with: "I wish they'd sort the thing out and leave us in peace!"

Marten tells us what he'd do: "I don't want the Turks to say 'Damn it, let's just give in and say the word "genocide."' If they're going to recognize the genocide, let's do it right. Anyway, I'm a musician, and politics goes in one ear and out the other." Marten's about to say something else about the Diaspora when he cuts himself off: "Don't write any of that. There's no need for me to get myself into trouble."

And so it is that his words go in one of my ears and out the other. Marten's already grabbed hold of a microphone and begun singing, as he does every night at his *meyhane*:[14] *Bende olan*

14   A traditional "winehouse" serving alcohol and meze, where the patrons often sing along to live music.

kalbi başkalarında unuttun . . . ("You've forgotten my heart in the hearts of others").

Once he's done with his repertoire of old romantic Turkish songs, Marten moves on to dance staples—the kind of music that gets hips undulating and arms uplifted, in both Armenian and Turkish. Once he gets going, he pulls first an Armenian woman to her feet, then, despite my protests, me. The woman and I are able to exchange only a few words in French, but when the refrain begins we smile at each other in the language of Anatolia: *Şinanay yavrum şinanay nay!*[15]

So, try to explain—try to explain any of this to third countries now deeply involved enough in this issue to be passing laws "recognizing the genocide"—and what do you tell them? Any Armenian, no matter how much they hate Turks, would understand what I meant if I said, *Şinanay yavrum şinanay nay*—would understand the bittersweet euphoria in our smiles and in our hearts. But how to relate this moment, this refrain, to the third countries entangled in the dispute between Turk and Armenian?

Is this issue nothing more than a question of political checks and balances for those third parties? And how can a politics utterly devoid of *şinanay* truly engage and absorb Armenians and Turks? What's the point of laws passed in foreign languages if they fail to take into account the fact that, even if Armenians and Turks have forgotten each other's faces and languages, they still trace their roots to the same soil?

Where do third countries in general, and the West in particular, fit into *şinanay*? I'm reminded of something a film director once said: "The West doesn't want our films; they want our carpets." I've seen the way *kilims* are marketed in the tourist shops of Turkey. It's quite a spectacle. They're tossed up into the air and rolled out on the floor. Convinced that they won't be getting their money's worth unless they're sufficiently

---

15   "Şinanany" is an exclamation of joy while singing and dancing.

amazed—and in a constant state of amazement for that very reason—tourists in white sports shoes set down their plastic water bottles to gape. Where these flat-weave carpets come from is not important. In fact, if that *kilim* swirling through the air, filling the shop with the heavy scent of wool, seems to have materialized out of nowhere from some undisclosed location in the mysterious East, then so much the better. The reality is that *kilims* are woven on looms set up in gloomy rooms on the narrow side streets of provincial villages in eastern and central Anatolia. And in these tiny rooms where girls who have never been sent to school toil like assembly-line workers, music reverberates full blast. This most Eastern of arts is invariably accompanied by throbbing Western music, often listened to on walkmans. The headphones in the ears of that nimble-fingered village girl may well be pumping out Britney Spears. These are not "Anatolian women pouring their hearts into their work, knot by knot"; these are girls consulting the sheet of paper at their side as they copy an oriental pattern furnished by a city merchant. Still, those kilims sailing through the air and settling at the feet of the tourists come with a story, a tale of flying carpets, Aladdin's lamp, belly dancing and Turkish delight. The tourists are presented with a tulip-shaped glass of apple tea, a beverage I have never known a single Turk to consume. It doesn't matter—they've saved up for this and they'll be leaving Turkey not with a documentary, or even a film, but with a *kilim* that whispers fantastic tales. Anatolia is whatever the tourists are buying this year.

The East is defined by the buyer, who passes it along via the merchant and the intermediaries to the girls watching MTV as they re-weave Anatolia. And, like it or not, those *kilims* have become the "real" Anatolia. And, just like those *kilims*, the stories of the Armenians and the Turks sail through the air and land before the white sports shoes of the West. The Armenians and the Turks, those rival merchants, proclaiming the superiority of their own corpses and their own suffering. But does the buyer really care about the pain knotted into those *kilims*, those death *kilims* bought and sold, bought and sold, both sides scanning the latest sales figures to see what's selling this year in order to re-weave ever more desirable patterns for the foreigners? How do you interpret the true story of Anatolia? How do you express pain in words that won't translate? What's lost in translation? What's gained? The Armenians are probably best placed to appreciate this. But on the question of those *kilims*—where they come from and the stories they tell—who is better placed to understand that than two women in the middle of Paris, one of them Armenian, one of them Turkish, dancing away with tears in their eyes to *Şinanay yavrum şinanay nay*?

Chapter 14

"If only this thing would get resolved"

"I HAD TO pay a lot of money for that. I wish that hadn't been the case."

These are the words of Arto Kilimli as he shows me his grandfather's carpetbag, which is hanging on the wall. His isn't the Westerner's lament at having had to fork out good money for a *kilim* saddlebag. Hanging above the stairs leading to the second floor of this home in a wealthy Parisian suburb is a saddlebag his grandfather once used as an attaché case, and into which the Armenian characters for "Kilimliyan"—the original form of Arto's family name—have been woven. It's a family heirloom, but it was purchased from an antique dealer! "My grandfather would drape that bag over the back of his donkey, like this . . ." Arto begins pantomiming before I stop him with, "I know, I know." We both laugh. He's accustomed to having to explain things at length to foreigners. He's pleased to be understood—it reminds him that we come from the same place. As he points to and relates the story of the other antique carpets and *kilims* lining the walls, he suddenly refers to the previous night.

"How about last night!"

"It was great," I say, "but I suspect Marten doesn't reflect the general attitude of the Diaspora in France."

He waves his hand in that typically Anatolian gesture of dismissal. "Don't pay any attention to the hardliners. Most of them have never been to Turkey. They're afraid to go. They think something will happen to them because they're Armenian. I had a wealthy friend who finally went to Turkey after many years, and he was so scared of trouble that, instead of telling the waiter his beefsteak was a bit off, he ate the whole thing. What would have happened if he'd complained? Absolutely nothing!"

Arto is still doing business in Turkey. He collects carpets and *kilims* in Istanbul and Anatolia and sells them in his shop in Paris. Despite his proclamations that "absolutely nothing" could happen, he still warns me: "Careful what you write, better not get them angry with me in Turkey." In the same way that Marten was concerned he might disturb the Diaspora in Paris, Arto is worried about ruffling feathers in Turkey.

I'm struck by the way our two communities have forced these two stateless men to choose their words with such care. There are so many things they have to consider. It was different in Armenia; but here it's about more than the betrayal of one's community. Marten and Arto also have to consider the sensitivities of a community in which they don't live, but to which a part of them belongs. Those are my thoughts as Arto takes me on a tour of his big house. Is there some way to explain certain truths in a way that's acceptable to everyone? Will a single language suffice—one that doesn't need interpretation, one that isn't diminished and doesn't require enhancement during the translation process? Is there a way to express things that, even if it's displeasing to some, encourages everyone to treat your words with respect, perhaps even to listen? I'm thinking not only of the Diaspora, but of myself as well; not only of the Turks who aren't interested in hearing about what I've seen, but also of Armenians, the French, and people in other countries. Is it possible?

"If only this thing would get resolved," says Arto, interrupting my thoughts. It bothers him—this thousand-year-old matter bothers him as much as though it's just happened and demands instant resolution. "Never mind all that," he sighs, "Come, let me show you the world's smallest chapel." We step out into the garden. Arto is indeed the owner of a chapel for two. It's full of artifacts from Anatolia: Turkish coffee cups, candles, icons, and, above a tiny altar, a darkened mirror.

"The mirror contains a hazy silhouette of Jesus. I tell people, 'He appears only to true believers.' You should see how happy they are when they see Jesus!" He laughs. Arto isn't particularly religious, or particularly Armenian for that matter. "If only people could talk," is all he says, "without shouting and without keeping quiet." He pauses for a moment, clearly troubled. "Those who were born here and grew up on terrible stories are angrier. But it's different if you know Istanbul and have friends there. It's not so easy to shout when you like a place and its people."

I'm leaving the house when something occurs to me: "The 'Kilimliyan' surname on the *kilim*—was the -yan dropped before your family name was passed on to you?"

Even as he smiles and waves his hand in that circular gesture of dismissal, his eyes fill with the same sadness I saw in the Armenian woman's eyes the previous night. He shrugs it off: "I'm taking you to a bookshop. Samuelian Bookshop. It's famous."

As we take the train from the suburbs back to the city center, I think about shouting versus silence. Can a single voice be heard among the din of shouting voices? As a method, it certainly doesn't offer much hope of helping to solve any of the world's problems. But there's really no alternative. As a word, "hope" seems to take one for granted. It's a slippery term. Become overly dependent on hope, and it's certain to desert you mid-journey. But you'll get nowhere without it either. I've always put greater trust in determination and insistence. When you know something's right, persist and never submit. Speak up. Don't allow yourself to be defeated by the professional noise-makers, or to lose heart and fall silent. Poke a stick into the wheel of the world—just to be stubborn.

"We're here. You should go inside and talk to them," Arto says, as we halt in a street somewhere off Odeon. "H.

Samuelian" is engraved on a dark green signboard. "We've got another appointment, Arto, we can't stay for long," I say.

"But you have to meet them," he insists. The three of us go inside. As always, Yurttaş keeps his threatening camera concealed. An elderly man and woman, clearly the proprietors, are speaking in a mixture of Armenian and French to another elderly Armenian, a customer who's arrived just before us. Ever the nimble merchant, Arto manages to squeeze past the customer and whisper something to the woman. The man and woman exchange looks; Arto assumes a pleading expression. He must be referring to "the two Turks." The elderly faces freeze in displeasure. A few words are sternly expressed in French, and they're no longer looking at Arto. I'd already retreated several steps at the sight of their souring faces: no, this is not the time or the place to "insist" on speaking. "I don't understand," says an abashed Arto, "they suddenly became incensed."

"Thanks anyway," I say as we step outside. Arto's more upset than we are, and I find myself consoling him. "It's hard, Arto. People may not want to share their most painful stories, on the hoof, with a couple of journalists they've never met. I can't blame them. Just forget about it."

"Maybe later," Arto murmurs, still upset by the anger in his community. "Maybe," I say. We leave Arto behind as we rush off to our next interview.

Arto Bülent Kilimli, the anonymous poet who told us how stories of the genocide had overshadowed his childhood; Isabelle; Marten—it seems to me that a growing number of people within the Diaspora are choosing neither to shout nor to remain silent. Perhaps they're not as visible as those seeking to pass laws in the name of the Diaspora, those doing the shouting. But they're there, and they don't approve of the ones bellowing on their behalf, or the ones who choose to say nothing at all. But who will be their voice? And who will be the voice of those Turks who don't wish to shout or shut up—the ones who, through their silence, are assumed to be on the side of the shouters? How do we get these two groups to talk to each other? For it is only when these two groups begin to talk that a new language will develop and take hold. And it is this language of friendship that will resolve whatever can be resolved. Just like what Hrant's doing in Istanbul. But is it working? Does taking a stance like Hrant achieve results?

★

"That must be them over there," says Yurttaş. A man and a young woman are looking at us with an air of amiable expectation. Burçin Gerçek works as a journalist in France and Switzerland, but she also produced *Nous avons bu le même eau* ("We Drank the Same Water"), a film shot in 2006 by Serge Avédikian, the director we're about to interview. Serge Avédikian is a middle-aged man with frank, friendly eyes and a vigor that belies his shock of gray hair. In 1915 his ancestors immigrated to France from what is now Turkey. He himself grew up in Armenia, before moving to Paris with his family when he was fifteen. We've barely begun talking when we share a laugh. I mention that I've come to Paris because of the "genocide denial" law, and Avédikian immediately says, "The French didn't pass this law on account of our beautiful brown eyes, you know. Not that our eyes aren't beautiful, mind you, but that's another story!"

Avédikian has earned the right to send up the hardliners. He knows the Diaspora and Armenia, and he's made films exploring the relationship between Armenians and their past. Furthermore, he knows Turkey, had the courage to speak out while he was there, and has striven to find a new language to express himself. "I first went to Istanbul in 1987. My grandfather was from a village called Sölöz, near Bursa. It was a mythical place for me. It's like that for families from Anatolia, the myth of the homecoming. That's why this film is called 'The Return' in Turkish. It's the latest trend in Turkish tourism: people going back to find their grandfathers' villages!" Avédikian laughs again, and makes me laugh too. "It wasn't easy, of course. When I got down to filming, the mayor obstructed me. They didn't want me to film the tombstones. I understand—they were frightened. They thought something would happen. It's normal. So I waited for seventeen years. I noticed how much Turkey had changed when I was invited to the Bursa Film Festival in 2003 for the screening of my short film *Ligne de vie* ["Line of Life"]. This time the villagers in Sölöz were eager to talk to me and to tell me their own stories. That village is inhabited by the Pomaks, who came to Turkey as part of the compulsory population exchange with Greece. They too know the meaning of exile. They'd like to meet the grandchildren of the Armenians who once lived in their houses. I proposed we set up a foundation, and that we keep the past alive by bringing together the villagers and Armenians. And that's how I set off for a village to tell the story of my grandfather but found myself making a film about the reactions of the local people to my grandfather's story. That's how *Nous avons bu le même eau* was made."

Film maker Avédikian and his beautiful brown eyes

Avédikian wishes to speak with the living, not the dead, and he wishes to speak of things unsaid. "The Armenians who left my grandfather's village, Sölöz, as well as those who left Gemlik and Gürle, didn't go because of the genocide. It was the population exchange that forced them to leave. If that mutual expulsion in 1920–23 hadn't taken place, those Armenians would probably still be living there. The eastern Anatolian Armenians survived the genocide by fleeing or converting. But my grandfather was among the Armenians who continued to live, as Armenians, in Western Anatolia. That is, there were Armenians who continued living in Turkey after 1915. Do you see what I mean? The Diaspora doesn't say much about that."

I see what he means, but I don't fully understand. Why would anyone continue to live in a country where their people had just been massacred? It's incomprehensible to me. But Avédikian isn't finished yet. "Naturally, some of the villagers are afraid that the Armenians are going to come back and reclaim their homes. There's no need to be afraid. People who have settled in Paris aren't going to go back to that village. But, if the houses were restored, there are Armenians who'd like to see where their grandfathers once lived and meet the locals. What Armenians expect is some kind of symbolic gesture—a gesture that doesn't necessarily contain the word 'genocide.' It's a matter of honor and dignity. And I'm well aware of the pathological results of being a member of the Armenian Diaspora in France."

That's where I stop Avédikian. "Mr. Avédikian, don't get yourself into trouble with the community here!"

"It's true," he says as he explains further. "When I use the word 'pathological,' I'm thinking of people who have based their entire existence and identity upon the genocide issue. But I also say, once again, that recognition of what happened is a matter of honor and dignity for us all. I can illustrate what I mean. Every time I go to Turkey for a film festival, journalists say to me, 'It was war. It's over. People died.' And I respond: 'Do you think I'm bringing this up for the fun of it?' I too have been worn down by the genocide issue. And that's why it's important to find a new way to talk about it. And that's why I choose to make the films I do."

Avédikian quotes the French philosopher and writer Jean Baudrillard: "'The Armenians are a very special case. They spend all their time proving they were killed. And they do it to prove that they're alive today.' I think there are better ways to reach a resolution. And that's why I want my films to be screened in Turkey."

Avédikian believes that the Diaspora and Turkey have the strength to confront their shared history. "We've got to trust the people," he says.

But what is there for the Diaspora to face up to?

"The Diaspora will find my film insufficiently forceful," he says, once again illustrating his point: "When the film was shown in Armenia, the host of a TV program said, 'In your film, you refer to good Turks too.' That was meant to be provocative. So I responded, 'Yes, I did. And I hope we talk some more about them. About Celal Bey, the governor of Konya, risking his life to save Armenians; about the governor of Aleppo; about other Turks who came to the aid of Armenians.' I didn't say this to please Turks. I said it because it's true, and I'll say it again."

"Mr. Avédikian," I say, "on the way here I was thinking about how hard it is to be heard unless you shout. Both because it's easier to hear the shouters and because it's much easier for them to find words. What do you think?"

He smiles. "They're speaking on behalf of the Diaspora. They have to talk tough. But we have to speak out on our own behalf. And I don't think we're all that few in number. We may not be the majority, but we're not alone either. Getting back to that law—as citizens of France, the Armenians here don't need that law; but as Armenians, what they secretly want is to shake things up and for the truth to emerge. The Armenians need to do this because Turkey hasn't taken a single step. And it's difficult to be in the Diaspora—you need to create an identity, something to hold on to, both culturally and individually. For some, the Diaspora is a country; for others, it's exile. You've got to understand how difficult it is. But when the younger generations start talking, they need to know that they're not guilty. Why don't we all come together and blame the government? There's no point in accusing individual Turks or Armenians, one by one. In my film, for example, people were sincere when they told me they'd never heard the Armenian story. They'd ask, 'Is that story true?' Yes, it's true, and we can talk about it among ourselves, and we can resolve this. That's what I say."

That's what Avédikian says, yes. And it's what I say. If Marten were here with his bottle of Yeni Rakı, he'd say the same, as would Arto, who'd join us carrying his grandfather's *kilim*. Isabelle seems to be saying something similar. And I know Hrant would agree. There's no doubt that Arto Tunç Boyajian and the playwright in Yerevan would add their voices to ours. And there was Haygaram, and Lilit, and Lilit's daughter, Arax, and others . . . How many are we? How loud would our combined voices be? That's the question.

People of conscience willing to speak up have always been in the minority. Why can't these ideas be shared with everyone? Why is it so often the case that the larger the crowd, the more strident the tone? There has to be a way for us to speak together—for all of us to have our say.

"Okay, that's enough for one day," Yurttaş announces. "We're going to get something to eat and drink with Özgür."

And that's what we do. As I'm submitting the humorous version of the day's events and reach the part about the bookshop, Özgür laughs. "It's no wonder they didn't talk to you. My God, what an unfortunate encounter!"

But why?

"Because that woman has family who died in 1915. Years later, the poor woman went back to Istanbul to see where her family had lived. But the date she chose was the unluckiest one possible: September 6–7, 1955!"

"She was right not to talk to us," I say. "We made her life hell."

"We?" asks Özgür. That's right, what did I mean by "we"? We joke among ourselves about the image of "the terrible Turk," but what do we mean when we say "we." Who are we? Getting away from the epic tales of the Turks we're fed at home; our defensive Third World response to the condescension we face abroad; the wrongs committed at home in the name of Turkishness; and the slights received abroad because of Turkishness: once we're disentangled from all that, who are "we"? And how can we manage to take a stand and to stand tall?

Suddenly, the shoe is on the other foot. I'd come here to understand the Armenians, but I now realize that I first had to understand who "we" were. For the first time, I was able to put a name to my strange reluctance to go to Paris. It was time to look past the flattering image Turks have of themselves, and past the terrible image of the Turk prevalent among the Diaspora. I would have to look past those twin distortions as I took a hard look into the mirror. Much harder than I'd expected.

Chapter 15

The daughters of ghosts

I WAKE UP exhausted. I realize that for some time now these interviews and this journey have taken on a life of their own, voices of their own—as though I've been speaking with shadows, speaking with the myriad voices of a single heart. And, for some time now, I've been talking to myself more than to the people I've been interviewing. They're haunting my dreams. I admit that this morning, the first time I've done so since I arrived in Paris. And there's only one day left before I return to Turkey. I'm suffocating, probably because the only way I'm able to move around this tiny hotel room is by shifting the suitcase and chair. I can't keep up with the thoughts swirling through my head, running through my mind, disappearing down a black hole. And when those thoughts do reappear, it's always the same refrain: "Children—the children of ghosts . . ."

Yes, they seem like the children of ghosts, all of them. And when they talk, those ghostly whispers seep through to the present—these children of ghosts with no place in museums. In the throes of death, a legacy of good and evil is transmitted to later generations, to the children of ghosts. So few of the people I've interviewed have used their own words. Their words belong not to them, but to those tormented ghosts, and that's why they've been so furious with "us" right from the start. It's the fury of the ghosts, not theirs. What do they want from us? What do the ghosts want? Do they even know? Do they know they're the children of ghosts?

★

"It's not only the Diaspora—there are ghosts in the Turkish community too."

Hélène Piralian is a petite woman with curly gray hair. She and the building in which she lives, with its wooden banisters and antiquated lift, seem to have grown old together, gracefully. When she speaks, her voice is like her hair—soft curls and undulations. Sandwich cream cookies have been set out with tea; chocolate cookies. A kindness, ready and waiting. Music unfamiliar and soothing; walls covered with oil paintings. Both the flat and Hélène Piralian herself are so exquisite that it somehow seems appropriate to enter her life and her home on tiptoe. And that's exactly what we do, without realizing it: Isabelle, me, Burçin Gerçek, who's arranged the interview, and, of course, Yurttaş. She's kindly made us feel completely at home, and I'm so tired that I don't feel like asking any questions. I begin talking of the things that were running through my head that morning, delirious and fragmented. She quietly listens, perhaps because she's a psychoanalyst, perhaps because the author of *Génocide et Transmission* is genuinely interested in the thoughts and feelings of a "Turk." As I talk I can feel the weight of the past few days lifting. The look she gives me isn't unlike that of Silva Gabudikian in Armenia.

She smiles, pauses for a moment, and finally addresses my ghosts. "Ghosts are hovering over the people of Turkey too. With the departure of the Armenians, the Turks lost a big piece of their lives and their people. Perhaps you're right—perhaps Armenians are 'the children of ghosts.' But if they're haunting us, they're haunting the Turks as well."

It might be the dimly lit room, the sudden solemnity, the smell of cookies, just like in Gabudikian's home: whatever the reason, the conversation is taking on a dream-like quality.

The words of four women embrace and entwine, forming sentences that mingle and build upon each other; Isabelle occasionally murmuring, "That's true," Burçin interpreting and explaining what it feels like to be a Turk living in Europe.

Women have a special way of communicating with each other. They wait until a sentence is nearly finished and add their words, as though to support each other's voices, to keep that sentence alive and aloft—like the games we played as children, all in a ring, hand-in-hand, rhythmically chanting songs together; or the dream-summoning lullabies sung by women.

And into this dreamlike conversation Hélène Piralian introduces the words of Turkish author Nedim Gürsel, something he's written about Anatolia, about the corpses littering the lands of Anatolia, where, even in death, fingernails grow longer, breaking through the soil of a land in which the dead are more alive than the living.

"But, with so many dead," I ask, "how do we talk?"

"Just like we're doing now," says Piralian. I reflect on the women in my country who wrap the corpses, who wash corpses and bathe babies and are intimate with life newborn and bodies lifeless. Those wise women are familiar with the cycle of life and fearless in the face of death. And I'm reminded of those women as I sit with these women, as though we too are gathered here together to wash bodies. Hélène Piralian has dismissed the shouting men for a moment and is talking to us, to women. "We need to get beyond the historical and political dimensions. We have some mourning to do. Together, we need to mourn the dead we've been unable to mourn."

The sensation of being in a dream is deepening. We're in Anatolia, washing bodies together, and as we wash we begin to remember each other's languages. As we wash, we forget that we speak different languages. Hélène's no longer speaking French to me, and even when I leave her flat I imagine, for a long time afterward, that we spoke in Turkish, or in some other language I didn't know I knew.

Hélène talks about what her people can do about this inter-rupted mourning. "The members of the Diaspora should have their childhoods psychoanalyzed. They've been traumatized by the stories they've heard as children. And Turks should agree to listen to them, because their stories will help to resolve the fear and pain Turks have failed to identify within themselves.

"I don't feel guilty," I say. "Perhaps," she responds, "you, as a people, are suffering trauma induced by constant accusa-tions of wrongdoing." Well, maybe . . . "A guilt complex is one possibility. Another possibility is the feeling of numbness you mentioned, the complete lack of feeling. Guilt can manifest itself in later generations as apathy or numbness."

The assistant director of the Genocide Museum in Yerevan pops into my head. I'd had "zero feelings" at the museum, but assumed it was only because I was being coerced into a display of emotion. Still, I had been surprised by my own lack of feel-ing. Hélène might have a point.

"That's it," murmurs Isabelle, unaware that she's speaking aloud. Awakened by her own voice, she feels she needs to share the rest of her thoughts with us. "When the people in Turkey start to see the buildings of Armenians, they'll begin to remem-ber and to ask questions. They've begun to see the buildings they pass every day. They're starting to feel things."

Hélène returns to the Armenians. "The Turks have been traumatized by constant accusation; the Armenians, by constant victimization. There are two communities suffering different conditions resulting from the same event. It is, of course, an injustice to divide a people into "deniers" and "non-deniers." There are Turks whose reactions to the Armenian story fall into neither category—and it's only when their reactions are given voice that we can end this impasse. At the moment, both communities are being ruled by their fears."

I point out that current policy is rooted in these fears, and that it's resulting in the passage of penal code amendments, bills, and laws. I ask Hélène how we can possibly reconcile our differences in the current political climate. "The French law and others like it stem from the victim psychology of the Diaspora. The members of the Diaspora imagine that these laws will protect them from their fears. Due to the stories of their childhood, they still feel endangered."

Fear and love. The Diaspora is in love with the same country they fear. Piralian tells me that the fear of Turks among the Diaspora is real and unresolved, and that what they feel for the land they left behind is also an unresolved love. It seems odd that an issue we've viewed as strictly political has such an obvious psychological dimension to it, that our policies have been rooted in pathologies that could still be driving policy ninety years from now. "Yes," agrees Piralian, "and that's why we need psychoanalysis."

I know all too well that people can fear the resolution of their fear. A lifetime informed by fear could seem suddenly meaningless if that fear is suddenly removed. When I mention this to Hélène she tells me about her own experience. "I was afraid of Turks, too. But I realized later that it wasn't Turks I feared—it was the emotions they'd awaken in me. They may not realize it, but the members of the Diaspora who vehemently oppose dialogue are afraid of themselves, afraid to be freed of their fears." She takes a sip of tea. Our tea is lukewarm now, like the tea given to children. "What they're most afraid of is being deprived of an enemy."

Men harnessing the rage of ghosts in order not to lose their enemies; women washing the dead and wishing to put ghosts to rest. A picture is forming before my eyes, but when the tea and cookies come to an end, so does the dream. As we prepare to go, Hélène says, "I'd like to work on this unresolved mourning with a woman in Turkey"—as though she's sending me back to Turkey with a message to all the women wishing to silence ghosts, seeking to dress wounds with other wise women on intimate terms with birth, death, and evil.

And me? "Us"?

This isn't about Turks or Armenians, Kurds or Europeans. It's about wounds and healing. It isn't about genocide or reparations. Even if reparations are paid one day, certain kinds of pain won't go away. This is about something else: about "us"; about a past swallowed up by fairytales; about getting the old stories straight; about bathing our ghosts and laying them to rest; about how to heal rage by sharing our tears with anyone willing to talk without shouting. No one needs to feel guilty. In order for us to accept the dead as our own, there's no need for those who haven't killed to feel guilty. We simply need to talk and to listen.

Isabelle and I step out into the street. It's my favorite time of day: Paris in purple—the hour at which all the colors of Paris are tinted a darkening violet as the sun sinks below the horizon and, suddenly, color is gone. I don't know why she does it—perhaps because we sipped lukewarm tea together over life and death, history and land. Isabelle suddenly embraces me, and I'm embracing her back. We'll be in touch, of course—and if you ever come to Istanbul one day . . . I'm not sure to what extent we believe our own words; certainly, neither of us knows what awaits us. No, Isabelle and I are simply exchanging the assurances of a friendship quickly made and as quickly ended.

That's how the journey ends. I don't even want to think about what will happen when I return to Turkey and write about my trip to Paris. I do jot down some thoughts in my notebook, though, as I do at the end of every journey:

> It should be something like women who comb and comb their hair as they weep, who weep and weep until all the knots are smoothed out . . .
>
> Who knows—you may be saying the things I said before I went to Paris: "What's it got to do with me? Why should I feel anything?" You have a point. Why should you feel anything about evil committed by a government long before you were born? But let's consider this for a moment; let's have the courage to give it some thought. Today, when we hear about Hutu

slaughtering Tutsi, we feel terrible. When we watch films depicting Nazi concentration camps, there are scenes we can't bear to watch. Our blood freezes at the sight of a Chechen "Black Widow" vowing to avenge the death of her husband, a Palestinian child throwing a stone, an Iraqi woman beating her breast in front of her destroyed home, bombs falling on a school in Lebanon ... These images all inspire feelings of one kind or another; so, tell me, why is it that on this particular subject we feel nothing at all? It's strange, isn't it? Someone far away tells us, "Our grandmothers and grandfathers vanished from those lands." Do we close our ears in order to distance ourselves from a "crime"? If we were able now to take even the tiniest of steps, perhaps the ghosts of these lands would disappear forever; perhaps the rage would subside much faster than we'd thought possible. And then, finally, the living would talk, not the dead. Death would fall silent and life would be heard.

★

When I got back to Istanbul, those were the final words of the series of articles I didn't write, was unable to write, and finally wrote. There was a huge uproar, of course—as well as those

Tens of thousands mourn Hrant Dink in Istanbul

oddly silent readers, of course. And I would call Hrant again, of course. Another dinner, more gossip and news. Another suit would be filed against Hrant. For a crime he hadn't committed, of course—and this time it was "Insulting Turkishness." "God," I'd say. "Damn it!" The days would pass, and we wouldn't meet. Another bill calling for "recognition of the Armenian genocide" would be introduced in the US. It would be time for us to meet, to talk over what was happening in America; it looked like I'd be going there. We'd drink *rakı*, of course. He'd talk about his own story for the first time, tell me things I'd never heard. As we drank we'd feel more sorrowful, and we'd drink more to forget our sorrows. "Write a book," he'd tell me, and I'd mention "İsmail," and say I couldn't write a book. "You'll write it," he'd say. I'd dig in my heels. "And you need to go to America. I'll persuade you; you'll write it." I wouldn't take his words seriously. "Drop by next Wednesday," he'd say.

Chapter 16

"A land of dead doves"

"*EZUUU! EZUUU!*"

I thought Hrant Dink's wife, Rakel, was saying *su*, the Turkish for water; I thought she was wailing the word *su*. Only later did I learn that *ezu* is a Zazaki lamentation.

I call out to the others: "Bring water! Quick! Water!"

Someone runs through the crowd and brings water back to the stairwell. I hand Rakel the glass. The back of her hand smashes into it: against the wall, water and shattered glass. She's sitting on the stairs looking at me, but seeing someone else—something dark, I think. Her screams are shattering: "I don't want it! We're fine, thanks. Take care of the state! Don't let anything happen! Take care of the state!"

Rakel looks at my face and screams. Her daughter, Sera, sinks down next to her mother, on the stairs, enfolded by Rakel: "*Ezuuu! Ezuuu!*" We're all as one, shattered—the crowd silent, weeping in the stairwell. Lifting her face from her daughter's face, Rakel screams, her eyes on each of us, one by one: "The state's pure! Our state's even purer now!" Her son, Arat, so like Hrant. A man's face, crying, until, finally, it's the face of a child whose father's just died: "Ohhh! Ohhh!" Arms wrapped around his body, in front of the door. Hands pressing against his chest, his heart; his wound still fresh. Sera's scream slashing the silence. Rakel's hands, clawing the air, clutching at the screams, falling to her side: "Is your blood purer now?!"

Sera lifts her face from the marble stair. "Give me back my *baba*! My *baba*!"

Rakel turns to me, to that person in front of her, whoever I am. In that voice, hoarse and dying: "We trusted you, we stayed in this country! We trusted you! And now this?"

My face, splitting into pieces. Leaning down to shake off the pieces. Looking down at the blood on my shoe. My friend's blood. My guilt. Hrant, lying outside, near the front door, on his back, in the street, in his blood. And we're all gathered in the stairwell, looking at our shoes.

★

January 19, 2007, 2:50 p.m. The *Agos* newspaper meeting ended, and editor-in-chief and columnist Hrant Dink went into his office. His mobile phone rang. He spoke, and hung up. Hurriedly, without a word to anyone, he ran down to the street without taking his phone or his coat. As he exited the building at approximately 3:00 p.m., three 7.65mm bullets pierced the back of his skull. According to the statements of eyewitnesses, a lightly bearded young man in a white knitted cap fired a gun and shouted, "I killed the Armenian!" Eyewitnesses say that Hrant Dink's last words were, "Don't do it, son, stop!"

All of the television networks switched to live coverage; many of the correspondents were openly weeping. At some point the growing crowd gathered in front of the offices of *Agos* newspaper decided that crying wasn't enough. A group composed mainly of intellectuals, journalists, and Hrant's friends decided it was time to take action. By evening, the crowd had swelled to 8,000 people. It was raining. Amid the tears and the shouts, the slogan that would shake Turkey was born: "We're all Hrant! We're all Armenian!"

Finally, everyone went home. A decision was made to hold the funeral four days later, on January 23. Hrant was still on all the TV channels.

★

Unable to maintain her composure, the anchorwoman smiled bitterly and demanded to know: "Mr. Kerinçsiz, how do you manage to have a clear conscience?"

Kemal Kerinçsiz, the attorney who'd cited Article 301 in a criminal complaint against Hrant for "denigrating Turkishness," was also on all the TV channels, expressing his "sorrow" even as he suggested that the gunman might have been Armenian. Rare footage of all of Hrant's interviews was aired repeatedly. The press heaped scorn on the government's clichéd statements. Newspapers and TV screens displayed the image of Hrant, lying in the street with a hole in the sole of his worn-out shoes.

The man in the street, people who didn't know Hrant, who'd never heard of *Agos* newspaper, learned certain things in those days:

He was a man who loved his country.

Look at the tears in his eyes when he says "my country."

He was a good man.

Look at them all! His wife and his children and all the people who loved him.

He had a hole in his shoe when he died.

Which means he wasn't on anyone's payroll. He was only defending his beliefs.

He was unfairly convicted.

He never said "The blood of Turks is poisonous." He said the hatred some Armenians feel for Turks is "poisonous."

He didn't insult Turkishness.

Did you hear how his voice trembled when he said, "How could I insult the people I live with!"?

Someone had ordered a child to kill him.

Did you see that boy on TV? They say he's connected to intelligence and the police.

Once Hrant was dead, they began to listen to everything he'd said while he was alive. They kept broadcasting the last article he wrote. The article, in which Hrant mentioned death threats, ended like this:

Yes, I know the uneasiness of the dove, but I also know that in this country people don't touch doves.

Doves are free to live in the city, even among the crowds.

A bit uneasy, yes, but just as free.

(*Agos*, January 10, 2007)

It was in those days when Hrant's words were being repeated on TV and in the newspapers that some people began saying, "We killed him by being unable to protect him." It wasn't "we" who killed him; but it's true, perhaps, that we weren't strong enough to take a stand against the forces eliminating the men and women who think and speak freely in Turkey. We were defeated that day in the heart of Istanbul, in broad daylight. That's what was behind our fury and our frustration. We held a mass mourning. That period of mourning and the slogans it produced would later cause serious divisions in Turkey. Hrant Dink's death had opened old wounds, and what followed would surprise us all.

On the morning of January 23, 2007, a crowd 100,000-strong marched past the front of the building where Hrant was shot. The scab had been torn off.

★

The crowd was streaming toward the Sebat building, which houses the offices of *Agos*. There was a deep silence. Hrant's wife, Rakel Dink, stood on top of a bus, microphone in hand, addressing everyone gathered to bid farewell to her husband. Her speech would take its place in Turkish political history. These words spoken by Rakel would be much discussed in the following days: "No matter who the murderer is, and no matter how old he is, seventeen or twenty-two, I know he was a baby once. Nothing will be accomplished, brothers and sisters, unless we examine the dark forces that would transform a baby into a murderer."

★

Hrant Dink's daughters, Delal and Sera, at the
Agos newspaper offices, on January 23, 2007

Hrant masks; people looking out through the eyeholes of Hrant masks; 100,000 people wearing Hrant masks. I can't bear to look. They shout: "We're all Hrant!"

Who are these people? What do they feel? Until just a few days ago, most of them had never heard of Hrant, his articles, and the things he said. Did Hrant realize how many people were behind him? How could he? No one ever said anything. What exactly are these people mourning? The death of a man they never met? Or the damning remorse of knowing that we'd been unable to protect "our Armenian"? The pain and grief of knowing that men who love their country and aren't afraid to speak out are still being killed? We were all tired of living in a land of dead doves.

They were angry. They were angered by living in a Turkey in which Hrant could be killed, and by the anguish it was causing them. They were angered by that crushing sense of being unable to change things. The pain was so intense, and so connected to their sense of country and self, that they felt just as I had when Rakel screamed: they wanted to die—instead of Hrant. And that's why we were shouting, "We're all Hrant! We're all Armenian!"—meaning, "Come and kill us too!"

Perhaps that's the way crowds remember. The latest death brings them back to earlier deaths and, along with the loss of Hrant, they grieve this unstoppable wheel of death—not just the deaths of Armenians, of Turks, Kurds, Assyrians, leftists; these people grieve for all of these deaths, and for this country founded on death.

So, who are these "Turks"? Why are their shoulders slumped? Because of the bodies they bear on their backs, grieving Hrant and those before him—reminded by a bullet of all they'd tried to forget, tired of being killer Turks. And along with the dead bearing down on the slumped shoulders of this crowd is the weight of the killers. They're Turkish: they're the ones who stormed the gates of Vienna, who live in a land of shish kebab and moustaches, of Turkish delight and *kilims*, who "rough up Kurds and kill Armenians." It's them—Turks who are tired of having their Turkishness shoved down their throats; so weary of death that they're ready to die, all of them, as together they shout: "We're all Hrant! We're all Armenian!"

They want the "poisoned blood" to flow forth, just as Hrant said. They want it to flow forth and flow away, so that they can live among people who don't kill and aren't killed. They wish to be not killer Turks, but Turks who are able to shed tears for the dead. They want to be themselves. They want the bloody past to end and a bloodless future to be built. They don't want history to repeat itself—they want it gone, and they want it to leave Turks in peace. They don't want to share the Turkishness of Turks who kill their Armenians. They don't want to share a country with those who kill Kurds and who kill fellow Turks for being insufficiently Turkish.

Nineteen-fifteen: there must have been a woman, about my age, in Van, Malatya, or Sivas. There must have been a lot of Turkish men and women who stopped and watched as their Armenian neighbors were leaving, and who felt like I do: defeated. There must have been a woman who felt what I feel now. As Agavni Hanım and Hovannes Bey, along with their children, Efronia and Agop,[16] were rounded up and taken away, they must have looked on with horror as others came and settled in that vacated house; there must have been people who felt helpless to stop it, who felt deep shame at being unable to protect their neighbors, who felt defeated and helpless in the face of savagery, just like us.

They existed. They were there. They cried as we cry now for Hrant. They were like that, they were like us. But other stories have been written, not theirs. Perhaps they were always in the minority, these people. And perhaps that's why our stories never tell us that they lived in these lands once and that we are descended, too, from people who wished to save doves, just like we do. We've never learned the story of those people so like the people marching for Hrant—the ones who would risk death to protect brother and neighbor.

16   An Armenian family hypothesized by the author. [Translator.]

Later, Turks were killed too—Muslims. But one death doesn't absolve another. Our shoulders still slump, and ghosts still roam among us. Until we condole with our ghosts and lay them to rest with our tears, until we speak out and mourn as one, it is our fate to reside in a land of angry ghosts.

Is it enough to say, "We're so sorry"? If we were able to say, now, "We're sorry. We were unable to protect Hrant, and all the others"; if we also apologize to our own dead; if we say, "We used you to cover up the deaths of others. Forgive us"; if we were to say, "May you all rest in peace"—what would happen? If ghosts no longer stalked, and we found peace?

It's evening, and everyone goes home with the weight of a past and a present that are too much to bear alone. And everyone understands the depths of Ararat as they contemplate the depths of their own pain.

Once again, cracks have appeared in our constructs of self and country. Ararat is crashing down on us.

★

I see those children in a dream—the ones in the museum under the Fortress of Little Swallows in Yerevan; those rows of ancient children staring out at me from the photograph lining an entire wall. I study their faces, one by one. They're in the countryside; water is flowing somewhere. Hrant stands in the corduroy suit he always wore, hands deep in his pockets. Perhaps this is the paradise Rakel referred to. Hrant stands in the middle of that group of children and smiles. I go up to him. "I've seen those children—I saw them . . . in Yerevan," I say. For some reason, we laugh. I tell him about my experiences in Paris. We laugh some more. We're too happy for me to tell him that 100,000 people marched in his cortege. The dream fades to black and is gone.

★

The days pass. New headlines begin appearing in the morning papers. That's when we begin to see what was festering under the scab torn off by Hrant's death. The headlines scream: "We're all Turks!" It's as though they know, somehow, exactly what we're thinking. They know we want an accounting for the murder, and to put our ghosts to rest. It's as though they've even invaded our dreams and are shouting, "Come to your senses! You're not Armenian!" It's fine to proclaim that "We're all Palestinians!" or "We're all Iraqis!" But Armenians! That spoils the narrative, and once that happens—you die alone.

And so began the backlash—the flash-fire of ultra-nationalist sentiment sweeping across the country. It grew more intense with the funeral ceremonies held for our martyred soldiers in the southeast, so intense that nationalist teenagers began shouting in front of the buildings of neighborhoods where Kurds lived: "Come out!"

Darkness fell over Turkey, just days after Hrant's death. People had seen the hole in the sole of Hrant's shoe. They knew someone like them had been killed. This time, they'd seen an Armenian killed before their eyes: that was the danger. A hole had been torn in the "traitorous Armenian" invective, and through it oozed suspicion, guilt, anger, and pain. What if people started asking questions? Questions about Ararat, our Ağrı?

★

And people *had* begun asking questions, little questions in hushed voices. Those little questions had to be smothered with grand sentences. That's why the headlines changed from morning to morning: the cracks had to be plastered over with ultra-nationalist mortar. Hrant had been buried in the depths of this land they so love. It'd happened just as he'd said:

"Yes, I *have* got my eye on your land. Not to take it away, but to be buried deep down in it!"

Ararat was now deeper than ever. Ağrı—the highest mountain in Turkey!

★

A few days later, there appeared on one of Turkish TV someone who'd criticized Hrant's approach to the Armenian issue as overly conciliatory; someone whose views on Armenian-Turkish relations were nothing like Hrant's; someone I'd interviewed in Paris. Once again, a figure from the Armenian Diaspora took it upon himself to speak for all Armenians.

I could see that the sight of 100,000 Turks marching and weeping for Hrant threatened to open up cracks in the solidarity of the Diaspora in the same way it had opened cracks in the Turkish approach to the Armenian issue. It was as dangerous for the Diaspora as it was for the official position of Turkey. For the man on the street, Hrant's death had shattered the image of the "traitorous Armenian"; the image of the "terrible Turk" was also crumbling. In the same way Turkey had clung to the image of the "traitorous Armenian" in order to stifle talk of its past, the Diaspora relied on the "terrible Turk" to maintain unity and keep their identity intact. And, judging from the Armenians speaking on television on behalf of the Diaspora, Turkey wasn't the only one busily plastering over the cracks.

Boston, 2007

PART III

*"I'd like to set out on a journey,
too, and get to know the Turks"*

Chapter 17

No laughing matter

STEPPING THROUGH THE front door of the upscale Italian restaurant in Los Angeles is a well-dressed man past middle age with a yellow folder under his arm. He's apparently on intimate terms with the elderly maître d', a figure straight out of *The Godfather*. They whisper conspiratorially. The maître d' indicates our whereabouts with a meaningful shift of his eyes. The well-dressed man walks over to our table with brisk steps.

We're just rising to greet him when he's suddenly upon us, both hands planted on the table: "Let's clear up the ground rules first. You won't reveal my name, you won't attribute any quotes to me, and you won't hint at my identity in any way. And no photos, of course."

After a moment, my mouth, which I'd opened to say hello, snaps shut. He knows he's thrown me but he misinterprets the reason. "You know the meaning of the expression 'ground rules,' don't you?"

"I do," I assure him. I pause before adding, "But I didn't know they were imposed unilaterally."

He's not about to moderate his tone. "Look here, young lady, I'm not all that interested in talking to you, and unless you agree to my terms I have no intention of sitting down at this table. So tell me, do you agree or not?"

I freeze for a moment, a moment in which various thoughts swirl in my head.

★

After Hrant died, everything seemed to become a bit meaning-less. Which is why I'd seriously hesitated to go to America. I'd begun to think that we had no chance, that people like Hrant, people like us who believe in dialogue, would be as unwelcome as ever and find it even more difficult to make our voices heard. And it wasn't just the Armenian issue: every initiative supported by Turkish intellectuals to advance the process of democratiza-tion had been thwarted and suspended. The political discourse was being defined on ultra-nationalist terms. We'd lost more than Hrant. Over a very short space of time, gains made in the name of freedom of thought had been unraveling in Turkey. The gun pointed at Hrant had taken aim at minds as well as hearts.

As a journalist writing about the Kurdish issue, political pris-oners, hunger strikes, political Islam, nationalism, and many other thorny problems, this is what I'd observed: no one kills the hardline sectarians positioned on opposing sides of the same game. It's the ones who refuse to be a part of the game that get killed. Their existence threatens the game and its players, on both sides. And so they're eliminated.

Political assassinations also target the groups represented by the victim. Writer and poet Musa Anter was shot in 1992, and a brave voice on the Kurdish issue was silenced. Uğur Mumcu was blown up in 1993, and that was the end of any more pioneering investigative journalism on the shadowy relationship of the state-politicians-mafia triangle. There were others, always others . . . And, finally, Hrant died, and with him an opportu-nity for Turkey to confront and question its past.

Those dissenting voices were silenced one by one, until silence prevailed. That's what Turkey felt like in those days: a land of muted voices. Even worse, the sense of loss over Hrant's death was being replaced with a sense of resignation. I was in no shape to go to America, especially to talk with the most combat-ive members of the Diaspora. But it was right around that time that I received a phone call. It was Isabelle, in Istanbul, and we

exchanged greetings just as we'd done in Paris. We arranged to
meet.

Pain isn't always sharp-edged; sometimes it flows through
you, warm and smooth. Pain isn't always icy; sometimes, shared
by two people, it's more like the sensation of passing through a
warm current in a cold sea. Isabelle and I immediately embraced
each other without a word. Hrant had gone, changing everything. Those he'd left behind were now embracing each other.
This embrace was also a silent form of communication. "I
know," it says. "I hurt too."

It was warm outside and gypsies were going from *meyhane* to
meyhane, playing music. Balmy night was descending, a bittersweet violin was playing, and we were talking about a funeral.
"Hrant has turned into something else," I said, "a symbol."

Isabelle looked somewhat peeved. "That may be true here.
But it's completely different in the Diaspora. They've transformed him into something else, someone else. If Hrant saw
what they were doing he'd be furious." I told her about the
man I'd watched on television just after the funeral, speaking on
behalf of the Diaspora. "That's what I mean," she said. "Them.
The very men Hrant advised to overcome their hatred of Turks
are now doing all the talking. The ones who wouldn't talk to
Hrant when he was alive have declared him to be the latest
martyr of the genocide. Hrant's become something he'd always
opposed."

I won't go into any details except to say that we cried together,
again. And then we embraced. Through Hrant, again. And as I
made my way home, I guess I was suddenly furious.

Fury isn't always a bad thing. It galvanizes; it helps you stand
tall. I decided to go to America—if for no other reason, so
Hrant wouldn't be on his own there. This was to be the most
difficult journey Yurttaş and I had ever taken, harder to bear
than Lebanon after the bombings or the sight of the tortured
Kurdish children of the southeast. Hrant was ever-present, and
we couldn't have anticipated what was lying in wait for us. We

sat now, pain still raw, as "the rules of the game" were being shoved down our throats.

★

"So, tell me, do you agree or not?"

I nodded in the affirmative. And that's when this extremely influential figure in Armenian lobbying circles, to be known henceforth as "Mr. Brownian," sat down at the table. Yurttaş got up and left, both because he couldn't bear this treatment and because he wasn't permitted to take photos. I expected things to pan out in the usual way. Those who are most reluctant to speak invariably end up having the most to say; I wanted to listen to Mr. Brownian, and I wanted to understand what makes his kind tick. We were expecting a second guest, prominent not only in Armenian circles but on the national political scene as well. He soon appeared in the doorway. Well-spoken and with the air and manner of an intellectual, he too insisted on the same rules: "Mr. Smithian" was ready to be interviewed.

It was Mr. Brownian, the one who'd declared his reluctance to speak to me, who got things rolling the moment he sat down. "Turkey's refusal to recognize the genocide is what binds those of us in the Diaspora. Were the genocide to be recognized, it would probably be the end of us."

Mr. Smithian believes it's more complicated than that. He'd like to explain in detail the stages his community has gone through in America. "The first ones to arrive here changed their names so they'd be more easily accepted by American society. The men married American women. But later, among the members of our generation, there was an Armenian awakening. People even changed their Anglo-Saxon surnames, from Thomas to Thomasian, for example. They'd decided to become Armenians again. They wanted to return to their ethnic identities."

The reluctant Mr. Brownian is anxious to speak again, and does so at length. "Our parents were focused on becoming

Americans. That's why they changed their names and their surnames. It was the rise of a better-educated, wealthier generation that led to a greater interest in things Armenian. That generation was concerned with becoming Armenian. Before them, no one ever talked about being Armenian. Americans had no idea what an Armenian was. I'm going to show you what I mean, and you'll be the first Turk to see it." Mr. Brownian pulls a DVD out of his folder. He jabs his finger at the cover, which depicts a scene from the Wild West. "Do you know who these people are?"

"Who?"

"Indians from Fresno!"

Meaning?

"Armenians!"

He chuckles as he tells me the story of the first group of Armenian immigrants, who settled in the town of Fresno. "They were making a cowboy film in the 1930s. When the producers couldn't get any Indians, they had the entire Armenian community brought to the set. Everyone became an extra in that film or got a part. So, today there's a cowboy film with Armenians playing Indians." Mr. Brownian becomes serious all of a sudden. "That's how alien Armenians were to America. They couldn't tell an Armenian from an Indian. But now, thanks to the powerful, wealthy members of my generation, people know about Armenians."

Mr. Brownian has the triumphant look of a man who has succeeded at last in proving the existence of himself and his people to the Americans. The finger pointing at the Fresno Indians wears the ring of a top university. He's played by American rules and he's won.

Everyone now knows who they are: Armenians, not Indians. That said, there are various categories within the community. According to what I'm told by Mr. Brownian and Mr. Smithian, there's a certain amount of "foreignness" among the various groups of Armenian Americans. For example, "The

Boston Diaspora is different from the one in Los Angeles," they
say: the Armenians identify themselves as "East Coaster or West
Coaster." The ones in Boston are more European, the ones in
LA more . . . American! The Armenians from Istanbul, known
as the "Bolsohays," are more "European/cosmopolitan," while
the Armenians from Armenia have it the worst. They're still
considered "Russians" by the Americans.

As Mr. Brownian runs down the categories and subcategories,
he touches upon an even more surprising distinction: "The ones
from Van [in southeastern Turkey] are considered 'the Jews of
the Armenians.' The ones from Harput are the best-educated.
The ones from Bitlis are good at making money."

All of a sudden, in this chic Italian restaurant in Los Angeles,
the names of cities in Anatolia are being reeled off. All of these
cities are pronounced in an American accent, and when their
Armenian names are used it's impossible for a Turk to know
which one they're referring to. Interestingly, distinctions that
existed a century ago among the Armenian communities of
what is now modern Turkey have been preserved to some
extent right here in Los Angeles by men like Mr. Brownian and
Mr. Smithian. I find it hard to believe. It's only later that I'll
appreciate the truth of what they tell me.

Right from the beginning, Mr. Smithian has approached the
subject in a fairly balanced way, and in sociological terms. He
returns to his experience of the Armenian awakening: "When
we were growing up my mother and father spoke English even
at home. In the 1950s, our parents subscribed to the dominant
model of that time, the great melting pot in which differences
would be eliminated as everyone was Americanized. That view
began to change with the rise of the black movement and the
growing recognition of ethnic diversity as a form of cultural
richness. Most people my age, including me, learned to speak
Armenian only as adults. This awakening opened the door to a
kind of psychological nationalism. Today, we enjoy increasing
influence over policy and politicians because the people who

went through this awakening are now middle-aged and politically active, with rising incomes, good educations, and high social standing."

As we talk about American policy and politicians, the subject of 1915 is naturally laid on the table. They don't go into any details about what happened in 1915. They don't even attempt to explain what they think about it, what happened, or why. Mr. Brownian gets straight to the point: "We don't want land, we want money!" Just like that! Blunt as can be! A real American! He explains, "That's the message we want to give. The message we want you to convey. We can agree on a price. There are experts who can determine the exact amount. And anyway, if Turkey agrees, Europe and America will provide the money. I mean, nothing's going to come out of your pocket."

This isn't like Europe. What happened; why it happened; what can be done to change the intertwined destinies of our two peoples; how this issue affects our societies—we don't address any of those issues. And that's when I understand that, no matter how often these two men bring up the towns of Anatolia, I couldn't be further from home. No one at this table wants to talk about dialogue, or mourning, or messy details of any kind. The message they've arrived at is this: "Turkey can buy peace!"

As I sit there, astonished at the speed with which talk has turned to money, they move on to figures. Millions of dollars. They tell me exactly how many millions of dollars will seal the deal. They explain how the figure was calculated. Mr. Brownian repeats himself: "Peace can be bought."

Buying peace—I think about how removed this sentiment is from the Middle East, how foreign it is to Turkey. "Have you ever been to Turkey?" I ask Mr. Brownian.

He grows irritable. "I won't go to Turkey. When the cruise ship stopped at Kuşadası I didn't even get off the boat."

I turn to Mr. Smithian. "I wouldn't feel safe in Turkey," he says. "I wouldn't go." But then he says, "I'm learning Turkish, though. Can you recommend a good grammar book?"

There's something strange going on here. They're so removed from Turkey they'd never visit, and they'd consider this issue resolved so long as they received reparations. But one of them talks of being from Harput, the other of being from Bitlis. They're American enough to dwell only on money matters, but there's something very Anatolian about them as well. They're close enough to want to learn to Turkish, but far enough away to stay on the boat at a Turkish port of call. I'm still thinking this through as talk returns to money, yet again.

Mr. Brownian does a quick audit of profit and loss for Turkey. "According to my calculations, the money Turkey spends in America on lobbying for its denialist policy would be enough to cover reparations." The look he gives me expresses the astonishment he feels at my inability to grasp the logic of his calculation, of this profitable investment.

The talk at our table is so centered on money that I decide not to ask any of my other questions. As I get up to go, Mr. Brownian says, "You should convey this message to Turkey. We expect a finite figure for our infinite pain. You understand, don't you?"

I do, I do . . .

I also understand what Vartkes Yeghiayan, the man who arranged this interview, meant when he said, "The people you're going to meet are nothing like the ones in Europe." I knew from an earlier meeting with Mr. Yeghiayan that he doesn't necessarily agree with them either. Not to say that the meeting with him was much easier.

★

"Turn right in 350 feet. Then turn right in 150 feet. After five feet . . ."

We keep getting lost because Yurttaş keeps getting fed up with the droning GPS directions and switching off the device with a muttered, "Ehh!" And then, because we keep getting lost, Navigation Lady is reactivated and Yurttaş starts quarreling with her again. The line that irritates him the most is: "Recalculating!"

As we lose our bearings amid the tangled freeways, exit ramps, and flyovers, our nag of a Navigation Lady recalculates and recalculates. If there really is a seaside city called Los Angeles, it's in hiding. There's an ocean somewhere, but no scent of salty sea air, no low roar of crashing waves. For a few days now, Yurttaş and I have been living on an alien planet specially designed for cars and non-smokers. We flee our mistake of a hotel, a true dive that we learn too late has earned the accolade of "perfect spot to have a secret rendezvous," jump into our car, the only place we can smoke without getting crucified, and begin searching for a place the inhabitants of this planet call "Glendale," which is where we're meeting with Yeghiayan.

When we finally enter the sleek offices of Attorney Vartkes Yeghiayan, who'd agreed to meet with us only after being supplied with numerous references, we see a framed article that appeared about him in Turkish daily *Hürriyet*: "The lawyer who filed the Armenian insurance claim!" Yeghiayan finds us looking at the wall, and greets us with an amused smile. He's nothing like the gruff, combative man I'd expected. He has the cultured, jaunty air of a *beyefendi*—an Ottoman gentleman—and seems to be the kind of person who chooses his words carefully and prefers to brush off the cares of this world with an anecdote.

He immediately informs me of his little act of espionage: "I googled you."

"I'm not surprised," I counter. "The minute I began researching the Armenian issue I realized I'd become the one being researched most of the time."

He smiles and, standing there in front of the *Hürriyet* clipping, launches into an account of the case that made him famous both in Armenian circles and in Turkey.

After switching from pre-med to history at Berkeley, Yeghiayan graduated from Lincoln Law School and would spend the next thirty years working as an attorney. One day, the things he read in the memoirs of Henry Morgenthau, US ambassador to the Ottoman Empire from 1913 to 1916, would inspire him to conduct further historical research, thus laying the groundwork for his leading role in that famous class-action suit.

"A conversation between the ambassador and Talat Pasha is recorded on about page 200 of that book. Talat Pasha tells Morgenthau that none of the Ottoman Armenians who'd taken out American insurance policies were alive, for which reason the policies had reverted to the Empire. He also requested that a list of policy holders be supplied. It was that brief exchange that caused me to begin my research. I'd worked for the Nixon administration, so I first sent a letter to the Department of the Interior asking if they had any information on this subject. They told me that there might be a record of the policies in the National Archives. I wrote to the archives and received a response ten days later. They informed me that they had a lot of microfilmed records and asked me to pay a service charge. That's the quickest I've ever paid for anything in my life. Microfilm of 590 pages of documentation arrived not long afterward. When World War I began, New York Life, the insurance company that had sold the policies, withdrew all its operations in Anatolia. For that reason, the Armenians began paying their premiums to the US embassy. And that's why there was a record of the claimants in the US National Archives. I followed a paper trail that led me from Istanbul to Washington to New York Life. I asked the insurance company how much those policies were worth. They told me: $10.8 million. Now that I'd found the money, it was time to track down the claimants. I placed an announcement in an Armenian newspaper published in America. It was a mistake, of course. Hundreds of people came to me with photographs, unrelated documents, and accounts of all they'd lost. But that crowd of people also included a ninety-year-old woman. For some reason, she'd kept the original records of an insurance agreement for all those years. The descendant of a claimant, she'd been trying to collect for thirty years. The insurance company told her she'd have to produce a death certificate because she wasn't the original policyholder. But there'd been a genocide; there were no such records, of course. That's when I decided to turn this into a cause. I hadn't expected a ninety-year-old to agree to such a long and difficult legal process. But I was wrong. She banged her fist on the table and exclaimed, 'I've always tried to understand why God has kept me alive for so long. Now I know.' Actually, she died soon afterwards, but her brother, Martin Marootian, agreed to take her place as our leading plaintiff."

Yeghiayan tells me how the statute of limitations was also an issue, describing how he had to act like a "deer hunter" and wait patiently until the right target appeared. "There's no statute of limitations for genocide, of course; but there is one for insurance policies. The Jews had managed to have a provision introduced. It extended, until the end of 2010, the statute of limitations for claims similar to ours. I needed a new law. I spoke to some Armenian senators in the California legislature and explained. Six months later, in 2000, state regulations allowed lawsuits in California for claims arising from the Armenian genocide. I did all this as quietly as possible. If the insurance companies had got wind of it, they'd definitely have blocked it."

Yeghiayan filed his class action suit and eventually settled for $20 million. He then placed ads on the internet to find the beneficiaries. Of a total of 2,300 policy holders, 1,600 came forward. The payout due to the missing 700 claimants was donated to Armenian charities. Yeghiayan filed a similar suit against French insurance company AXA (formerly L'union vie), which was settled for $17.5 million.

For both Armenians and Turkey, the most important aspect of this complicated legal process was the designation, for purposes of the law, of "Armenian genocide victims." Even more significant was the possibility that the success of the insurance claims would be used as a legal precedent for reparation claims by the American Diaspora. According to Yeghiayan, a team of economics professors was formed to calculate the current value of all the premiums paid to the insurance companies active in the Ottoman Empire during that period. Yeghiayan says the same methods can be used to calculate the total material losses of Armenians living in Anatolia prior to 1915. The successful case filed by Yeghiayan has produced "the price of peace" for the Diaspora. But would it work?

For all his references to settlements and legal decisions, Vartkes Yeghiayan personally believes that these methods don't have that much meaning for either side: "Rulings and resolutions recognizing the genocide are actually meaningless unless they bring the two sides together. Many countries now officially recognize the genocide. And the result? Not one of them has caused Armenians and Turks to come together to solve the problem. Even worse, Turkey's reaction to these resolutions is so vehement that the issue has become even more highly charged." A disillusioned smile on his lips, Vartkes Yeghiayan outlines the rules of the game here in America and across the globe: "Everyone's making money from this. This dispute is making some Armenians and Turks rich. It's become a financial matter. 'Give me money and we'll get your law passed!' That's what's been going on for fifty years. Lawyers and politicians in the US; lobbyists in Turkey—this is lucrative for them all."

Yeghiayan is a lawyer. He doesn't need to get into arguments over what happened; he simply follows the rules of the game, according to law, in order to do whatever it takes to win. Weary, perhaps, of talking about this, the more cynical side of the fight for justice, he gets up, walks over to the bookshelf, and pulls out one of the many files. His expression softens as he carefully opens the file and removes a photograph. It's a picture of a child—a boy or a girl, it's hard to tell. A sepia photograph of a barefoot child in an Arab-style white headdress, wearing what looks like a long nightdress and a lambskin, and holding a staff.

The look on that face is that of a child who's forgotten how to cry. "Pretty, isn't she?" chuckles Vartkes.

And then his voice softens to match his face, as he gazes at the photograph. "That's my dad." He pauses. "At the age of fifteen, after he'd walked through the desert and made it to a city in Syria, he went to a photography shop and had that picture taken. 'I haven't got any money,' he said, 'but I'll work and I'll pay for it. You should take my picture because I'll keep it for the rest of my life and I'll always remember.' Don't ask me for the details, but my father died in Ethiopia. And I'm Ethiopian."

He laughs at my surprise, but when I open my mouth to ask a question, he silences me with a wave of his hand. He really meant it; he doesn't want to go into details. "When my father died in Ethiopia this photograph was in his wallet. At first I had no idea who it was. I'd never seen it before. So I asked my mother. 'That's your father,' she said. 'But why did he keep it in his wallet all these years? Out of anger with the Turks?' I asked. 'No,' she replied, 'so he wouldn't forget how he was saved.' And now I keep that photo so I won't forget."

After all the lawsuits, and in light of his father's story, how does Vartkes Yeghiayan feel about Turks? Yeghiayan is a man who prefers to respond to a question with a story. He moves on to his own story. "I studied at the American Missionary School in Cyprus. Again, don't ask me for any details. Back then I was famous not as a lawyer but as a young athlete! I was a good tennis player. When I became the Cypriot tennis champion, the *Armenian Mirror Spectator* came to interview me. 'Are you proud to be Armenian?' the reporter asked. Annoyed, I responded, 'The Turks trained me, and I'm trying to beat Greeks. What's any of that got to do with being an Armenian!' The reporter went and complained to my principal, who sat down and wrote a letter to my father. The letter my father then sent to me went something like this: 'The reporter asked you that question so you could inspire other Armenian boys to be as successful as you. Armenians may not have done anything for you, but you can do a lot for them.' So, I guess that answers your question."

It did. After we left Vartkes' office I looked at the old photo he'd given me. Those eyes—eyes that would never forget hunger. I thought of my grandmother. I was reminded of a story she was fond of telling me, for some reason: "We were so poor that when we had fish for dinner I'd take the bones to school in my lunch pail the next day. When no one was looking, I'd squat in the corner and gnaw on those bones. And that's why you're never to complain about food."

Privation and pain: most of the people who've passed through Anatolia have known both. And if that's why Vartkes Yeghiayan seems like a brother to me, it's also the reason I feel so remote from those men and their calculations in the Italian restaurant. As remote as I feel from the deafening speeches made by Turkish nationalists. Sometimes I feel like we're a little community of our own—we, the ones with a sincere desire to share our stories without any of the shouting and shriek-ing. A people bound together by tales of Anatolia. Children of people who have gone hungry. And when they begin exchang-ing stories, these people, they'll change not only the way Turk views Armenian and Armenian views Turk—they'll change the way the entire world looks at the Armenian-Turkish issue. Our people have scattered, to Armenia, France, America, and who knows how many other places—members of a Diaspora even in their own countries. Turks who have mourned the loss of what's best about their country are part of this Diaspora. And so are those who marched and wept in Hrant's funeral cortege. And today, as I stare at that photograph of a hungry boy, I believe, truly believe for the first time, that stories are more powerful than shouts and roars. And stories will last longer.

Chapter 18

What do mothers love more than their children?

"THESE PEOPLE ARE becoming more and more like the grandmothers and grandfathers we never knew."

Ruth Tomasian pushes back a lock of graying hair and shows me another old photograph of a young couple. The deference with which this engaging middle-aged woman shows me the black-and-white images of these men and women reminds me of the veneration shown to the elderly. Ruth is one of those women you might come across anywhere in the world, women who have found a story they believe in and patiently pursue until it becomes their life. She seems older than her years—perhaps because she's been studying the faces in these pictures for so many years.

She softly tells me her story: her father's Armenian heritage, her American mother, and "Project Save," the archive of memories to which she's devoted her life. "I used to design costumes for the theatre. One day, I began collecting photographs of Armenians as research for a play. Up until that day I'd always considered myself to be American. But when I found those photos in our attic, I began a journey into the past—both my own and that of the Armenian people. When other families started sending me their photos, I realized something. They'd always tell me the story behind the photo, and what I realized was how peaceful I felt as I listened to tales about my father's ancestors. And I said to myself, 'I'm not going to make any money chasing after stories, but it's not like I'll make any in the theater either. So I might as well do what makes me happy!' And that's how these photos and the stories of their owners began to accumulate. What you see here is an enormous Armenian family album."

Project Save is housed in a hushed room on the top floor of the Armenian Museum in Watertown, an Armenian neighborhood in Boston. The moment you step into the large, dimly lit room, you're greeted by somber faces in large oval frames lining the walls. Newlyweds, a girl in a white frock seated at a piano, a middle-aged couple—these are the people, long gone, whom Ruth describes as "the grandfathers and grandmothers we never knew."

I'm reminded of a line from Bertolucci's *The Dreamers*: "We compare our mothers and fathers to our friends' parents, but our grandmothers and grandfathers are always unique." What makes them so unique is their unqualified, doting love. But what makes the grandparents you never knew unique?

We make conversation, looking not at each other but at the photographs. As we wander through an Armenian neighborhood of the 1920s, Ruth points to the "upstanding American citizens." "Back then, the most important thing was to become American. That's why most Armenian men took American wives. Others kept to tradition and traveled to Lebanon and Armenia to find brides. That's made something of a comeback these days: many of the young men prefer to have a wife from Armenia."

The room seems to fill with the scent of memories, of houses and people. Ruth smiles when she catches me sniffing a few photos, as though trying to get a whiff of the past. Now, along with America's "upstanding citizens," we see the occasional snapshot from Anatolia—pictures of the "other" ones. Men being lined up and taken away, turning round for a split second to look at the camera. Women whose men have been rounded up; in these, perhaps the first and only photos of their lives, they haven't had a chance to comb their hair. I recognize some of the cities: Sivas, Malatya, Elazığ . . . Some of the landmarks are unchanged, and identifiable even today. I find myself visualizing what happened, the streets and roads along which the Armenians were led and driven. The more closely I study the faces and places, the more vivid are the scenes playing out in my mind's eye. I can almost hear them. Could those people in the photographs have known that their lives and their stories would lead, one day, to the word "reparations"—to the betrayal of their friends, the loss of their homes and loved ones, the way they were sacrificed at a tumultuous point in history? Could they have imagined what their grandchildren would say one day, the descendants who don't speak their language and whose faces resemble foreigners more than their own?

As they trudged along roads of no return, their black-and-white images frozen forever at the click of a shutter, could they have known that very moment would be so carefully stored away one day? Those eyes staring into the lens seem to be staring into the future, into the eyes that will one day gaze back into theirs, deep into their eyes . . .

The words burst out of me: "This'll never be resolved. Sometimes I feel as though . . . It's become a huge industry. Not just politics and money; a psychological industry, too, for both sides. An industry of anguish."

When a Turk and an Armenian meet, details don't have to be explained at length, and Ruth immediately understands what I mean: "An industry of anguish? Interesting, that's the first time I've heard anyone describe it that way," she says. She pauses, and then she looks at the photos with a pained smile. "That's right. An industry of anguish."

She picks up a photo between her fingertips and sets it on the other side of the table to make room for the next photo— slowly, as though handling something wounded, careful not to jar. When she speaks, she too begins mid-thought: "The Armenians had such rich lives. We diminish ourselves by focusing exclusively on the genocide. But we need a country as well. The land of Armenia captured in these photos is gone, so we're building a country out of our memories."

Girls in white lace dresses, thick black hair gathered into chignons. Wristwatches and dusty button-up shoes. Heavyset boys struggling to maintain heroic poses. A group of men and women, weary but standing tall in front of a house still under construction, in front of horse-and-buggies . . . They're in America!

"That's the reason I started doing this. There's a lot more to the Armenians than genocide. These photos are being collected in order to understand these people and to show how they lived." As Ruth pulls open another drawer of photographs, she tells me about the famous Armenian picnics. There are panoramic shots of huge groups of picnickers in the 1920s. "They arrived here before 1915. Judging from the photographs, picnics are where they did most of their socializing. Look, they're all dressed in their finest clothes." We scan the smiling faces, and Ruth draws my attention to the girls: "The picnics were where they met their prospective husbands. That's why the girls are always so beautifully turned out."

The sense of sorrow and longing so intrinsic to the word "diaspora" dissipates as we look at these photos. I consider the story of the Armenians who arrived here before 1915. A reading of Armenian history shows that the themes of exile and migration have always been integral to Armenian identity. But, prior to 1915, the myth of the "old country" wasn't part of Armenian identity, even if they had suffered massacres at various points in their history. In the faces I'm scanning right now, I detect ambition and hope—theirs is the expression of the "American dream," not of the trauma following 1915. As the descendants of the people in these photographs sought an identity as members of the Armenian Diaspora, they must have internalized those later events, and made the later suffering their own. As they sought to remain a distinct community and to remember who they were, the stories of massacre would have bound them more tightly than accounts of picnics. In an adopted land, where the locals couldn't even tell you apart from an Indian, you'd have needed a compelling story for yourself and your children.

From the archives of Project Sate: Armenians in Kimonos

As we move along the table, to the unopened drawers and new pictures on the walls, Ruth points to a photograph. "Not everyone went west!" I squint at the picture. I do a double-take. "Surprising isn't it? Armenians in kimonos! Some of them went to Japan, and India."

"Scattered like pomegranate seeds," I murmur. "That's right," she agrees, "like pomegranate seeds."

She shows me a group of musicians. The instruments and the men have stepped out of old Istanbul, but the caption reads "Buenos Aires." A memory pops into my head. "That's funny, I'd forgotten all about that. My first tango instructor was Armenian, at the Armenian Tango Center in Buenos Aires." He was a white-haired man, with white skin, dressed head-to-toe in white. Even though I knew he was Armenian, I hadn't thought to ask how he'd ended up in Argentina. But I'll never forget what he told me: "Señorita, you're trying to lead the dance. This dance is led by men. In order to tango you must learn to surrender!" I share this story with Ruth and we joke about "women who don't know how to surrender."

As Ruth and I journey together through the past, she isn't Armenian and I'm not Turkish. She's a person pursuing the stories of the people from my country; I'm a person pursuing the stories of the people in her country. We don't put a name to our stories, but we tell them with compassion, and we listen with understanding. The tone will be very different later that evening. It's April 24 and, naturally, a memorial ceremony is being held in Boston.

At her desk, Ruth jots down the address of the ceremony venue as I continue to look at the portraits hanging on the walls, those Armenians of old—the grandfathers and grandmothers. As I'll do so often, here in America, I talk to Hrant. Through him, and through his absence, everything has taken on new meaning. There's one thing everyone talked about in Armenia, in France, and, now, in America: the absence of grandfathers and grandmothers. I remember how Hrant mentioned the same thing the night he poured out his heart and told me his life story.

Armenians and Turks represent themselves and their lives in very different ways. In describing their societies, Turks tend to look forward, Armenians back. The lyrics of an old Turkish march adopted in recent days by young men and women reacting to the rise of political Islam run through my head:

> We've always emerged unsullied
> Ten years after every war
> And in ten years we have created
> Fifteen million youths of every age . . .

That's from the Tenth Anniversary March of the Republic. It's still being sung in Turkey today. I remember remixes being played at summer discos, and everyone joining in. The lyrics ringing in my ears haven't taken on new meaning: " . . . unsullied . . . fifteen million youths of every age . . ."

We Turks are always young, and always wishing to be younger. I glance over at Ruth. I think about the various Armenian women and girls who are younger than her. At a very young age, they start out in life in the company of the aged, listening to the stories of another age. In Turkey, we're raised to be younger, faster, more dynamic. Yes, we memorize a few dates and a few marches. But even the tales told us by our grandmothers begin with the founding of the Republic. How difficult it will be for these two communities to understand each other. And yet, how easy it's been for these two women, me and Ruth, to share stories of our common humanity.

"I'll see you there," Ruth says as she hands me the address and a brochure. The program is to begin with a religious ceremony, followed by a screening of *Voices*, a documentary by the artist Apo Torosyan, and then a panel. According to the brochure, the panel participants are calling for more research, much more research, into the past. I scan the list of the twenty-six groups participating in the event. One of them is "Armenians of Aintab." That is to say, Antep, the city in southeastern Turkey. It happens to me all the time. I'll see a Turkish or Armenian word transcribed into French or English and fail to recognize it. The names of people can be particularly disconcerting: it's strange to read a name derived from a Turkish word "in English." But many of the first immigrants to America and Paris must have considered their names too strange for their new countrymen, and chosen to leave their Turkish names behind, in Anatolia. How am I supposed to write their names now? The way they spell it in English, or the way it's written in Turkish? I ask everyone I interview. Most say I'm free to spell their names any way I choose, but some prefer the version transliterated into a foreign language. A few of them even allow me to use Turkish characters, like "ç" and "ı." I look at Ruth's surname. Her story seems to be one of addition, not subtraction, as though "-ian" was added to "Tomas" when she become interested in her Armenian roots. Even the names in the Diaspora have a subtext fraught with meaning.

As we're walking out of Project Save, an elderly man walks in—one of the project employees. When he hears me speaking Turkish with Yurttaş, his face lights up. "*Hoşgeldin*," he says, in Turkish. "Welcome." Before we can ask, he's already telling us, thrilled: "*İskenderunluyum ben.*" So, he's from ancient Alexandretta, in modern Turkey's Hatay province. He takes our hands and squeezes them, and squeezes some more. He doesn't want to let go. Finally, embarrassed by his own show of delight, he releases our hands. We walk away. I glance back at this old man so excited to have met people from the old country. His face dims as we step through the door. The joy on that old man's face and the sorrow in the e-mail that elderly man sent me after the Armenia articles appeared aren't part of the narrative in the abbreviated version of a story that some have reduced to the single word "reparations." Mr. Brownian said we could "buy peace." But what of that sorrowful grandfather or that joyous old man? Who's going to "lobby" for them? I realize just how much we've lost with Hrant's death and his advocacy of a "third way," of the development of a common language of reconciliation for both Armenians and Turks. What we've lost, along with Hrant, is a human dimension in which sorrow and joy would have colored our language. Can we find enough people on both sides to develop a new way to speak together? Are there mothers willing to transmit the past to their children not in Turkish and Armenian, but in a language of good will and understanding? What would happen if children grew up speaking this new language?

But, then again, people will never tire of raising their children to carry on the fight.

There's something I've always wondered, above all else: Do mothers love their children less than they love their communities, their religions, and their states? The mothers of children sacrificed to a sense of identity; the women who haven't yet given birth—will they refuse one day to give their children to a cause?

The ceremony later that evening seems to anticipate my question.

Chapter 19

"May the air ring with our stamping feet!"

THE ROOM FILLS with the sound of stomping boots.
The door opens onto the packed auditorium of the Watertown Armenian Cultural and Educational Center, and they come marching in. Leading the way are two teenagers, side by side, carrying the Armenian and American flags; lined up behind them are boys and girls in scout uniforms, arranged oldest to youngest, children as young as seven struggling to ensure their stamping feet are heard. Bringing up the rear are the spiritual leaders. In the silent auditorium, the sound of marching footsteps gets louder and louder. When they all reach the front of the stage they come to a halt. Men of religion from six different churches stand in front of the stage, praying in Armenian. I recognize the Armenian for "genocide" and the name "Hrant." The little soldiers of the Armenian Youth Federation stand at attention. I take in the scene on the stage: religion, flag, children and "genocide"!

Here, in the conference room of a city in a country of jeans and Coca-Cola, MTV and the Statue of Liberty, hippies and Wall Street, a people are willing themselves into existence. A highly disciplined people are using their new language, English, and the mother tongue they seek to preserve, Armenian, as they redefine themselves. Religion, country, "genocide," and discipline . . .

Religion, country, the War of Liberation, and discipline—somewhere in Turkey, at this very moment, children the same age might be involved in a similar ceremony. They too are struggling to stamp their feet as loudly as possible. And they're singing a march:

> On our brows, the garland of enlightenment
> We're Turkish youth, advancing towards the divine light
> Turks, unparalleled on the face of the earth
> A race that knows no fear . . .

Or:

> The sun is rising on the horizon
> Let's march, my friends
> Be heard by earth, sky, water
> May the air ring with the sound of our stamping feet!

Why "stamping feet"? What's wrong with normal footsteps? Perhaps nations or peoples want everyone to know when they've arrived. Or perhaps the sound of their footsteps confirms their own existence. Or maybe, by having their little children march like soldiers—*rap, rap, rap*—the community is convinced that they're all possessed of an iron will, and are indestructible. "We're bringing up new soldiers," they're saying, "and, for ever more, we'll continue to give birth to soldiers, for our people, for our cause." Whatever the underlying reason, one thing is clear: these footsteps are not meant simply for walking along the ground. There's something else, and it has nothing to do with walking or with children.

A young woman takes the microphone. In a tremulous voice she sings the American national anthem, followed by the Armenian national anthem. As preparations are being made for the video screening, I try to arrange some interviews for the following day. The first person I find is Apo Torosyan, the painter and artist whose video we're about to watch. After I mention my letters of introduction and references, he agrees to speak with me. Then I move on to others, one by one. Every time I introduce myself to someone, they turn to the person I've just spoken to, with questioning eyes. If that persons nods, the second person agrees to talk. And that's how I silently and steadily gain admittance to the community. Everyone hands me one of the brochures made available at the entrance to the hall. I've nearly arranged all the interviews I'll do in Boston when I spot Ruth. She brings me a calendar entitled "Armenians on Stage." It features amazing pictures and in-depth information on the Armenian actors and theater troupes in America at the turn of the last century. I flick through the pages. The panelists on stage continue droning as I smile at the photos. The bundle of glossy brochures slides off my lap. One of them documents the steady increase in bilateral trade between Turkey and America since 1980. It also lists the dates of various events, including Ronald Reagan's mention of the "Armenian genocide" in 1981, as he was talking about the Holocaust; the approval in 1984 of a US House Joint resolution proclaiming April 24 a day of memorial for the Armenian geno-cide; the adoption in 1996 by the US House of Representatives of a resolution barring the use of American economic aid to fund "denial of the Armenian genocide"; a law forbidding the use of American aid to fund Turkish lobbying activities . . . They're all there, in chronological order, but the volume of trade between the US and Turkey has risen steadily. That must be the argument presented by the Armenians to profit-oriented American foreign policy-makers: "Don't worry about the economic consequences of recognizing the genocide; it'll be business as usual." Another brochure is headlined: "Thank you, members of Congress!" It goes on, "Listed below are the names of the members of Congress who have taken a favorable position concerning recognition of the Genocide. Please pick up the phone and follow the instructions below as you thank them: a receptionist will answer the phone. Say you want to speak to an official from the State Department, and then read the following message . . ."

I stick the brochures between the pages of the calendar Ruth gave me, covering the faces of smiling Armenians with brochures on money. *Voices* begins on a large screen: photographs too horrible to contemplate; images of children who've starved to death; bodies swinging from nooses; Talat Pasha, Cemal Pasha—the Committee of Union and Progress. Five elderly men talking about what happened in the late 1800s, in the early1900s. They're crying. The story of 106-year-old Yeghsapet takes place in Harput. His entire family gone, he was left with a Turkish family, as was his sister. Yeghsapet was later reunited with his family in America, but his sister didn't want to leave behind her husband and five children to join him. Today, somewhere in Harput, there's probably a woman my age who doesn't even know that her mother's mother was Armenian.

Next, Sossos, who was born on Lesbos in 1919 after his family fled İzmir (Smyrna), talks of his visit to the Aegean town of Ayvalık many years later. One of the old men he met said, "Brother, you went away. But when you left, you took the abundance of this place with you."

There are photographs in the documentary of the spacious houses of Ayvalık. I remember touring the coves of Ayvalık the previous summer, and the captain repeating what so many of the Western Aegean Turks say: "When the *Rum* were here, it was full of vineyards. And when they went, what did the Turks do? They didn't tend the vines, and the islands turned barren."

Those ruined buildings on the islands don't seem to await anyone; they have no past; not much is said about who built them, about how or why they were abandoned. What little we do know belongs not to the recent past, but to olden times. Most of us don't stop to consider that there are women the same age as our grandmothers who left those houses and went off to a new life. Kayaköy[17] is like that—a ghost town on a moun-

17 Kayaköy, located in southwestern Turkey, was abandoned by its Ottoman Greek inhabitants as a result of the 1923 population exchange between Greece and Turkey, according to the terms of which an estimated 2 million people were mutually expelled from their lands of birth.

tainside, its cisterns still damp, its hundreds of stone buildings in ruins. No one goes into those houses anymore. The doors and windows have been removed, and the village stands there, like a corpse picked clean. The Turks living in the nearby villages will tell you how decent, knowledgeable, and skilled the old Anatolian Greeks were. It's not in the history books, but go to any abandoned Greek town in and around İzmir province and you'll soon appreciate the true affection the locals still have for their old neighbors. But when it comes to the Armenians . . . Until the books I read before I came to America and the documentary I'm watching now, I didn't even know there were any Armenians in İzmir. And not much is said about them in eastern Turkey either. What's behind this amnesia? Why, even though we still talk of having driven the Greek army into the sea, do we never talk about having "driven" Armenians anywhere? I was born and raised in İzmir and can reel off the names of the old Greek quarters. But I don't know any Armenian ones. That's the deep silence Hrant was talking about—and it's something far more disturbing than a refusal to say "genocide": "We were here. Why can't you remember?"

As an Istanbul Armenian, he insisted, "I'm here. Why don't you see me?"

And what of those marching children? What would he say about that? "Try to understand," he'd probably say, "that they're trying to stay together, that their past and their identity are more important to them than to Turks, who have a state."

And what would he have said about the addition of his name to the "Genocide Memorial Prayer?" The rounding up of about 600 Armenian politicians and intellectuals on April 24, 1915, is memorialized today as "the beginning of the genocide." What would Hrant say to being memorialized as one of those 600? What would Hrant, who criticized an Armenian identity resting on the status of "perpetual victim," have said to becoming one more element in that victim identity? Isabelle was right when she said, in Istanbul, that Hrant had become someone else. In a last-ditch effort to reinforce the mortar of nationalist Turkish identity with Hrant's blood, extremists had suggested "Hrant might have been killed by an Armenian."

And now, here in America . . . "Did you enjoy it?" Apo Torosyan is asking me about his documentary. I'd been so preoccupied with the scouts, the marching, the images of dead children, and the prayers for Hrant that I'd found it increasingly difficult to follow the ever more complex stories of the elderly people on the screen. "Pain," is all I say. "Pain," he echoes. We stand there, looking at each other. "I'll be expecting you at my workshop," he says. "There are some things I'd like to show you." The following day we'll be going to Apo's house, and the day after that to other houses and offices. We've listened to many stories, and we'll be listening to more. As I leave the auditorium I'm thinking to myself, "Why are they telling me all this?" and I continue to ponder this question as Yurttaş and Navigation Lady quarrel in the streets of Boston over the location of a restaurant. And I wonder, once again, what it would have been like had I arrived in their midst as a reporter from Alaska. Would they have narrated their stories any differently? Would I have listened any differently? How have I been listening to them in Yerevan, Paris, Los Angeles, and Boston?

At that moment, I gain a clearer understanding of the way I've been communicating with Armenians: by simply opening my eyes and listening, without contradiction or objection. Some adopt a combative tone from the start, expecting to be challenged. When they see that I'm listening without endorsement or contradiction, they begin to speak more calmly. The anticipation of contradiction has fueled their anger as much as the stories they're telling, I now realize. They need to talk, and they need you to listen—that's all. And as you listen, their tone softens, and most of them even end up talking about the "good Turks" as well—as though, while you listen, the tone of their stories slowly strikes the right balance and temper. It's different if someone is making their case to you on a personal level: it's no longer a story; rhetoric is employed, and you find yourself thrust into the position of someone who has to "deny" or "recognize" genocide. When it's established that I represent no one but myself, the rhetoric is abandoned and the personal narrative begins. Simply listening to someone may not make them feel better, but it does improve your relationship with them. A willingness to listen without judgment helps to smooth away tensions and alleviate the burden of these conflicting versions of a shared past. What I mean to say is, sometimes it's better not to talk; sometimes it's better to let others do the talking and to know how to listen in silence. That's what they need; I sense it every time. Even for the people in America, who are so far from Anatolia, who now have so little connection to Turkey and the lands of which they speak—they need it too; I feel it every time I listen to them.

Even though the Greek restaurant doesn't have *rakı*, Yurttaş and I are ecstatic at being able to order ouzo. But when the waitress brings vodka glasses full of straight ouzo, Yurttaş mutters in Turkish, "You can go to the moon, but you don't know how to drink *rakı*!" Our dismayed response to the American-size plates of meze, to those mounds of shrimp and *tzatziki*, is also typically Turkish.

The night ends with us getting into the car clutching paper cups of ouzo, returning to our hotel on the riverbank. Enis Batur's book[18] pops into my head, and I ask myself, "Okay, America's a big joke—but just how long can we keep laughing?"

18   A reference to Turkish author and essayist Enis Batur's *Travels in New York: America's a Big Joke, Dear Frank, But Just How Funny Is That?*

Chapter 20

"Locked horns"

A S I WAS arriving at Apo Torosyan's home in a suburb of towering pine trees and houses decked out with American flags, the last thing I expected was a discussion about the poet Nâzım Hikmet. Even more surprisingly, Apo also spoke of the artist Bedri Rahmi Eyüboğlu and the folk singer Ruhi Su.

"We'd meet up at Narmanlı Han. Bedri Rahmi Eyüboğlu was my teacher at Akademi, the Academy of Fine Arts. Back then, we were all trying to imitate Western painters. One day he came into the atelier and gave us this look. 'You're all sitting around like a bunch of old ladies at your knitting. Do something you can truly call your own,' he said. I'll never forget it."

Upon graduation from the academy, Apo moved to America, where he's been living for the past forty years. In his art, he depicts the things he hasn't forgotten over those forty years. We go up to his atelier on the top floor of his two-story home, and he shows me his "Anatolia" series. Embedded on canvas are slices of bread, square and circular. "My ancestors died from bread," says Apo, "either from a lack of it or from the bread itself." Then he adds, "I have this bread baked by an Italian cook."

As I ponder whether the baking of Anatolian bread in America by an Italian chef is the tragic or the comic side of his story, Apo explains: "In 1915, my father Hrant was five, my aunt Repekah fifteen, my uncle Hovhannes seventeen. My uncle dressed up as a woman and fled to Marseilles at around that time. Rounded up along with all the other Armenian men one day was Sarkis Agopyan, the man who was to become my aunt's husband. He was told, 'You're being inducted into the army,' and taken out of the city, where they were put to work digging trenches. Then they were killed, and filled those same trenches. The rifle misfired when it was Sarkis' turn, but he was able to throw himself into the trench and play dead. He lay in that makeshift grave for three days and three nights. Then he fled to Bulgaria with my aunt. My father was five when he was forced to resettle. When I'd ask my father about those days, the only thing he'd say was, 'There's no God. If there were a God, those days would never have been lived.' He never wanted to talk about it."

Behind the paintings on the easels in the second–floor work-shop are aerial photos of Kınalı Island in Istanbul and snapshots taken on the islands in the 1970s. There are smiling photographs of his father, "handsome Hrant," and his mother, "Greek girl Marie," taken on Kınalı Island in the 1950s. Which is to say, Apo is from an Armenian family who remained in Turkey after 1915. So, if he and his family stayed in Turkey, and if his father and mother didn't tell him much about 1915, where did Apo get his accounts of what happened that year?

"In Turkey, I wanted to be accepted by the Turks. 'I'm not one of those bad Armenians,' I'd say to myself. I wouldn't even read anything in Armenian, and most of those books were in that language. Books on the genocide were kept secret in Turkey. And I saw them as propaganda." Apo points to the family's tiny house in the photograph of Kınalı Island. "The new owners aren't looking after it very well," he says, before he resumes his story. "I completely denied my identity. Then, in 1964, the train I was taking to Europe passed through Sofia. I'd arranged to meet with Sarkis, my aunt's husband. I looked over and there was this skeleton of a man, holding a sack. The clothes on his back were about fifty years old. I was wearing jeans. He handed me the sack, then he gripped me by the arm and said,

'Apraham, don't go back there, they'll kill you.' I guess he was still living in the past."

I ask Apo how he learned the stories of his ancestors. "Over many years," he replies. "After my mother died I became preoccupied with the subject. It was 1999. I realized that she was going to die soon, and I started reading. I read history books. Then I remembered the letters my uncle had sent me years earlier. I found them in the garage. Amid all the cares of everyday life, of making a living and of the children, I'd totally forgotten about them. The letters told the stories of our family. The bread I use in my paintings comes from those stories, and from the sack Sarkis gave me at the train station in Sofia."

Apo leads us downstairs and continues telling his story as we eat the kebab with garlic-yogurt sauce he's made for us. "I didn't open that sack when Sarkis gave it to me at the station. But when I got on the train and looked inside, I saw it was full of bread. He'd presented me with bread. My grandmother Elizabeth died because of bread. After she was forcibly resettled, she was taken to a hospital near Aleppo. She'd had nothing but bread to eat for so long that her flesh had become like bread. She died there. My other relatives died on the road from a lack of bread. That's why I say my ancestors died from bread, or from a lack of bread. And that's why bread is at the center of my art." He glances over at his wife Jennifer, who is of Irish origin. "They knew what starvation was too. People who have known hunger recognize each other."

As I eat my kebab, I consider how difficult it is to talk about hunger in a place like America. The people of Anatolia believe bread is god-sent and sacred, and would understand what he was saying; but how could Americans, in whose movies children are shown having food fights, possibly understand? How could you explain to them that Anatolian children are taught to pick up any bread they see on the ground, kiss it three times, and put it to one side? How could they grasp the keen awareness of starvation instilled in Anatolian children who are told that any leftover crumbs of bread "will be swept up in the next world with your eyelashes"?

Apo tells me about going to visit Edincik, his grandfather's village near Bandırma. I'm reminded of what Serge Avédikian said when we spoke in Paris: "It's modern Turkey's latest tourist activity: Armenians coming back to see the villages of their grandfathers."

He doesn't cry when he talks about his village or his family's painful history; but when the subject of his friends comes up, his eyes fill with tears—not while talking about land, or home, or "accounts of the genocide," but only when referring to the friends he left behind in Istanbul. When, in middle-age, after his mother's death, he belatedly discovered the stories of 1915, perhaps those photographs taken on Kınalı Island, now in his atelier in America, started to mean something else. Perhaps those memories of 1915, which were relatively new to him, have caused a shift in his perception of the country in which he was born and grew up. But when it comes to his friends, they're the same as always, close to his heart and warm. When he sees people from the "mother country," a different language bursts forth and he excitedly begins to recite the poems of Bedri Rahmi Eyüboğlu: "Did you know he was talking about an Armenian girl when he wrote 'my black mulberry; my black grape'?"

Armenian artist Apo, who is trying to explain hunger here in America—land of plenty and of eating more, and still more—tells us that he learned to make kebab with yogurt from his older sister. The yogurt is Greek, the *pide* on which it is served is the pita bread sold in Europe and America, and as for the tomato sauce . . . But we eat it because it's good. We eat, and then we eat some more.

★

"Would you like something to eat?"

"No, thank you."

We're back at a restaurant in Los Angeles. This time, Attorney Vartkes Yeghiayan is going to introduce us to some of his friends.

Yeghiayan has taken us to one of the regular weekly meetings he holds with some of the leading names in the Armenian Diaspora. Wealthy businessmen and lawyers, poolside. Most of them smoke long, thick cigars. The men sitting around the table are the very picture of the "sitting pretty" Armenian Diaspora as painted in Turkey. They've finished lunch and are chatting over coffee. After the rather inhospitable reception I received at the Italian restaurant in Los Angeles, I have no expectations from this "table of the well-heeled." Rising from the table is cigar smoke, exaggerated American accents, references to figures and dollars—I'm dismayed by the thought that this will be a repeat of the earlier "You can buy peace" dinner. But—"*Hoşgelmişsiniz!*"

Attorney and Islamic Law Professor Berj Boyajian is welcoming me to the table, in Turkish and with a smile. He puts down his cigar to clasp my hand with both of his. "You'll have to excuse us, our Turkish is vulgar. Village Turkish, isn't it!" It's an incredible sight. It's impossible not to laugh. That an extremely polished, extremely American, extremely wealthy-looking man would speak to me with a Turkish accent you would only hear in a village in eastern Turkey, and that it happens poolside in Los Angeles ... I laugh, and I'm not alone—Berj Boyajian laughs along with me at the preposterousness of the situation.

Vartkes Yeghiayan introduces me to Berj with, "He's one of the three people who distributed the settlement from that life insurance class-action suit."

Boyajian, who was born in Syria, continues to speak in Turkish. "Can we speak a little Turkish? Mine's a bit rough, but ..." In broken Turkish, he struggles to remember each and every word, because there's a story he wants to tell. "My father and mother spoke Turkish at home. 'Why do you speak Turkish with your wife?' my father's friends would ask. Baba would reply, 'Speaking Turkish adds a different flavor.' And it does. It's got a flavor all its own."

So Berj Boyajian and I continue speaking in flavorful Turkish. Vartkes briefly outlines for the benefit of the others what I've set out to do. What I have learned from my contact with Armenians, a community completely closed to Turks, is that they too are rooted in a Middle Eastern male tradition: you need to be introduced to the community by a notable member of that same community. In fact, you might even need to gain the "approval" of not just one but several people simultaneously. As Vartkes explains, Berj takes a thoughtful puff on his cigar and opens his mouth to speak—in Turkish of course: "Now, how did that saying go? Animals . . . butt their heads. What was it? Ah, their horns! But we human beings—we do the same thing by talking. I've got my own pain. My father was from Antep, my mother from Urfa. Why don't I have a grandfather? Because . . . well, you know why. But you have to get over the pain. Life goes on."

I tell Berj that I've have had more difficulties in Los Angeles than anywhere else, that being from Turkey didn't present nearly as many problems with the Armenian communities in Armenia or in Paris. He laughs: "We're living in luxury here, of course. We have no ties to Turkey. Everyone speaks their mind."

At that point, Mr. Kartalian, another of Vartkes' friends, joins in. Born in Egypt, he's a lawyer too: "There's a tradition in Armenia of taking an interest in Turkey. Most of them migrated from Van, so they know what's going on there. No one here is that interested in Turkey."

Talk turns to Hrant. I try to find out what happened in the Armenian community in Los Angeles after he was gone. Vartkes is the first to speak: "We're far from Turkey, and we can say anything here. But Hrant was talking in Turkey. Those who killed him couldn't have done Armenian nationalism a greater service. His death poured gasoline on Armenian nationalism, fanned the flames."

The others nod in agreement. Then they criticize Armenian nationalism and those who frame the issue in harsh terms: "It was easier for the Germans to acknowledge genocide. It's not at all like that for Turkey, of course. There's the obvious issue of land. But the fear of losing land doesn't change facts. For me, it's a matter of principle. The actual number of people killed isn't that important. What's important is to acknowledge that those people were once living in those lands. Don't they ever wonder why east Anatolia is so barren now—why it's a dustbowl?"

Berj returns to Hrant: "When Hrant died, Turkish nationalism was the big loser." He takes another puff on his cigar: "But there's something you probably understand: it's all about money here. Over there you all think that the Turkish lobby is much weaker than the Armenian lobby. That's not the case. They spend many times what we do."

Vartkes interrupts: "In your opinion, what percentage of Armenians would say 'An apology is enough'?" When Berj doesn't respond, he answers his own question. "Sixty per cent of the Armenians in America would accept a simple apology." Kartalian and Berj nod in agreement. Vartkes continues: "Even if they did give us land, no one would go back. My father would have gone, but I wouldn't."

I can't believe they're even discussing this. I don't see how they can even begin to compare life in an Anatolian city to the lives they're leading in Los Angeles. I ask whether any of them has ever been to Turkey. They've all been to Turkey. Vartkes says, "Some say they won't go to Turkey. It's laughable." They laugh.

And as they laugh, I suddenly realize that I've spoken only to men in Los Angeles, and that I don't have any appointments with any women. Berj tells me about his sister, clinical psychologist Maral Yeranossian. "You must see her," he says.

"I really must," I agree, "because do I ever need a psychiatrist after all these Armenians." We all laugh.

As I rise from the table, Berj Boyajian speaks Turkish one last time: "We talk like Kurds, don't we?" Without waiting for a reply, he turns to his friends and continues in English: "That's what they said the last time I went to Istanbul. Apparently, we don't speak very genteelly."

Cigars in hand, they laugh; a cloud of smoke hangs over the table.

Chapter 21

Do Armenians get to play golf?

WE'RE WREATHED IN clouds of smoke. As we all puff away, I feel as though I'm in the Middle East, not America. We're sitting in the Boston offices of *Hairenik*, a newspaper with a circulation of 5,000, in the company of a group of men who are decidedly less American than the ones we met in Los Angeles. There's editor-in-chief Khajag Mgrdichian, who is originally from Beirut; his assistant, Zaven Torikian; and the editor of *Armenian Weekly*, Khatchig Mouradian, the person responsible for introducing us to the others. I expect our conversation to go more easily, partly because they're members of the east-coast Diaspora, partly because I know their newspaper has a leftist slant, but mostly because they're rooted in Middle Eastern culture. And indeed, things start off smoothly enough. Mgrdichian gives me a rundown on the newspaper, talks of his eight years on the committee that organized the previous night's ceremony, and provides some general information. When he mentions the committee, I ask, "Isn't it wearing to be involved with genocide all the time?"

He's suddenly grave. "Genocide is why I live here. Genocide is the reason I don't have a grandfather. Genocide is the meaning of my life. I can't live like other Americans who expect nothing but fun out of life." The languid cloud of Middle Eastern cigarette smoke is swept away by that all-too-familiar Middle Eastern acrimony.

I see, once again, that 1915 is connected not only to personal, political, historical, and communal identity; it can also define an individual's moral framework, easily furnishing the ideological underpinning of a sectarian politics.

I'm mulling this over when Mgrdichian explains further: "I studied electrical engineering. But because I'm Armenian, I didn't become an engineer. There were always more important things for me to do."

"You mean you needed to transmit suffering to others, as it was transmitted to you. Is that it?"

"Yes."

"For how long?"

"Forever, if need be. Until there's a just settlement."

"A just settlement?"

"Let me ask you something . . ." Mgrdichian is poised to ask his question as Yurttaş draws my attention to a map on the wall that isn't visible from where I'm sitting. I lean forward and take a good look: a map of Greater Armenia![19] I now know what Mgrdichian is going to say even before he says it. "Do you think I have the right of return to the land of my grandfather?"

"Of course you do," I say. "But as a Middle Easterner you know that land disputes are always resolved with blood."

Mouradian steps in to simplify: "Think of it as a rape, and then answer the question," he says.

I smile and say, "As a Marxist, surely you're aware how inappropriate that analogy was, in terms of the relationship between quantitative and qualitative change . . . ?" My little attempt at humor falls flat. I ask Mouradian the same question I asked Mgrdichian: "Isn't it tiring to live like this?"

19 The Armenian Revolutionary Federation (ARF), an Armenian political party that is influential among the Diaspora, advocates the establishment of a "Greater Armenia" that would incorporate much of northeastern Turkey, the historical homeland known as "Western Armenia," which has been under Ottoman or Turkish control since about 1500 CE.

Mouradian replies, "I keep pictures of genocide at home. When you explain 1915 to the kids here in America, they always compare it to the Holocaust or to what's happening in Darfur. That's the easiest way for them to understand the frightening events of those days. They see Darfur in the American media, and they understand what happened to us."

Deputy editor-in-chief Zaven Torikian talks about his own child: "I didn't have to sit down and explain anything. His teacher told me something the other day: on April 24 my son raised his hand and asked to give a five-minute talk on the Armenian genocide. His teacher told him he'd have to ask the principal first. But he ended up making that presentation. Children learn about it one way or the other. We all did."

Mgrdichian has a different story. "Sometimes grown-ups are forced to tell their children. When I asked my grandfather how he knew Kurdish, he had to explain where we were from and how we got where we were."

Mouradian changes the subject. "You're right in thinking it's shaped our lives. I remember the writer Peter Balakian saying, 'I want to be able to play golf one day without feeling guilty.'"

I mention how Hrant said that proponents of dialogue on both sides are being thrown to the wolves. I also point out that Hrant's name had been added to the prayers at the April 24th memorial ceremony. "It's no secret that the genocide is the force binding Armenians," Mouradian says. "Yes, Hrant's name has been added to the list of people we pray for. The people here see him as the latest member of the group of Armenian intellectuals killed on April 24, 1915."

That's when we leave Mgrdichian and Torikian, who says he'd love to come to Istanbul. We accompany Mouradian to his offices in the same building, because he tells me that if I'm going to write about Hrant I should see the issue dedicated to him in *Armenian Weekly*. Once we're in his small office, Mouradian pulls out a magazine with a black cover. Set against the black are a white dove and the outline of a closed mouth. The dove represents Hrant; the mouth, silence. Across the bottom of this sketch by Zareh is scrawled: "To leave 'boiling hells' and go to 'ready heavens.'" I know what inspired that: it's from something Hrant wrote when he was receiving death threats. He said that, instead of going to the "ready heavens" the Diaspora had prepared for him in the West, he preferred to transform the "boiling hells" of his own homeland.

As I leaf through the magazine, Mouradian talks about Hrant. "After Hrant died we made some changes to the April 24th memorial service so we could include him. People were affected by two things: the savagery of the murder and the size of the funeral. His death brought Turks and Armenians together."

"Possibly because Armenians saw that Turks were weeping for an Armenian, too," I suggest. Neither of us speaks for a moment. I add, "Hrant didn't say anything as harsh as the conversation we all had a moment ago, and he always criticized the Diaspora's hatred of Turks. What was the general opinion of him here before he died?"

"No one was angry at Hrant personally," Mouradian says, "but it was well known that he couldn't speak openly in Turkey. One thing his death changed was that Turks also came to some of the events we held here. I saw a young Turkish guy. We were talking about Hrant and he started crying. It was moving."

"What kind of events are you talking about?"

"Let me introduce you to two of my friends," Mouradian says, "this evening, at Café Pamplona."

★

A Harvard Square coffee shop with a European feel, Café Pamplona has an illustrious leftwing past. Established by a Basque woman in 1980, it's run today by a couple from Beirut. Khatchig tells me that among the luminaries who have been spotted at its cramped little tables are Al Gore and Spike Lee. His friends arrive: Sevag Arzoumanian and Jason Sohigian.

Sevag talks a mile a minute, is originally from Beirut, and has dark skin and curly hair; Jason seems displeased at my presence, and says not a word. With his dark eyeglass frames, black hair carefully combed to one side, and freshly pressed shirt, Jason reminds me of a '50s frat boy. The moment Sevog sits down, he gives me a rapid-fire rundown on the one-day symposium he helped to organize a month earlier, and hands me a brochure entitled "Armenians and the Left." The Armenian Revolutionary Federation, the most hardline leftist organization in Armenian political history, is listed on the brochure as the organizer. Topics for discussion include "The Media and Social Injustice in Armenia" and "Turkish-Armenian dialogue in the wake of Hrant Dink's Assassination." Because the symposium was organized by a nationalist movement, and because Sevog was among the organizers, I'm ready with my first question: "How do you manage to reconcile leftist ideology with nationalism?"

Sevog is eager to explain. "If I'd been born in a normal country in a normal society, I wouldn't be a nationalist. But you can describe me today as a leftist nationalist—like the liberation movements in Latin America, like Bolívar. Armenian nationalists don't claim to be superior to other people; we simply demand equality. In any case, nationalism has been a progressive force at times, in Italy and in France. I consider nationalism a progressive force for the Armenian nation."

I turn to Jason to see if he'd like to add anything. He's icy and tight-lipped. Does he even know why we're here, I wonder to myself. I break the silence with a question about the scouts at the April 24th memorial service—the marching feet, the blend of militarism and religion. Sevog laughs. "I was a scout in Beirut until the age of sixteen. Look, if we were living in the time of the Third Reich, you'd be right to be uncomfortable. But don't forget that we're members of a community that's afraid of losing its identity."

"Does that make any difference?" I ask.

Sevog explains, "Children were enrolled in youth organizations in Germany to prepare them for the army. Today, in the US, no one takes orders from anyone. If you tried to impose that kind of fascist hierarchy they'd spit in your face."

I shift my gaze to Jason. Signs of life stir on his face. This time I wonder if he's too much of a nationalist to speak to a Turk. Khatchig realizes that Jason's determined silence is making me tense, and explains once again who I am and what I'm doing here. He pauses and adds, "She'll only report what you say!"

Because I'm a Turkish journalist, assurances have to be repeated a few more times. After Jason sees my visa he utters a single sentence: "It's the social standing of Armenians in America that makes them do it."

Khatchig turns to me and says, "Ask him about his political views."

Before I have the chance to ask: "I'm an anarchist!"

He's certainly the most presentable anarchist I've ever met. "But he went to Armenia to get married," Khatchig teases. Okay, I can understand the contradiction between nationalism and Marxism. But an anarchist on the hunt for a bride of his own ethnicity!

Jason loosens up at last. "Our parents considered themselves to be Americans, not Armenians. They worked for America; I'm working for Armenia. I was born in America, but when I went to Armenia I felt like I belonged there more than here. Individualism threatens the American family; everyone's getting divorced. That's why I chose to marry a woman from Armenia. We've got a two-year-old baby now."

"But isn't the sanctity of marriage something an anarchist . . ."

I drop my question mid-sentence. Jason's still talking, anyway. "I'm a traditionalist anarchist. The only reason I'm collaborating with the socialists is that I can't find a political group I'm close to."

I decide to engage nationalist-socialist Sevog and traditionalist-anarchist Jason on the subject of reconciliation. When I ask them for their thoughts on Turkish-Armenian dialogue, Jason responds first. "It doesn't interest me. It doesn't matter to me, even if it is important to most Armenians. I don't care what Americans say either. This is between Turks and Armenians. And it's up to Armenians to decide what solution will satisfy them, and when."

Sevog develops the point: "It's not healthy to get fixated on whether America or any other countries recognize the genocide. And it doesn't really serve the Armenian cause. It's begun to seem as though the only thing the Armenians care about is lobbying the US Congress to pass laws and resolutions. It's degrading. It's degrading to make policy like a bunch of lab rats. That's why we're organizing these panels and events, so Armenians can create new ways to shape policy, and so that we can form alliances among like-minded political groups."

The empty coffee cups are whisked away, the tea arrives, and the subject changes. Sevog tells me he's envious of his Kurdish girlfriend, who's from Van. Why? "Because I've never been able to see Yozgat, the place my family's from."

This politically active young Harvard graduate is sitting here in Boston talking about Yozgat as though it were the most beautiful spot on earth. I can't help laughing. "Consider yourself lucky!"

Sevog's not laughing. He's dead serious: "I wish I'd been born in Burunkışla village, in Yozgat province." He tells me how his father was raised by a Turkish family, how his father later wandered with his uncle through various countries until, while working as a stonemason in Beirut, he met his mother. "They told me all this when I was eleven," he says, "because I asked about it one day."

Students stream into Café Pamplona. It's getting difficult to talk above the chattering voices. Jason reveals that he's co-chairman of the "Armenia Tree Project," which aims to plant half a million trees at 625 different sites in Armenia. "We're going to plant a 53,000-tree forest for Hrant."

"Hrant would be pleased," I tell him.

The heading on the brochure, "Armenians and the Left,"

catches my eye: "Armeno-Turkish Relations: Pitfalls and Possibilities Following Hrant Dink's Assassination." How would Hrant have felt if he'd seen he was the subject of a panel discussion? If he'd seen these young men, socialist and nationalist, anarchist and traditionalist? As I reflect on the discussions I've been having since morning, which included "demands for territory," I think back to the story Hrant told as a panel speaker, in a trembling voice:

> Beatrice left Anatolia in 1915, but she'd return to her birthplace of Sivas every year. One summer, the elderly Beatrice closed her eyes for the last time in that village in Sivas. An old man in the village managed to reach Hrant and ask him to inform any next of kin that might be in Istanbul. Beatrice's daughter was contacted, and the next day she rang Hrant from the village, in tears. She said she wasn't bringing the body back to Istanbul and handed the phone to an old man, who said, "It's her mother, her blood. But if you ask me, let her be buried here—water finds its way back into the cracked earth."

And that was the ancient Anatolian saying to which Hrant was referring when he lifted his hands into the air and thundered: "Yes, we have our eyes on this land. But not to take it away— just to be buried deep within it!" He was moved to tears when he said that. How moved would he have been to see that he'd become a "panel heading"? Well, he would have been happy about the trees—I have no doubt about that. Café Pamplona has become unbearably crowded. We all leave.

Chapter 22

"A velvet purse"

WE STEP OUT of the café and into the desert heat. Actually, "flee" would be more accurate. Never, here in Los Angeles or anywhere else in the world, had we been treated like that, and Yurttaş and I were both highly annoyed. "Enough!" Yurttaş shouts. "We weren't put on this earth to put up with this!" He is right to be angry. As much as I've tried to understand the hatred and rage some Armenians feel for Turks, that exchange a moment earlier, in that faux French café in Los Angeles, had me seething.

The interview with Zaven Manjikian, arranged by a mutual friend, had started badly and ended worse: "Journalists are for sale. And Turkish journalists come cheapest of all!" At which we put down our cups of coffee and walked out. Mr. Manjikian's wishes had come true: he'd been rude, and he could now sit alone in the café and gloat.

Yurttaş had never warmed to Los Angeles, but after this latest incident he absolutely loathed it: "Los Angeles is a big lie!" And indeed it was. The Kodak Theater, where the Oscars are handed out, is housed in a mid-size shopping mall; the imprints of the feet and hands of the stars are found on a tiny stretch of cement in front of a Chinese restaurant; the famous Hollywood sign is impossible to photograph and inaccessible by car; the only action at the Hollywood Walk of Fame are tour buses touting trips to the homes of the stars and the antics of Spiderman,

Supergirl, and Superman, that trio in spandex willing to pose for a picture so they can take their tips to a nearby stand and gobble up hamburgers. Oh, and Supergirl smokes like crazy. The ocean is out there somewhere, but we never manage to get to Venice Beach: Navigation Lady is determined to keep us away from the water at all costs. "Is there even a place called Los Angeles?" Yurttaş howls. Life isn't worth living. We have hours to kill until our next appointment, and we keep getting lost.

★

"Did you have any trouble finding it?"

Greeting us at the door is Boston businessman Harry Parsekian. "It's not that hard to get around Boston," he adds. We'd met at the April 24th memorial service and been invited to his home for coffee after dinner one night. His thirty-four-year-old wife, Helen, stands just behind him as we're welcomed into their beautiful home. The moment we're inside we see a map on the wall. "This one's different," he says.

"You're right," I agree, "it's a *National Geographic* map!" That wouldn't have been funny anywhere else and under other circumstances, but after all the talk of maps and land, it makes me smile. Next to the map is a picture of a flower emerging from the snow. "*Kardelen*," I say in Turkish, because I don't know the English for "snowdrop."

Parsekian nods: "I took that picture on Mount Ararat." And that's how he begins telling me about his adventures in Turkey. "I first went to Turkey for two days in 1967, with my mother. She's from Efkere village, in Kayseri. They call it Bahçeli today. I went back in 1985 to climb Ararat, but we couldn't get permits because of PKK terrorism. So I climbed it for the first time in 1986, with a French group. I also visited some of the villages in Kayseri. My mother told me she'd lived on Demircilik Caddesi, and I was able to find it. They'd poured asphalt over all our memories, of course, but it was still amazing to walk along that street, to touch those memories."

Helen brings us Turkish coffee, served with a piece of Turkish delight—just like in Istanbul or Beirut. "Helen's from Lebanon. But her family's from Everek village," Harry Parsekian tells me. He pauses for a moment, then speaks in Turkish: "That's where Mt. Erciyes is!"

"So you speak Turkish?"

He makes a "so-so" hand gesture, but responds in Turkish: "It's happening . . . slowly, *yavaş yavaş*. I come from Anatolia!" Parsekian is aware of how much more meaningful that last sentence is in Turkish, and has managed to express himself beautifully. Then he pokes fun at himself: "I am *yavaş yavaş* learning!"

I tell him he speaks with a Kayseri accent, and how strange it is for me to hear someone switch from American-accented English to Turkish with an Eastern accent. He laughs: "It's a good accent. It shows I'm from Anatolia."

Helen serves us "*sütlü*" when she means to say "*sütlaç*." Her solicitous Middle Eastern manner and baked rice pudding soon have Yurttaş and me feeling better than we have for days. I ask Parsekian what it felt like to be in Anatolia, and mention that many of the Armenians in America are afraid to visit.

"The *Midnight Express* syndrome!"[20]

He laughs and jokes about the Turkish clichés: "I'm a left-winger, which makes me an internationalist." I'm about to bring up the conversation at Café Pamplona, but don't want to interrupt Harry Parsekian as he sums up his feelings, again, beautifully. "I was born Armenian. I could have been born Turkish. That's how I see things. The world's my country. I wouldn't say I'm atheist—that would be overly bold. But I'm an agnostic."

"Can you explain," I ask, "why the April 24th ceremony had so many religious leaders and such an overtly religious tone, even though most of the organizers are leftists?"

---

20 *Midnight Express* is 1978 film that tells the story of an American sentenced to thirty years in a Turkish prison for drug smuggling. William Hayes, the author of the book, and Oliver Stone, who wrote the screenplay, both publicly apologized to the Turkish people for the racist depictions in the movie version of Hayes' ordeal.

Helen answers. "The church is our state; the priests are our leaders. Armenians don't go to church just because they're religious; they're there as members of the community. That's why you'll always see a school and a cultural center next to a church. Our lives are entwined with the church. Harry says he's an agnostic, but you can't really take religion out of what it means to be Armenian."

Harry Parsekian had become quite emotional as he talked about Anatolia; I ask him about Armenia. He describes his trip there in 1998, to help out after the earthquake. "I got a better understanding of the Armenian people. They had no power, no food; but they had a sense of solidarity and cooperation. Try cutting off Americans' gas for five days: they'd lose their minds. But the people in Armenia managed to keep going, hungry and poor though they were."

"Armenians are designed for survival," I say, and Harry and Helen begin laughing.

Harry tries out his Turkish again: "I went to Ararat, and there I slept. In a sleeping bag!" Every time he manages a sentence in Turkish, he congratulates himself with a smile.

We continue in English: "I've been to Armenia many times, but going to Anatolia . . ." He's thoughtful. "Going to Anatolia is like visiting my mother and father." I ask him whether he spoke to the villagers when he went to his mother's birthplace. "Of course I did. 'Where did all the Armenians go?' I asked. They pointed to a bridge and said, 'They went over that bridge.' No one told me what happened after that." Harry interrupts his own story: "*Oldu, oldu!*" He probably means to say "*olan olmuş bir kere*"—what happened, happened. He changes the subject. "We have a special place in our hearts for old people because we've never seen our own grandparents. I go once a year to sing songs to the elderly—in Turkish!" He bursts into song: "*Kadifeden kesesi /* A purse of velvet . . ."

"That was my grandfather's favorite song," I tell him. Then I sing the next line. Harry joins in, and the words of that old Istanbul folk song echo in a living room in Boston.

He stops midway through the song and says, "Your Turkish is European. We don't speak that kind of Turkish. We only know Anatolian Turkish."

We sip our coffee and Helen, like any woman in Anatolia, presses us to accept more, more, more . . .

★

"Would you like another coffee?"

"One more and I'll have a heart attack." Because we'd already had scores of coffees in cafés across Los Angeles in the hours before our appointment with historian Levon Marashlian, both Yurttaş and I turn down his kind offer here at Glendale Community College. I mention the unfortunate events of that morning—the way we had to quit the café and how the Armenians here are nothing like the ones in Armenia and France. Marashlian interrupts me: "That's the perception—that the Armenians in Armenia are reasonable and the ones in the Diaspora are trouble."

Marashlian goes on to say that this is the distorted picture created in Turkey. Levon Marashlian is a historian whose books have been published in Turkey. He has participated in joint conferences with Turkish historians. I ask: "The Turkish government has recently called for historians to come together and debate this issue. What are your thoughts on that?"

Marashlian replies, "Imagine a 'debate' on the existence of the Turkish War of Liberation. Which Turkish historian would participate in something like that? Armenian historians already know what the Turkish ones will say; Turkish historians know what the Armenian side will say. Your government's proposal was politically motivated; our rejection of it was also grounded in politics. If you ask me, successive Turkish governments have forced the Turkish people to continue bearing the burden of the atrocities committed in Ottoman times. If the genocide were recognized, it would become a subject taught in history lessons, just like the Holocaust in Germany. Have you ever seen Jewish people holding demonstrations against Germans? You don't, because the subject's been closed."

Marashlian seems to appreciate the political dimensions of this issue, so I ask him about the "genocide recognition" resolutions the Armenians are trying to have passed in foreign countries. He is critical of the Turkish media: "The only time the Turkish press takes any notice of this issue is when one of those resolutions is passed. And even then, they turn historical fact into a current affairs issue. If it weren't for those resolutions, there would be no mention of genocide in Turkish newspapers. Have you ever seen a single article about a book published by an Armenian author? No. Turkey's able to ignore historians, but they're unable to ignore the political implications of genocide recognition."

I bring up the representatives of the Diaspora who advocate a financial settlement. Marashlian says it's more complicated than that: "Some might think that way, but this is principally about a general process of restitution, of making amends. The specifics of how that is to be done are secondary. Right now it's strange, of course, to sit down and talk about dollars and cents. If, by some miracle, Turkey recognized the genocide, we could then work with Turkey to decide what form compensation would take." Marashlian pulls a Kleenex from the box on his desk. "Even if they said they'd give us this tissue, that would be all right. It's a matter of principle."

"Is there a form of compensation that you'd recommend?" I ask.

He thinks for a moment. "That's a matter for politicians and diplomats, but in the final analysis, Armenians won't get everything they want—but Turkey can't just walk off as though nothing has happened, either. We've been robbed of more than money and property. The culture of a people has been destroyed. The genocide is also the reason Armenia's in the state it is today, landlocked and impoverished. The intention was to eliminate Armenians as a regional power—and they succeeded.

I think compensation should include Armenia's free access to the Black Sea."

Marashlian is aware that this solution won't satisfy many of the hawks in the Diaspora, but he's not overly concerned about it. "Politicians can hammer out the details. It's justice I care about. Whatever the agreement that's reached—if the genocide is recognized, Turkey's headache will be over. If a meaningful and just solution is reached, Turkey will have gained something far more valuable than money. Turkey will also have taken away the political genocide card played by its neighbors. It's always the same."

What is?

"Neither side will be completely satisfied by a solution, whatever it is. We have to recognize that."

Marashlian races off to his class. I think about the issue of money as we leave the campus. Mr. Manjikian had told us this morning that Turkish journalists "come cheap." How much money would it take to make him stop hating? Would this money from Anatolia make Harry Parsekian feel any differently as he traveled to Anatolia to commune with his mother? Which of us could dare to say that Turkey's "national headache" would be over if we paid reparations to the Armenians? We get into the car. We've had a long day, and go straight back to our "perfect spot to have a rendezvous." I skim the daily newspapers. There are write-ups of the May Day demonstrations: Mexicans sprayed with tear gas, children affected. The very first sentence of the article estimates the cost to the city of Los Angeles. I've never seen anything like it. It's in Los Angeles that I learn for the first time that there's a "price tag" for a demonstration.

Chapter 23

"When in Rome . . ."

"**W**HAT CAN YOU do? This place runs on money, of course!"

As Tatul Sonentz-Papazian, editor of the magazine *Hai Sird*, sits in his Watertown, Boston office talking about Armenian and Turkish lobbyists, he doesn't seem all that pleased about their emphasis on money. With connections to the Armenian Revolutionary Foundation and the vice-chairmanship of the Armenian Relief Foundation, Papazian is a prominent figure not only in the Armenian community in America, but throughout the twenty-five countries where his organization is active. As this elderly man tells me how many states have passed "genocide recognition resolutions," the number of members of Congress who support the Armenians compared to the number siding with the Turks, the budget for such activities, how he got involved in lobbying, and how the Jews have been more successful lobbyists than the Armenians, he pauses in the middle of a story: "Americans didn't know a thing about the genocide. They still don't know that much. But at least we can say we've created a certain 'brand familiarity.'"

Brand? That's too commercial a term for a story of suffering. "Couldn't a word like that get you into trouble with your own community?" I ask.

And that's when he says, "This country runs on money. You know what they say: When in Rome, do as the Romans do!"

Tatul carries Ararat in his heart

The shade of regret in the midst of his sarcasm emboldens me to protest, in a tiny voice: "But you're *not* Roman!"

At this point, thirty minutes into an unemotional discussion of dry matters, Papazian suddenly asks, "Do you mind if I smoke a cigar?" and breaks into song, in Turkish: "*Nane suyu nane şeker / Benin canım seni çeker . . .*"[21]

I stare. This happens to them all time. I'll be discussing a contentious issue with someone whose family is originally from Turkey and, all of a sudden, unaware perhaps of what they're doing, they'll recollect the "old brotherhood" and launch into Turkish, as though sending out a signal flare of some kind. Papazian takes a long drag on his cigar and smiles wistfully. "My grandmother used to sing me that lullaby. I'll always remember it."

Tatul was born in 1929. The man who a moment ago was speaking in an American accent about figures, money, and lobbying is gone, replaced by an elderly man with a story to tell—a man with a far-away look in his eyes and an air of vulnerability. He takes a few deep drags on his cigar, holding the smoke in like an Anatolian man, and tells me he was born in Cairo, but his mother was from Van, his "real" country. His father, from the Black Sea port of Bartın, worked as a deckhand on ships bound for the Crimea. His grandfather was from Trabzon. Tatul slowly comes to his own childhood: "I didn't hear about the genocide from my mother or my father. But everything you have goes with you as you walk off. And later, between the lines and in the words of songs, you hear about what happened. And you carry what you've learned for the rest of your life. Then, one day . . ." He stops, clamps the cigar between his teeth, and pulls a file from the shelf. He takes out a poem and puts it on the table. "I wrote that for my grandfather."

21 "Mint juice, mint candy / It's you I want ..."

Allow me to call you Hovseph
since I am your elder now
and in my mind you are
and will forever be
the young father
of my mother
loving husband
of my grandmother . . .

Hovseph—
headless silent forebear
forever spouse and parent
yet a mute and blind memory
 . . . of a lost grandfather.

I finish reading it. "The face of my grandfather . . . has been an obsession of mine for years. What was he like? He was twenty-five when he was murdered. I've been thinking about him for years, thinking of his face."

"Isn't that exhausting?" I ask.

"It's emotionally draining," he agrees. "I'm not all that interested in recognition of the genocide by other countries. It's hard to explain. Recognition by Turkey has become the reason for my existence. I've had a long life, and what I've come to realize is this: there's something more important than freedom—and that's justice."

"But were Turkey to recognize it, you'd lose the reason for your existence," I say.

"We're homeless," Tatul says. "You should understand that." His eyes swim with tears. "I sang you a silly little song a minute ago. A silly little song! But it's my childhood—I've forgotten Turkish. I can't remember anymore." He's overcome for a moment, then continues. "The ones in Armenia don't understand this. Hrant was talking at home. But it's different for us. We're living with the threat of obliteration."

He speaks now of the reasons Turkey should recognize the "genocide." I note the change in his expression, his voice, the words he chooses. Speaking with a Turk does the same thing to them, every time. Just like Tatul, they get angry but they also want to pour out their sorrows. They're angry and they're full of pain, but it's not pure anger or pure pain. I remember what Hélène Piralian said in Paris: "If you're Armenian, you fear an encounter with Turks because you're afraid of what you'll feel when you meet one." I understand how emotionally draining it must be, and I know that if an Armenian has found the courage to talk, you should listen. As you listen, some of the anger and pain may be alleviated. I've sensed it every time—that if they are able to open up and talk to me, it does them good. Is it simply because I'm a "Turk"? Is it because a Turk is listening to them and never once questioning what happened? I suspect that it might be because I'm from "the old country." Speaking to someone from the land of ghosts might take them back to those fabled lands they heard about as children.

I'm thinking about all this as Tatul finishes what he was saying. I catch the last line: "The more threatened, the more rigid Armenian national identity becomes." Tatul pulls other files from the shelves and takes out more poems to give me. I sense he'd be happy for me to stay a while longer. But we're already late. As I leave his office, I entertain the fantastic notion that this problem could be resolved if every Turk listened to every Armenian—just listened. If we replaced "dialogue" with a different word: listen. Listen in silence until they've said all they need to say. Would it do any good?

★

"Of course it would—but listening isn't as easy as people think."

I'm walking in the rain on the riverbank in Boston with Phil Gamelian and Ceren Ergenç. They're telling me about the "Turkish-Armenian Dialogue" initiative they organized in Boston in 2005, in a sincere effort to foster dialogue. Phil is earning a master's degree in Conflict Resolution from Brandeis University, while Ceren is a graduate student in International

Relations at Boston University. Phil approached some Armenian students, and then he set out to recruit some Turkish students in the Boston area. He met with little interest, at first. Many of the Armenians also had second thoughts, and insisted on a single precondition: "The Turkish participants have to recognize the genocide!"

Having made little headway, Phil visited with some of the leading names in the local Armenian community and, having received their support, was able to launch the initiative with Zeynep Civcik, a Turkish graduate student at Brandeis University. "Our plan," he explains, "was to engage in confidence-building activities and to form relationships before taking on any controversial subjects. The second step was to discuss stereotypes. And, finally, to sit down and talk about history."

So, did things pan out as planned?

"Zeynep and I were the group facilitators. But once we started talking I found that my personal feelings, my feelings as an Armenian, were very intense. It was harder than I'd expected. I'd assumed I could distance myself."

Ceren also learned some surprising things about herself when she attended the dialogue group. She mentions realizing that she had never considered the implications of the Armenian roots of a former neighbor—a "madam," as Christian women are often addressed in Turkey. It's similar to the way many Turks fail to consider the significance of the "Armenian" buildings, or the fact that there aren't many Armenians left in Turkey. "Just like Madame Anahit," I say. Ceren knows who I mean, but I have to explain to Phil. Madame Anahit used to wander among the tables in Nevizade and Balık Çarşısı, an area of Beyoğlu, in Istanbul, devoted to *meyhane*, meze, and *rakı*. She was always dressed in colorful gowns and had her raven hair pulled back into a bun. I never saw her without an accordion; I don't think anyone ever did. The most dignified lady in the city, she'd walk from table to table, playing tangos. The walls of the *meyhane* were lined with photographs of Madame Anahit posing with merrymakers. When she died, in 2003, the headlines mourned her passing with, "We've lost Madame Anahit." She was, of course, Armenian; Ceren has a point. I never consciously viewed her as an Armenian. She was always that incredible woman with the accordion, the one whose poise and stateliness could silence a table of tipsy men with a single look. Memory's a strange thing—so many things recorded but unnamed. I think about Madame Anahit, and I can hear the strains of "Yıldızların Altında" ("Under the Stars") as Ceren speaks.

"One day, a friend introduced me to an Armenian in China," she says. "She hated me so much she wouldn't shake my hand, and I had no idea why. But after talking to the other students in the group I have a better understanding of how that happened. I can empathize with Armenians. I have my own interpretation of history—that's different. But the group's enabled me to appreciate the feelings of others."

From what Phil and Ceren tell me, not everyone in the group was prepared to confront themselves and their memories. "I realized," Ceren says, "that some of the Turks in the group had internalized historical narratives and discourses different from mine. My approach was emotional, but some of them became more nationalistic. When we started discussing history, some Turks seemed to have a reflexive need to rationalize what had happened. Some of the Armenians were also a bit overemotional or reactionary at times. But what really struck me was this: the inability of some Turks to believe that this issue is a source of personal pain for Armenians. It was difficult to get them to realize that the Armenians in the group felt real pain."

Ceren summarizes the conclusion most of the Turks reached: "There was recognition that this is our common history, something that happened to us all, whether or not you use the term genocide or blame a particular side. We have to recognize that, on a human level, there is still great pain over what happened—for all of us."

Phil tells me how the Armenians in the group responded. "We'd write up a summary of each meeting. Once we'd all agreed on the wording, we'd post it on our website. I observed that, while some Armenians felt the meetings had been constructive, others were indifferent or felt they weren't doing any good."

Phil says that the groups were limited to the same fifteen or twenty people, and that three seminars were held to discuss the results of the meetings. When these seminars on a common history and memory had been completed, the group was dissolved. Ceren explains the difficulties of moving from a collective memory to a common history. "We separated the groups into Armenians and Turks, and asked everyone to develop historical timelines by writing down, in chronological order, events that had shaped Armenian-Turkish relations. We found that the highlights on the two timelines were completely different. Historical events of importance for one side had no meaning for the other side, or were ignored. We saw that we could create a common history only if we appreciated the importance of historical events on both sides."

That's what Hrant meant when he used to say that whatever happened had happened to us all, and that we shared the same history. I ask Phil and Ceren if Hrant's death has changed anything. Phil says, "Armenians always talk, write, and think about Turks. But Turks never talk about Armenians. When Hrant was killed, Turks finally started talking among themselves. The more hardline elements in the Armenian community took the view that 'Turks are killing Armenians again,' and their voices were loudest. But I'm certain not everyone thinks that way."

Ceren reflects for a moment, as I wait for her to answer. "Turks were affected by Hrant's death more than Armenians," she finally says. Then she turns to Phil and says, "I'm sorry, I shouldn't be speaking on behalf of Armenians." She laughs and explains: "That's one of the things we learned in the group—moving beyond our prejudices, and not speaking on behalf of others." She has more to say about Hrant. "I've had a lot of long discussions about Hrant with different people. Something strange happened. Previously, we Turks had thought more or less along the same lines. With Hrant's death, we found we were suddenly polarized, divided between those with a conciliatory approach and those without. The Turks here were divided."

As two people who have thrashed out so many issues together, Phil and Ceren are obviously comfortable with each other—two people, not just an Armenian and a Turk. Members of that little diaspora comprised of people from both communities—members of a "minority" who leave the shouting to others. "Talking does a lot of good, of course," Phil confides, "but it really isn't as easy as people think. You might think you're free of anger and hatred, prejudice and enmity—but you can never be sure."

They exchange smiles and Phil tells me a story, one they probably both know. "It took a strange incident for me to realize how much I've internalized. I'd known Ceren for about six months, and we'd become good friends. We were out on a walk one day, with my son, and I left him with Ceren while I went into Starbucks. I was ordering a coffee, and I suddenly thought, 'How could I have left my child with a Turk?' I still can't believe it. I'd never realized how ingrained they are, all these prejudices. And I'm someone who's dedicated to dialogue. Who knows what other people are thinking?" Ceren smiles, not taking it personally, having long since sorted out this kind of thing with Phil. They've been contacted by students in other cities who want to set up similar groups.

It starts to rain harder. We walk away from the river, and I watch as the two of them walk off, Ceren in purple boots and Phil, who, as a Yereventsi, still has something of a Soviet air about him. Who knows that they think of me? All the people I've spoken with, the ones who laughed and cried as they told me their stories—what did they think of me after we'd shaken hands and said goodbye? Once I'd walked off, was I no more than a "Turk" to them? Did they believe I was in pain over the death of an Armenian friend? Or would they always see me as a Turk who was unable to fathom the magnitude of their pain, no matter what we said to each other? Of course, I had no way of knowing something they themselves might never know. And what do I keep secret from myself? Why do I keep pursuing Armenians? As I listen to them, am I hiding something? Will I only ever see them as Armenians? With my country on the brink of disaster, why am I digging into the past? What's my problem? Once we've shaken hands and parted, who are they to me?

★

"That's a difficult question. I'll think about it."

It was late in the afternoon when I arrived at the office of clinical psychologist Maral Yeranossian Babian on Ventura Boulevard, in Los Angeles. She's the sister of Berj Boyajian, the attorney who'd told me, poolside at a luxury hotel, that he "speaks Turkish like a Kurd." He'd also given me Babian's business card. As we drove to our last interview, Yurttaş and I were both worn out. I'd been having nightmares ever since Hrant's death, and the hectic schedule over the past two weeks had compounded the fatigue I felt from those sleepless nights. The news from back home was bad. Nationalist demonstrations had led to back-street scuffles. The press claimed a big offensive against the PKK was imminent. Turkey was bubbling over, as always. I had a story to tell—a long one—and I was almost certain I wouldn't be able to get it published when I returned. Perhaps I'd embarked on this, the last of my three journeys, simply to be able to write a column entitled, "In loving memory of Hrant": "We have to continue to talk. You can kill people, but you can't kill humanity." Something along those lines. I'd felt burdened for months, and overshadowed by a cloud of mourning for Hrant. It was time for it to lift, but I knew it wouldn't. The intractability and reluctance to speak of the Diaspora in America was disheartening. As Turkey was being swamped by its own brand of ultra-nationalism, the image of the "shameless, murderous Turk" I'd confronted in America had led me to ask myself what I was doing, and for whom. I'd had it.

That's why I was so happy to sink into the red velvet armchair in Babian's office. Incense was burning in the small visitor's room, and Babian had probably been killing time after a long day as she waited for us to arrive. The moment we met, in a spirit of sisterly solidarity perhaps, I confided: "I'm exhausted."

Babian gave me a smile that was reserved but friendly: "You look it. Is it the Armenians that have worn you out?"

"No. Turks *and* Armenians."

We both laugh. Silence.

I don't have to mince words with Babian—I can tell from her manner. So I ask a direct question. "If a Turkish patient came to you, would your general feelings about Turks prevent you from treating her?"

Babian looks surprised by my bluntness. But, instead of responding with an easy "Of course not," she says, "That's a difficult one," thinks for a moment, and, a doubtful note in her voice, replies, "It would probably depend on the patient's problem." In her smile is the admission that she's avoided the question.

Babian, who arrived in the US from Syria at the age of twelve, specializes in adolescent psychology. Other than Turks, she treats patients from just about every ethnic group. I wonder to myself if adolescence is particularly difficult for Armenians. That would be about the time they begin hearing terrible stories of suffering, like a rite of passage. I ask Babian whether it's necessary or not to tell children those stories. She gives my question serious consideration. "It's extremely difficult for me to answer that strictly as a psychologist. I'm also an Armenian mother who has reared her own children. But if I look back—yes, we should tell them. They need to be told. We need a future. It's easy to be assimilated in this society. If we were living in the Middle East it would be different. But here—unless we planted the seed of reality in them, their identities would soon be wiped out here in America."

Seed of reality?

"The fact that they're Armenian."

And as a mother? How does the mother of a child feel as she tells these stories to her own child so that they can be reproduced in the next generation?

"This time, I'm considering your question both as a psychologist and a mother. Yes, it needs to be told, because we tell them everything. Since we tell them everything, they need to know this too—where they're from, how they got here. They see terrible things happening all over the world and learn a lot of painful realities. Why shouldn't they learn about this too?"

"Even in America, where children are protected from violence of all kinds and reared in virtually sterile conditions?" I ask.

Babian cites the example of a family she knows. "There's a newlywed couple. He's twenty-two, a recent university graduate. His wife is American. One day he sat his wife down to tell her about the genocide and show her photographs of those days. The next day his mother-in-law appeared at the door: 'How could you show my daughter those pictures? What are you trying to do?' she asked. He let it go—they had just got married. But I know the time will come when he'll tell her again. He has to, because that story is a part of him. He has no choice but to tell it."

"If 1915 is a part of you, aren't you a part of it? I suppose belonging to that story means you belong somewhere," I say.

Babian nods. "Our mothers and fathers didn't tell us much because they were building new lives here. There are priorities for immigrants. First comes the basic need to feed your family, then the need for information, then the need to belong somewhere. People would like to be talked about when they're dead—I think it has something to do with that."

"So you need to go through a form of trauma in order to belong, in order to be a part of the whole? You need to be added to that story of suffering?" I say.

Babian holds up the palms of her hands and looks at me as if to say, "That's the way it is—what can you do?"

"But how? How does she tell her children?"

"The children would come with me to the April 24th memorial ceremonies and chant slogans. But they didn't know what they were saying, of course. My daughter, Sonia, began asking me about it later, when her grandfather died. She was twelve. I think the story of the genocide had merged in her mind with the loss of her grandfather. Her grandmother had given her a Bible written in Turkish with Armenian characters. When she came to me with that Bible, I explained. She was unable to sleep that night, and for several nights afterwards. But my son . . ." She pauses and smiles. "He didn't seem to mind that much. On April 22, some Turks held a counter-demonstration in Washington to protest American recognition of the Armenian Genocide. I could see that he wasn't as angry as I was, that he didn't mind all that much. Now, the people my age—when we were young, we had no idea how to react to a Turk. When we'd meet Turks they wouldn't know how to respond to us either. But I think young people today are less self-conscious. They want to talk— that's what I've observed. And they approach each other more like Americans, less like Armenians."

"Is it worth it?" I ask. "Is it worth it to carry on traditions by handing down pain to a child?"

Babian bows her head for a moment. She straightens, purses her lips, and says nothing. I've assumed she's not going to answer, when she says, "Unless they learn about it, they'll be lost."

Perhaps the world is spinning so fast we need to cling to each other and to the stories that bind us together. Or perhaps the world's isn't going anywhere. There's been a story right from the start—we're incorporated into that story when we're born, and when we die we're simply replaced by the new ones, by the new faces. And still, today, we risk falling off the face of the earth if we're not part of a narrative: that's the meaning of being lost. Being alone must be worse than death for some people. If you're going to end up alone, it's better to become part of stories full of death than to have no story at all. Unless you're part of a greater whole, you might get lost—like the first humans, who knew better than to remain alone in the forest and risk annihilation. It's such a primal need that you might even want to kill anyone who tells you that the story you've been told, and of which you're a part, might not be true. The fear that you, everyone you know, and your story might be wiped off the face of the earth, could even cause you to kill—to kill one of the most beautiful people on the face of the earth, even. Even Hrant.

Perhaps the world isn't turning at all. Or perhaps it's spinning out of control . . .

The incense on the table has burned out, and it will soon be getting dark outside. As we step through the door, Babian clasps my hand in both of hers. "You know what, I'd like to set out on a journey, too, and get to know the Turks. I'd like to understand why they won't talk about it."

I clasp her hand in turn in both of mine, and say, "You really should, because once you set off on a journey, you begin to understand not only others, but yourself as well."

Yurttaş insists we see the ocean at least once before we leave Los Angeles. That endless expanse of sand . . .

Chapter 24

My Armenian Sister

THE SUN IS about to set by the time we've negotiated the tangled freeways and arrived at Venice Beach. A Latin American bodybuilder in a thong and roller skates juggles two balls and looks for someone to tip him for a posed picture. An Indian stands on his head, legs intertwined and immobile. A Rastafarian in a fantastic hat plays an electronic guitar as the metal wheels of his skates whir by. Black men do acrobatic dances, flying and feinting. Women with glistening skin bronzed at tanning salons are taking their overflowing breasts out for a stroll. These are the sights and sounds that make Yurttaş dub Venice Beach "a human circus." There's something for everyone in this country where nothing gets a second glance—but we have to drink our beer on the beach, the only place we're allowed to smoke. We take our cans of beer out onto the beach. Off in the distance, men beat drums as women dance, whisky bottles in hand. A police car is parked not far from this group of partiers, but they're lost in dance and song. Yurttaş and I don't need to say a word—we simply exchange smiles.

We sit down on the sand, in silence. Yurttaş suddenly breaks into a plaintive folksong.

That's when I see her—the young woman sitting alone a little further along. The moment the song begins, she recoils even as her head swivels to look at us. She's got wavy, light brown hair, like me. Her eyes are dark brown, like mine. We might even be the same age. Her nose, her mouth, her penetrating eyes—we have similar roots, it seems obvious. I can tell from her nose, her mouth, and her eyes—but most of all from the way she flinches at the sound of a folksong from the "old country." She's Armenian. She tenses; I see it. She feels troubled, irritated, and angry—then she refuses to let herself feel this way, and tries to let it go. I can read her emotions as if they're written on her face, one by one. The residual pain of something she hasn't experienced personally, nor her mother, nor perhaps even her grandmother, is running along her spine, and she doesn't know what to do.

Now, what can I say to you, Armenian sister of mine? What can I say?

Neither the stories of the Jews and Germans nor those of the black and white South Africans are like our stories. We can take neither the English and the Aborigines nor the French and the Algerians as our model. We need to find common ground, and we need to make it our own.

"We need to recognize that this is a matter of honor," Hrant would urge, "that the Turkish refusal is a matter of honor because they're unable to believe that their ancestors could have done such a thing, and that Armenian insistence, too, is a matter of honor because they've kept their suffering alive for a century."

It's easy for both sides, yours and mine, to confuse honor with pride. We come from a land that believes in cleansing through blood. And our histories are written by men.

We're the children of people who believe that, through our pride, we defend our honor. In fact, it's when we defend our pride that we lose our honor, and we both know that.

Over there, pride makes my people silent and unwilling to listen about 1915. Here, it's pride that makes you shout the names of your dead in foreign tongues. In lands far apart from each other, we continue to confuse pride and honor.

We don't have to live together anymore; we don't have to talk to each other. We don't have to apologize, and you don't have to forgive. No one has to do anything. The "proud" clamor and "proud" silence will continue. If we do choose to do anything, it will be in order to remove the yoke of our stories from around our necks. If we do anything, it will be because we want a better, brighter future for us all. Whatever we do, it has to come from our shared humanity.

I now understand that if a lie has been told in the past, a stain remains upon the children of that land—even if no one knows the whole truth. If life has become devalued in my land today, that devaluation began with your deaths. If my country has become inured to so much savagery, it began a century ago when they had to reconcile themselves to your people being taken away. That's not the kind of country I want.

You too understand that it falls to you to grant absolution for the pain of those who came before you. Who can possibly understand what a burden that must be? Neither do you wish for the pain of your people to be deified. You now want that imaginary land whose language you don't speak, and to which you'll never return, to become real for you, so that your attachment to the old stories will bring peace, not pain. You wish to free yourself of the hatred that makes you captive to the "terrible Turk."

Whatever we do, it will be for these reasons—not because we're forced to.

I say we need to talk, but I know that before people begin to talk, they need to know who they're talking to. You, my Armenian sister, will be talking to people who grieve the loss of their Armenian friend—the 100,000 people marching behind Hrant, the many people who watched on television and wept until their faces hurt. They know what loss is. They know what it is to feel eviscerated.

Who's going to talk to them? Children who now wish to be freed of their ghosts. That's you, isn't it? Have I understood right?

That's why I set out on a journey that took me to this expanse of sand on the other side of the world: to see who could talk to whom, and why.

It's your Ararat and our Ağrı. Your loss and our pain.

I don't want to prove that you died once upon a time. I want my country to remember that, once upon a time, you too lived in these lands. That's more important. That's what we need today.

I want my country to see that you're still living today. I want people to learn that pieces of themselves have been scattered to the winds.

Don't feel you constantly need to explain your heartbreak to people whose faces look nothing like yours and mine. The people of my country want to listen to you now. The men in ties might be too proud and too timid to admit this, but the silent majority still know how to suffer with honor. I want to believe that about my country, about my mad country. I have no other choice—and, I'm afraid, neither do you. This is our only chance. We were sisters once. Now our only chance is to become friends. We never chose to become sisters; we never chose not to be sisters. But you can choose your friends— friends who understand you, friends with much in common, like you and me.

I need to listen to you. You should tell me your story, one more time. You should set off on a journey toward my country and try to understand it a little better, try to find out what's here and why it's the way it is. Pain is always dumped on the wrong doorstep. Grieving falls to those best able to grieve. That's what will happen this time, too. The "guilty" and the "strong" won't share in the mourning, and they won't help us to heal this wound. We'll have to do it ourselves. Our voices might be drowned out by the shouters. It doesn't matter—it's not important that they hear us. What is important is that we hear each other. Voices mingle; you know that. People some-times come together until there are so many of them that they can no longer be ignored. I want history to record our voices, not just the voices of the shouters. I want our children to know that we were there too, you and me, and that we did what we could. If nothing else, I want our children to know that. I won't give birth to a criminal, and you won't give birth to a victim. I want us to have babies, and to teach them that our peoples can become friends again.

They were that simple, the things I wanted to say . . . But I didn't. I couldn't.

Yurttaş finished his song. Taking a final drag on his cigarette, he said, "Come on, the adventure's over!" We stood up. That young woman watched as we walked away. The sky was deepening, from gray to black. I turned and looked: her eyes on my back, still. Perhaps she too had things to say but had left them unsaid.

We returned to Turkey. The backlash following Hrant's death had reached fever pitch. Reasonable discussion was more difficult than ever. The rise of political Islam, the military, and the ultra-nationalist fervor whipped up by the ongoing clashes in the southeast had discouraged discussion of any kind. In the explosive political climate of the day, the country seemed to have no interest in the Armenian issue—a problem rooted in the past.

At a gathering of intellectuals one night, someone even said, "We should set up an emergency network in case something happens to one of us." We were scared, but were even more scared for our country. There was still this country that we loved and for whose problems we were seeking solutions. But which country was that? Was it the country we once knew, a country that seemed to be disintegrating before our eyes, smashed into smaller and smaller fragments? Who were we? When even the fragments of our country were gone, who would we be? Would we too turn into the children of ghosts? Like the Lebanese, Iranians, and Iraqis wandering through Europe? Or like the Armenians?

One day, a group of schoolchildren cut their fingers and painted a Turkish flag with their blood. The bloody flag was framed and sent to the General Chief of Staff. My picture began appearing in the press after I wrote a column arguing, "This flag's red enough without any more blood."

The caption appearing under my photo was: "Here's that hideous woman!"

And that's when I thought, even if I do love this country, what if it no longer loves me? I was afraid. Could someone continue loving their country under these circumstances? That's when I recognized the depth of the need to belong. Even if they're going to kill you, you still want to go home. Wherever home is—even if it's been reduced to ashes—you need a home. Hrant was right. Home may leave you, but you can never leave home. You're compelled to love your country, however heavy your heart.

Postscript

THAT OXFORD RAIN, seemingly suspended in mid-air, is gone. Spring has begun hitching up her skirt, inch by inch. But it's not the spring I know; it's indecisive.

I'm here in this distant country to get away from the stories in my subconscious, and to be able to look into the heart of the "other." I needed to put some distance between myself and my home. It's only when you leave home that you fully appreciate how much you've been shaped by the stories you've been taught. And now, far from home, I look into the heart of the "other" as I look deep into my own heart.

I know that the people of my country have begun remembering, even if they haven't put a name to it. Something unnamed has crept into the public discourse. You won't find it in the newspapers or at official meetings. But, I'm telling you, those terrible days are being discussed in living rooms and in side streets. The thing is, they're unsure what they should think about what happened, and they can't put a name to what they're feeling. What's begun, in the wake of Hrant, are the first whispers of a mourning process.

In Oxford, signs of spring have arrived along with the sepia light of early evening. The books are still stacked on the table. *Armenians, Armenian Genocide, Armenian Genocide Lie, Turkish Denialism, Lobbyists for the So-called Armenian Genocide*—all of them read through the rainy winter. I'll be going home soon, but time hangs heavy.

You find yourself among strangers, floundering in a foreign tongue. You're translating your story and the story of your home into another language. As you do so, both stories and words fall by the wayside. You're dismantling and reassembling yourself and your home, piece by piece, word by word. And when you are reassembled, you feel like a mechanical toy with an extra piece that won't fit anywhere: you're living with a malfunctioning tongue, an inoperative mind, a misfiring heart. You're diminished. And even as you think to yourself that it would be better to take that extra piece and limp home now than to continue living "out of gear," you know you have to stay and make something of yourself here in a foreign land. You can will yourself into existence only by repeatedly telling the same stories about who you are and where you're from. Sometimes they joke with each other, and you don't quite get it. You make a joke—but it's misunderstood, and the joke's on you.

You keep talking about your home, and the more you talk the further away it gets, until you're left with sand streaming through your fingers. Your home has been reduced to nothing as you struggle to describe it in a foreign tongue. And as you slot your home into a foreign language, it too is like a mechanical toy that doesn't work like it once did; it's malfunctioning. It's lost its flavor and its smell. That huge home of yours has shriveled up into a few memorized sentences spoken to foreigners. You're tired of it all, and you'd like nothing better than to sit at home, in silence, in your own language.

It's simple, really: you'd like to be with people who love you and with whom you never have to consider where you belong or who you are. When you can't remember the words of an old song, you'd like someone there to remember it for you. You'd like to speak your mother tongue when you're drunk, first thing in the morning, as you fall asleep, in your dreams, while you make love, when you're angry, and as you cry. It's that simple. You'd like to go cold inside at the sound of a curse.

A pile of books and papers on the table; deepening sepia light. Kanuni Garbis[22] singing: "*Ada sahillerinde bekliyorum . . .*" ("I await you on the shores of the island . . .").

"Armenians on 8th Avenue" is written on the album cover. These are Armenians who traveled to the other side of the world in 1915. All of their songs are in Turkish. If there's a point somewhere in that song where an Anatolian would sigh and exclaim, "Ah!" be certain that the Armenians of 8th Avenue would exclaim it at exactly the same place, in New York, in the 1950s. On the same cover, a woman is beating out a dance rhythm with a pair of wooden spoons. Another woman sits in the back, trying to smile—a smile that's died on her lips; the bruise of a smile. I study the faces of these women, who traveled from Anatolia to the other side of the world. How hard they're trying to remain upright. I understand now how difficult that is.

I don't feel personally guilty about the ones who came before me and who killed the ones who came before them. And I don't think I ever will. For what is death but the dust of Anatolia itself? That may sound hardhearted to outsiders, but the people in Anatolia, as well as those who left Anatolia behind, know well its bloody essence. Still, for the first time, I look at those women, those people on the album cover, trying so hard to stand tall and unblinking, those people on the other side of the ocean singing their songs from home—and at a time I myself am so far from home.

What's death beside homelessness? May no one be homeless. It's the pain they carry in their hearts and transmit to their children. The sepia light falls on them too as I see into their hearts.

★

22   Armenian master *kanun* player Kanuni Garbis Barkirgian is one of the artists featured on "Armenians on 8th Avenue," a collection of Turkish songs originally released in the US in the 1940s.

I'm in Paris, stepping into the Samuelian Bookshop. The same elderly woman and elderly man are standing in the same shop. A year ago, they refused to speak to me. I'm sure they don't want to see me now, either. The elderly woman is approaching. Does she remember me? She doesn't, and I'm glad. Because I no longer want to be a journalist who picks people apart with questions. All I want is a few books in English about Armenians. "Unfortunately, Mademoiselle," she says, "we have only one book in English." She ignores her stiff legs, climbs up to the top shelf, and removes a love story from among the history books: *Efronia*. The story of beautiful Efronia's love for a Muslim youth in the dying days of the Ottoman Empire, of an Armenian girl who'd remained behind while so many were driven from their homes in 1915. As I flip through the pages of the book, the elderly couple talk among themselves. We may be speaking a different language, but we recognize each other. They glance over from time to time, the old foxes, sprinkling their French with a few Turkish phrases, speaking just loud enough for me to hear. They speak a few words of Turkish and scan my face. I can see them out of the corner of my eye, my head buried in the book, a smile on my lips. They begin speaking Turkish together, a language half-remembered, bitter in flavor. I start laughing. So do they. I thank them in English, pay for the book, and walk away. When I glance back at them through the glass door, they're looking at me and smiling. A bruised smile is spreading across their faces. I can't explain; it's about home. I can't translate it; it's too Anatolian.

As I read the story of Efronia, I smile every time I remember that elderly couple. Then I begin smiling at things I come across in the book—the Turkish words. Especially *turşu*. It's always in italics. Even though I know that English readers are unfamiliar with this particular *turşu*, because their "pickles" are usually sweet—a kind of pickle someone from Anatolia would never eat—I still smile. Parts of yourself become italicized in foreign languages. I can't tick off all the examples here—there are so many, and they're so connected to home, so Turkish. A pickle may seem unimportant, but if you only knew how, over time, it is precisely these small, unimportant things that drain life of flavor.

I look at that book and at other books telling Armenians stories in foreign languages, and I'm amazed at all the footnotes and italicized words. Even the most basic things have to be explained at length as they tell their stories to foreigners. It's not that difficult to explain death and numbers, but when it comes to the story as a whole . . . If you can't explain a pickle, how can you possibly convey the full meaning of "homeland"—your home, the way it smells, the place it has inside you? How do you explain?

And now, in Oxford, they ask, "What's going on in Turkey these days?"—and something *is* always going on in my country—and you have no choice to but to start at the very beginning. And as you talk, your speech is sprinkled with italics and footnotes. And, after a while, our story seems so strange, so incomplete, so drained of flavor, that you don't want to explain anything at all. With the passage of time, people probably find that they're fading away, feeling lost. What's death? May no one ever become homeless.

In Oxford, I gain a better appreciation of what they must feel, and of what they must have felt. There's not much I can say about death; I've never died. But to find yourself homeless— incomplete and inadequate—that, I can understand. And that's what I apologize for. Nothing could be worse. I see that now.

Come what may, you want a home. You want a home that doesn't ensnare and isn't out of reach. A place you can go in and out of. A place you can return to and leave from. A bed in which you always sleep best. That's what a sense of belonging should be. Not a place in which we're ensnared by "patriot- ism," or from which we're expelled as a "traitor"—a sense of belonging that doesn't force us to reject everything we have in order to leave it behind; a home that doesn't consume us when we're in it. Because home is never composed entirely of evil and dark secrets.

And everyone . . . loves their home, I was going to say. But it's not love; it's something else. I don't have to define or translate what I mean. Everyone knows what I mean—I know that. And for that reason, as I sit here in a country where spring is not the spring I know, amid so many books and so much history, the sepia light of day fading away, I'm telling you that I'm sorry. I'm very sorry. My home is your home—please come one day. That's the kind of thing I want to say. I want to offer you more than an apology; there's so much else and so much more I'd like to say.

Actually, shall I tell you the truth? Marko Melkon is singing, "I drink *rakı* and I wander," and I'd like, one day, to be able to sit and drink rakı with you, un-italicized rakı, and talk about our history, whether it be "glorious" or "black," with light hearts and light words. I want us to put it behind us, and I want us to have children who don't have to know about what we're going through now.